D0041231

William Shakespeare

JULIUS CAESAR

Edited with a Commentary by Norman Sanders
Introduced by Martin Wiggins

PENGUIN BOOKS

PENGUIN BOOKS

Published by the Penguin Group
Penguin Books Ltd, 80 Strand, London WC2R ORL, England
Penguin Group (USA) Inc., 375 Hudson Street, New York, New York 10014, USA
Penguin Group (Canada), 10 Alcorn Avenue, Toronto, Ontario, Canada M4V 3B2
(a division of Pearson Penguin Canada Inc.)
Penguin Ireland, 25 St Stephen's Green, Dublin 2, Ireland (a division of Penguin Books Ltd)
Penguin Group (Australia), 250 Camberwell Road, Camberwell, Victoria 3124, Australia
(a division of Pearson Australia Group Pty Ltd)
Penguin Books India Pvt Ltd, 11 Community Centre, Panchsheel Park, New Delhi – 110 017, India
Penguin Group (NZ), cnr Airborne and Rosedale Roads, Albany, Auckland 1310, New Zealand
(a division of Pearson New Zealand Ltd)
Penguin Books (South Africa) (Pty) Ltd, 24 Sturdee Avenue, Rosebank 2196, South Africa

Penguin Books Ltd, Registered Offices: 80 Strand, London WC2R ORL, England

www.penguin.com

This edition first published in Penguin Books 1967
Reissued in the Penguin Shakespeare series 2005

1

Account of the Text and Commentary copyright © Norman Sanders, 1967
General Introduction and Chronology copyright © Stanley Wells, 2005
Introduction, The Play in Performance and Further Reading copyright © Martin Wiggins, 2005

Set in 11.5/12.5 PostScript Monotype Fournier
Typeset by Palimpsest Book Production Limited, Polmont, Stirlingshire
Printed in England by Clays Ltd, St Ives plc

Contents

General Introduction

Every play by Shakespeare is unique. This is part of his greatness. A restless and indefatigable experimenter, he moved with a rare amalgamation of artistic integrity and dedicated professionalism from one kind of drama to another. Never shackled by convention, he offered his actors the alternation between serious and comic modes from play to play, and often also within the plays themselves, that the repertory system within which he worked demanded, and which provided an invaluable stimulus to his imagination. Introductions to individual works in this series attempt to define their individuality. But there are common factors that underpin Shakespeare's career.

Nothing in his heredity offers clues to the origins of his genius. His upbringing in Stratford-upon-Avon, where he was born in 1564, was unexceptional. His mother, born Mary Arden, came from a prosperous farming family. Her father chose her as his executor over her eight sisters and his four stepchildren when she was only in her late teens, which suggests that she was of more than average practical ability. Her husband John, a glover, apparently unable to write, was nevertheless a capable businessman and loyal townsfellow, who seems to have fallen on relatively hard times in later life. He would have been brought up as a Catholic, and may have retained

Catholic sympathies, but his son subscribed publicly to Anglicanism throughout his life.

The most important formative influence on Shakespeare was his school. As the son of an alderman who became bailiff (or mayor) in 1568, he had the right to attend the town's grammar school. Here he would have received an education grounded in classical rhetoric and oratory, studying authors such as Ovid, Cicero and Quintilian, and would have been required to read, speak, write and even think in Latin from his early years. This classical education permeates Shakespeare's work from the beginning to the end of his career. It is apparent in the self-conscious classicism of plays of the early 1590s such as the tragedy of *Titus Andronicus*, *The Comedy of Errors*, and the narrative poems *Venus and Adonis* (1592–3) and *The Rape of Lucrece* (1593–4), and is still evident in his latest plays, informing the dream visions of *Pericles* and *Cymbeline* and the masque in *The Tempest*, written between 1607 and 1611. It inflects his literary style throughout his career. In his earliest writings the verse, based on the ten-syllabled, five-beat iambic pentameter, is highly patterned. Rhetorical devices deriving from classical literature, such as alliteration and antithesis, extended similes and elaborate wordplay, abound. Often, as in *Love's Labour's Lost* and *A Midsummer Night's Dream*, he uses rhyming patterns associated with lyric poetry, each line self-contained in sense, the prose as well as the verse employing elaborate figures of speech. Writing at a time of linguistic ferment, Shakespeare frequently imports Latinisms into English, coining words such as abstemious, addiction, incarnadine and adjunct. He was also heavily influenced by the eloquent translations of the Bible in both the Bishops' and the Geneva versions. As his experience grows, his verse and prose become more supple, the patterning less apparent, more ready to accommodate the rhythms of ordinary speech, more colloquial in diction, as in the speeches of the Nurse in *Romeo and Juliet*, the characterful prose of Falstaff and Hamlet's soliloquies. The effect is of increasing psychological realism, reaching its greatest heights in *Hamlet*, *Othello*, *King Lear*, *Macbeth* and *Antony and Cleopatra*. Gradually he discovered ways of adapting the regular beat of the pentameter to make it an infinitely flexible instrument for matching thought with feeling. Towards the end of his career, in plays such as *The Winter's Tale*, *Cymbeline* and *The Tempest*, he adopts a more highly mannered style, in keeping with the more overtly symbolical and emblematical mode in which he is writing.

So far as we know, Shakespeare lived in Stratford till after his marriage to Anne Hathaway, eight years his senior, in 1582. They had three children: a daughter, Susanna, born in 1583 within six months of their marriage, and twins, Hamnet and Judith, born in 1585. The next seven years of Shakespeare's life are virtually a blank. Theories that he may have been, for instance, a schoolmaster, or a lawyer, or a soldier, or a sailor, lack evidence to support them. The first reference to him in print, in Robert Greene's pamphlet *Greene's Groatsworth of Wit* of 1592, parodies a line from *Henry VI, Part III*, implying that Shakespeare was already an established playwright. It seems likely that at some unknown point after the birth of his twins he joined a theatre company and gained experience as both actor and writer in the provinces and London. The London theatres closed because of plague in 1593 and 1594; and during these years, perhaps recognizing the need for an alternative career, he wrote and published the narrative poems *Venus and Adonis* and *The Rape of Lucrece*. These are the only works we can be certain that Shakespeare himself was responsible for putting into print. Each bears the author's dedication to Henry Wriothesley, Earl of Southampton (1573–1624), the second in warmer terms than the first. Southampton, younger than Shakespeare by ten years, is the only person to whom he personally dedicated works. The Earl may have been a close friend, perhaps even the beautiful and adored young man whom Shakespeare celebrates in his *Sonnets*.

The resumption of playing after the plague years saw the founding of the Lord Chamberlain's Men, a company to which Shakespeare was to belong for the rest of his career, as actor, shareholder and playwright. No other dramatist of the period had so stable a relationship with a single company. Shakespeare knew the actors for whom he was writing and the conditions in which they performed. The permanent company was made up of around twelve to fourteen players, but one actor often played more than one role in a play and additional actors were hired as needed. Led by the tragedian Richard Burbage (1568–1619) and, initially, the comic actor Will Kemp (d. 1603), they rapidly achieved a high reputation, and when King James I succeeded Queen Elizabeth I in 1603 they were renamed as the King's Men. All the women's parts were played by boys; there is no evidence that any female role was ever played by a male actor over the age of about eighteen. Shakespeare had enough confidence in his boys to write for them long and demanding roles such as Rosalind (who, like other heroines of the romantic comedies, is disguised as a boy for much of the action) in *As You Like It*, Lady Macbeth and Cleopatra. But there are far more fathers than mothers, sons than daughters, in his plays, few if any of which require more than the company's normal complement of three or four boys.

The company played primarily in London's public playhouses – there were almost none that we know of in the rest of the country – initially in the Theatre, built in Shoreditch in 1576, and from 1599 in the Globe, on Bankside. These were wooden, more or less circular structures, open to the air, with a thrust stage surmounted by a canopy and jutting into the area where spectators who paid one penny stood, and surrounded by galleries where it was possible to be seated on payment of an additional penny. Though properties such as cauldrons, stocks, artificial trees or beds could indicate locality, there was no representational scenery. Sound effects such as flourishes of trumpets, music both martial and amorous, and accompaniments to songs were provided by the company's musicians. Actors entered through doors in the back wall of the stage. Above it was a balconied area that could represent the walls of a town (as in *King John*), or a castle (as in *Richard II*), and indeed a balcony (as in *Romeo and Juliet*). In 1609 the company also acquired the use of the Blackfriars, a smaller, indoor theatre to which admission was more expensive, and which permitted the use of more spectacular stage effects such as the descent of Jupiter on an eagle in *Cymbeline* and of goddesses in *The Tempest*. And they would frequently perform before the court in royal residences and, on their regular tours into the provinces, in non-theatrical spaces such as inns, guildhalls and the great halls of country houses.

Early in his career Shakespeare may have worked in collaboration, perhaps with Thomas Nashe (1567–c. 1601) in *Henry VI, Part I* and with George Peele (1556–96) in *Titus Andronicus*. And towards the end he collaborated with George Wilkins (*fl.* 1604–8) in *Pericles*, and with his younger colleagues Thomas Middleton (1580–1627), in *Timon of Athens*, and John Fletcher (1579–1625), in *Henry*

VIII, *The Two Noble Kinsmen* and the lost play *Cardenio*. Shakespeare's output dwindled in his last years, and he died in 1616 in Stratford, where he owned a fine house, New Place, and much land. His only son had died at the age of eleven, in 1596, and his last descendant died in 1670. New Place was destroyed in the eighteenth century but the other Stratford houses associated with his life are maintained and displayed to the public by the Shakespeare Birthplace Trust.

One of the most remarkable features of Shakespeare's plays is their intellectual and emotional scope. They span a great range from the lightest of comedies, such as *The Two Gentlemen of Verona* and *The Comedy of Errors*, to the profoundest of tragedies, such as *King Lear* and *Macbeth*. He maintained an output of around two plays a year, ringing the changes between comic and serious. All his comedies have serious elements: Shylock, in *The Merchant of Venice*, almost reaches tragic dimensions, and *Measure for Measure* is profoundly serious in its examination of moral problems. Equally, none of his tragedies is without humour: Hamlet is as witty as any of his comic heroes, *Macbeth* has its Porter, and *King Lear* its Fool. His greatest comic character, Falstaff, inhabits the history plays and *Henry V* ends with a marriage, while *Henry VI*, *Part III*, *Richard II* and *Richard III* culminate in the tragic deaths of their protagonists.

Although in performance Shakespeare's characters can give the impression of a superabundant reality, he is not a naturalistic dramatist. None of his plays is explicitly set in his own time. The action of few of them (except for the English histories) is set even partly in England (exceptions are *The Merry Wives of Windsor* and the Induction to *The Taming of the Shrew*). Italy is his favoured location. Most of his principal story-lines derive from printed writings; but the structuring and translation of these narratives into dramatic terms is Shakespeare's own, and he invents much additional material. Most of the plays contain elements of myth and legend, and many derive from ancient or more recent history or from romantic tales of ancient times and faraway places. All reflect his reading, often in close detail. Holinshed's *Chronicles* (1577, revised 1587), a great compendium of English, Scottish and Irish history, provided material for his English history plays. The *Lives of the Noble Grecians and Romans* by the Greek writer Plutarch, finely translated into English from the French by Sir Thomas North in 1579, provided much of the narrative material, and also a mass of verbal detail, for his plays about Roman history. Some plays are closely based on shorter individual works: *As You Like It*, for instance, on the novel *Rosalynde* (1590) by his near-contemporary Thomas Lodge (1558–1625), *The Winter's Tale* on *Pandosto* (1588) by his old rival Robert Greene (1558–92) and *Othello* on a story by the Italian Giraldi Cinthio (1504–73). And the language of his plays is permeated by the Bible, the Book of Common Prayer and the proverbial sayings of his day.

Shakespeare was popular with his contemporaries, but his commitment to the theatre and to the plays in performance is demonstrated by the fact that only about half of his plays appeared in print in his lifetime, in slim paperback volumes known as quartos, so called because they were made from printers' sheets folded twice to form four leaves (eight pages). None of them shows any sign that he was involved in their publication. For him, performance was the primary means of publication. The most frequently reprinted of his works were the non-dramatic poems – the erotic *Venus and Adonis* and the more moralistic *The Rape of Lucrece*. The *Sonnets*, which appeared in 1609, under his name but possibly without his consent, were less successful, perhaps because the vogue for sonnet sequences, which peaked in the 1590s, had passed by then. They were not reprinted until 1640, and then only in garbled form along with poems by other writers. Happily, in 1623, seven years after he died, his colleagues John Heminges (1556–1630) and Henry Condell (d. 1627) published his collected plays, including eighteen that had not previously appeared in print, in the first Folio, whose name derives from the fact that the printers' sheets were folded only once to produce two leaves (four pages). Some of the quarto editions are badly printed, and the fact that some plays exist in two, or even three, early versions creates problems for editors. These are discussed in the Account of the Text in each volume of this series.

Shakespeare's plays continued in the repertoire until the Puritans closed the theatres in 1642. When performances resumed after the Restoration of the monarchy in 1660 many of the plays were not to the taste of the times, especially because their mingling of genres and failure to meet the requirements of poetic justice offended against the dictates of neoclassicism. Some, such as *The Tempest* (changed by John Dryden and William Davenant in 1667 to suit contemporary taste), *King Lear* (to which Nahum Tate gave a happy ending in 1681) and *Richard III* (heavily adapted by Colley Cibber in 1700 as a vehicle for his own talents), were extensively rewritten; others fell into neglect. Slowly they regained their place in the repertoire, and they continued to be reprinted, but it was not until the great actor David Garrick (1717–79) organized a spectacular jubilee in Stratford in 1769 that Shakespeare began to be regarded as a transcendental

genius. Garrick's idolatry prefigured the enthusiasm of
critics such as Samuel Taylor Coleridge (1772–1834) and
William Hazlitt (1778–1830). Gradually Shakespeare's
reputation spread abroad, to Germany, America, France
and to other European countries.

During the nineteenth century, though the plays were
generally still performed in heavily adapted or abbrevi-
ated versions, a large body of scholarship and criticism
began to amass. Partly as a result of a general swing in
education away from the teaching of Greek and Roman
texts and towards literature written in English,
Shakespeare became the object of intensive study in
schools and universities. In the theatre, important turning
points were the work in England of two theatre directors, William Poel (1852–1934) and his disciple Harley
Granville-Barker (1877–1946), who showed that the
application of knowledge, some of it newly acquired, of
early staging conditions to performance of the plays could
render the original texts viable in terms of the modern
theatre. During the twentieth century appreciation of
Shakespeare's work, encouraged by the availability of
audio, film and video versions of the plays, spread around
the world to such an extent that he can now be claimed
as a global author.

The influence of Shakespeare's works permeates the
English language. Phrases from his plays and poems –
'a tower of strength', 'green-eyed jealousy', 'a foregone
conclusion' – are on the lips of people who may never
have read him. They have inspired composers of songs,
orchestral music and operas; painters and sculptors; poets,
novelists and film-makers. Allusions to him appear in pop
songs, in advertisements and in television shows. Some
of his characters – Romeo and Juliet, Falstaff, Shylock
and Hamlet – have acquired mythic status. He is valued

for his humanity, his psychological insight, his wit and humour, his lyricism, his mastery of language, his ability to excite, surprise, move and, in the widest sense of the word, entertain audiences. He is the greatest of poets, but he is essentially a dramatic poet. Though his plays have much to offer to readers, they exist fully only in performance. In these volumes we offer individual introductions, notes on language and on specific points of the text, suggestions for further reading and information about how each work has been edited. In addition we include accounts of the ways in which successive generations of interpreters and audiences have responded to challenges and rewards offered by the plays. The Penguin Shakespeare series aspires to remove obstacles to understanding and to make pleasurable the reading of the work of the man who has done more than most to make us understand what it is to be human.

                                                    Stanley Wells

The Chronology of Shakespeare's Works

A few of Shakespeare's writings can be fairly precisely dated. An allusion to the Earl of Essex in the chorus to Act V of *Henry V*, for instance, could only have been written in 1599. But for many of the plays we have only vague information, such as the date of publication, which may have occurred long after composition, the date of a performance, which may not have been the first, or a list in Francis Meres's book *Palladis Tamia*, published in 1598, which tells us only that the plays listed there must have been written by that year. The chronology of the early plays is particularly difficult to establish. Not everyone would agree that the first part of *Henry VI* was written after the third, for instance, or *Romeo and Juliet* before *A Midsummer Night's Dream*. The following table is based on the 'Canon and Chronology' section in *William Shakespeare: A Textual Companion*, by Stanley Wells and Gary Taylor, with John Jowett and William Montgomery (1987), where more detailed information and discussion may be found.

The Two Gentlemen of Verona	1590–91
The Taming of the Shrew	1590–91
Henry VI, Part II	1591
Henry VI, Part III	1591

Macbeth (revised by Middleton)	1606
Antony and Cleopatra	1606
Pericles (with George Wilkins)	1607
Coriolanus	1608
The Winter's Tale	1609
Cymbeline	1610
The Tempest	1611
Henry VIII (by Shakespeare and John Fletcher; known in its own time as *All is True*)	1613
Cardenio (by Shakespeare and Fletcher; lost)	1613
The Two Noble Kinsmen (by Shakespeare and Fletcher)	1613–14

Introduction

Shakespeare wrote *Julius Caesar* in 1599, a year that marked a turning point in his professional career: already a senior member of his acting company, with the building of the Globe theatre he became the part-owner of a London playhouse. The play, too, represents a turning point in his development as an artist. It stands between his most original contribution to 1590s drama, the masterly sequence of English history plays which had just come to an end with *Henry V*, and the major tragedies of the 1600s, which were to begin with *Hamlet* the following year. *Julius Caesar* is a play on the cusp, a double-visioned work sharing something in common with both genres: it combines, as I hope this Introduction will illuminate, the objective detachment of historiography with the personal engagement of tragedy.

LISTENING TO RHETORIC

More than any other Shakespeare play, *Julius Caesar* dramatizes the process of audience management through public oratory: politicians win and lose power according to their ability to influence the Roman people with their rhetoric. Brutus the conspirator and Caesar the ruler

whom he helps to assassinate both understand that, in
politics, a course of action cannot simply stand on its
own merits: a statesman must, in Brutus' words, 'Fashion
it' (II.1.30), present it in a way that imaginatively engages
the people. Often this is more a matter of winning hearts
than minds: such speeches usually sound impressive in
the heat of the moment, but will less often bear sustained
scrutiny. For example, Caesar's determination to go to
the Senate despite all danger is expressed to his wife and
servant in powerfully heroic terms:

> Danger knows full well
> That Caesar is more dangerous than he.
> We are two lions littered in one day,
> And I the elder and more terrible;
> And Caesar shall go forth. (II.2.44–8)

Yet this bears no relation to any sane perception of reality;
it is no basis on which to take a life-or-death decision. It
is up to the actor whether he plays Caesar at this moment
as dangerously deluded, his judgement 'consumed in
confidence' (II.2.49) as Calphurnia puts it, or, alterna-
tively, as a brave man trying to justify his courage to a
sceptical household; but the point is that the justification
invites such scepticism, from us as much as from the characters onstage. Shakespeare's pedantic friend and rival
Ben Jonson mocked him for having written in a later
scene, 'Caesar did never wrong but with just cause'. The
line appears in the published text as 'Know, Caesar doth
not wrong, nor without cause | Will he be satisfied'
(III.1.47–8), and the anomaly is sometimes explained as
a sheepish revision in response to Jonson's criticism that
it is logically impossible to have a just cause for wrongdoing. Yet, if that is what Shakespeare originally wrote,

perhaps Jonson had missed the point: such a line would
have been a coherent part of the design of the play,
another of the magnificent rhetorical non sequiturs with
which Caesar, to the very end of his life, tries to get his
own way.

Politicians' speeches collapse not only under the
weight of their own inherent overstatement or illogi-
cality but also through their failure to misrepresent reality
convincingly enough. Explaining his determination to
reject Metellus Cimber's suit and uphold his brother's
banishment, Caesar uses the metaphor of the unmoving
pole star:

> But I am constant as the northern star,
> Of whose true-fixed and resting quality
> There is no fellow in the firmament. (III.1.60–62)

But his fashioning himself in those terms, 'Unshaked of
motion' (III.1.70), is ironically undercut moments later
when he is murdered. Brutus' attempt to fashion the
killers' public image is no more successful, showing all
too often the inventiveness of a clever man who has
given himself so far over to theory that he no longer has
any sure sense of common perception. Perhaps, after the
assassination, he is just being inappropriately facetious
when he argues paradoxically that they are Caesar's
friends because they have 'abridged | His time of fearing
death' (III.1.104–5), but beforehand he sets himself a
difficult task in earnest:

> Let's carve him as a dish fit for the gods,
> Not hew him as a carcass fit for hounds.
> And let our hearts, as subtle masters do,
> Stir up their servants to an act of rage,

> And after seem to chide 'em. This shall make
> Our purpose necessary, and not envious;
> Which so appearing to the common eyes,
> We shall be called purgers, not murderers. (II.1.173–80)

Vivisection and animal sacrifice played an important part in Roman religion, which is why Brutus can imagine that the conspirators might be seen as sacrificers rather than butchers; but does he really expect either metaphor to predominate in the public mind over the visible actuality of a bloody attack on a human being?

Part of the point is Brutus' unbounded confidence in his own powers of persuasion. His proposal that the assassins should wash their hands and forearms in the spilt blood of Caesar can appear simply crazy – even, in some productions, to his fellow-conspirators. Its immediate effect is to give him something he must apologize for when Mark Antony arrives on the scene:

> Though now we must appear bloody and cruel,
> As by our hands and this our present act
> You see we do, yet see you but our hands
> And this the bleeding business they have done.
> Our hearts you see not; they are pitiful;
> And pity to the general wrong of Rome –
> As fire drives out fire, so pity, pity –
> Hath done this deed on Caesar. (III.1.165–72)

Its purpose is to lay the foundations for an apology in the rhetorical sense, a speech of self-justification, by clarifying what is to be justified: the killers make a savage spectacle of themselves so that Brutus can deny that savagery the more effectually. It says something that he is temporarily successful, with the plebeians if not with

Antony: in the play's structurally central scene (III.2), with power up for grabs, the two men compete oratorically for the public mind, and so for Rome, and crowd support goes at first to Brutus, before Antony wins them over with his altogether slicker performance in the public pulpit.

This is a crucial moment not only in determining Rome's political future but also in the play's management of its audience. So far we have witnessed rhetoric that is at best semi-public, directed at particular groups of people – petitioners, colleagues, potential enemies – rather than at a mass audience. But the two great political speeches of this scene work differently, and have a peculiar effect. In the theatre they are often addressed as much to the auditorium as they are to the onstage crowd – appropriately enough since, as we shall see, the play itself is doing something very similar to what Brutus and Antony are doing with the crowd. But this is not a straightforward process for the actor: Antony's speech in particular – 'Friends, Romans, countrymen' (III.2.74) – has the reputation of being a theatrical catch-22. There are, it is said, two fundamental mistakes that an actor can make with the speech: one is to play it to the audience; and the other is *not* to play it to the audience. The reason for the paradox is the doubleness of viewpoint which the play seems to demand of us. If the actor playing Mark Antony delivers his speech to the audience then, quite properly, he is involving us in the political action: like the onstage audience, we listen and respond to what is being said; the staging makes us, as it were, honorary members of the crowd, bringing us to a new degree of engagement. But of course we are not really Roman citizens living in 44 BC, so the outcome of events holds no direct, personal significance for us: for us, it's

only a play, and, however effectively that play may
engage our interest and sympathies, it is to be hoped that
Antony's sly rabble-rousing words will not turn us from
audience into mob and induce us, as they do the Romans,
to riot, burn down buildings and murder innocent poets.
In the end we need to see through what Antony says in
the same way that we saw through the rhetoric of Brutus
and Caesar. The play is written to maintain in its audience a fine balance of engagement and detachment; an
actor's delivery of 'Friends, Romans, countrymen' can
all too easily tip that balance one way or the other.

    Part of this effect is accessible to any audience of any
good production, but part requires an effort of historical
imagination: if Shakespeare wrote for playgoers, necessarily he wrote in particular for the late-sixteenth-century
playgoers he knew rather than for the unimaginable
inhabitants of future centuries. We can see both aspects
in an earlier moment when a politician addresses the
people, albeit with less dignity and less measured rhetoric: at the very start of the play. 'Hence! home, you idle
creatures, get you home', commands the Tribune Flavius
(I.i.i). This opening line can have a powerful impact
when played to an audience, rather than just to the onstage
characters. Before any live performance there is always
an atmosphere of pleasurable anticipation among the
assembled playgoers, which reaches its height as the actors
come onstage and begin the play. But the first thing to
be said in this play is an order to go away again. The
effect, startling in any century, would have been particularly acute at the Globe in 1599. We are used to theatrical
performances being mainly evening events, whereas in
Shakespeare's time they took place in the afternoon; if
you were an apprentice or artisan who wanted to visit
the theatre, you had to take time off work, or wait for

one of the period's infrequent public holidays. It is pertinent, then, that Flavius demands, 'Is this a holiday?' (I.1.2). There was many an antitheatrical zealot in London who would castigate plays in the same terms, for encouraging idleness and absenteeism, and as *Julius Caesar* begins it is almost as if one of those fanatics has invaded the stage and begun to harangue the 'idle creatures' who are wasting their time with something so trivial as a play. As the scene develops it becomes clear, as most playgoers must always really have known, that Flavius is a tribune from ancient history trying to send Roman revellers home; but it is important that the play also begins with a momentary frisson of the contemporaneous.

Julius Caesar is fairly rigorous in the way it uses contemporary references. That may seem a surprising assertion given that the play is often said to be rather slapdash in the way it creates and maintains its period setting. In contrast with the historically erudite and heavily footnoted Roman tragedies of Ben Jonson, Shakespeare's play is famous for its anachronisms: the Romans didn't have striking clocks like the one the conspirators hear at their meeting in Brutus' orchard (II.1.191), and their 'books' were scrolls in which you couldn't keep your place by turning down a leaf, as Brutus has done in the book he reads in his tent at Sardis (IV.3.271). Clearly, one cannot claim strict historical authenticity for this version of ancient Rome. But arguably it's not that sort of authenticity that matters: the play demonstrably doesn't correspond in every detail to what historians know of Rome in the first century BC, but what matters in a drama is how far the world onstage differs from the familiar, day-to-day lives of its audience. Such commonplace things as books or striking clocks can simply be taken for granted unless you have made a study of when they happen to have been invented; what an audience will notice are the ways in which the world of the play is *discontinuous* with the world in which it is being performed. It is to emphasize that discontinuity that the play usually offers its understated reminders of the contemporary situation in 1599.

There is a complex example in the second scene, when Cassius is first trying to persuade Brutus to join the conspiracy. He does it by appealing to Rome's history, and the part played in it by Brutus' famous ancestor, Lucius Junius Brutus, who expelled the city's kings in 510 BC:

> O, you and I have heard our fathers say,
> There was a Brutus once that would have brooked
> Th'eternal devil to keep his state in Rome
> As easily as a king. (I.2.157–60)

Those lines work to establish the difference between Caesar's Rome and Shakespeare's England in two ways. One is very obvious: England is a monarchy, whereas the Rome of the play has been a republic for more than four hundred years, and doesn't want its kings back now; these are two states with different histories, different forms of government, different political traditions. But the speech also distances Cassius more subtly, by inserting a sliver of irony between him and the Elizabethan audience: his words carry a meaning unintended by the character and irrelevant to the action, but all too apparent in 1599. For Cassius, the absolute undesirability of monarchy is defined in terms of an extreme state of affairs which, in contrast, was a present reality for the Protestant Englishmen for whom the play was originally written: in the 1590s the eternal devil *did* keep his state in Rome, in that the politico-religious iconography of the time portrayed the Pope, England's great Continental enemy, as Antichrist.

My point is not that this passing reference to the contemporary Rome of the Catholic Church provides some kind of key to a topical layer of meaning now lost to us. On the contrary, I suggest that to search for such topicality is to obscure the play's real concerns with *Roman* politics, with a conflict in which the audience has no personal stake, and so doesn't need to take sides, doesn't have the responsibility to vote one way or the other. The introduction of a contemporary reference into this milieu is what might be called a significant irrelevance: the playgoers of 1599 are reminded of their own habitual modes of political thought, and that reminder serves as a marker of their own distance from the Roman politics of the play. It's a moment that reinforces the detachment which is one of the two paradoxically opposed positions in which *Julius Caesar*'s audience is apt to find itself.

In a sense, the start of the play is another example of this process. Here too the audience is encouraged to remember its contemporary situation – this time its situation *as* an audience at a London playhouse, and so liable to the strictures of the theatre's opponents. What's unusual and uncharacteristic is that, uniquely, this moment does not have the effect of detaching the audience from the action; on the contrary, we are clearly being induced to take sides. Whatever the variety of incompatible opinions and personal philosophies to be found in any theatre audience, there is one thing which every member will have in common: some may like a tragedy and some may not, some may like Shakespeare and some may not; but none of them will disapprove of the theatre on strict ideological grounds – otherwise they wouldn't be there in the first place. So when, in the first few seconds of the action, the tribunes Flavius and Marullus are associated with sixteenth-century London's self-righteous antitheatrical moralists, and when they seem to address the assembled playgoers, insultingly, as 'idle creatures', an audience's natural response is one of dislike.

That response is reinforced in the rest of the scene: Marullus and Flavius prove eminently dislikeable. They are self-important in their assumed superiority as they reprove the onstage crowd for taking an unauthorized holiday. They cannot bear not to have the best of the encounter, and Flavius' bearing disintegrates all too easily into comical alliterative bluster when he can't get a straight answer from the recalcitrant cobbler: 'What trade, thou knave? Thou naughty knave, what trade?' (I.i.15). Perhaps most damagingly, they are guilty of complacency in their high public office: as Tribunes of the People they were supposedly elected to safeguard the interests of the very plebeians for whom they now show such deep patrician contempt. And, as the scene goes on to emphasize, these men are Caesar's political enemies.

If this opening scene strikes a keynote for our response to the rest of the action, if the aim really is to make us take sides, or even simply predispose us to prefer one faction to another, then it has to be said that the play is not working at a very sophisticated level of political judgement. The action at this early stage has given little overt attention to politics as such: the scene is much more about personalities than about the business of government. In that respect we don't have the information to make the judgement that we seem to be propelled towards: to assess a complex issue on the basis of personal feelings about the men who espouse one particular point of view is the politics of the Roman mob. Perhaps the audience has already been associated with the members of that mob by the rhetoric of the opening lines, with their momentary ambiguity as to the identity of the 'idle creatures' being addressed; yet later there is a stronger sense of the fickleness, then the savagery of the citizens in the aftermath of Caesar's assassination, which seems to justify Marullus' description of them as 'cruel men of Rome' (I.1.36).

Equally, a collective public response to individual politicians is often central to the workings of statecraft in any age: issues may be coloured, or even obscured, by the personal qualities of the men and women who espouse or oppose them. Casca admits as much when he urges that Brutus should be recruited to the conspiracy:

> O, he sits high in all the people's hearts;
> And that which would appear offence in us,
> His countenance, like richest alchemy,
> Will change to virtue and to worthiness. (I.3.157–60)

The conspirators may be sure in themselves that Caesar's death will be for the public good, but in the political arena it is not those civic reasons that will count, but the people's love and trust for Brutus – though in the event, of course, it is Mark Antony and the mass bribery of Caesar's will that sways the populace.

In soliciting an attitude to the two tribunes, the first scene gives the audience direct experience of this aspect of popular politics; but it does this using men who are very minor players, and whom we shall never see again. (The Flavius who briefly appears in Brutus' army in

Act V, scene 4 need not be the same man; in any event,
he is based on a different historical personage.) That's
important, because personalities are only one element
in the equation, and arguably the most trivial element.
In the second scene the play's political focus widens,
and the key politicians enter the action: Caesar, Antony,
Cassius and Brutus. The dialogue begins to concentrate
on the issues, especially at this stage as they are perceived
by Cassius. Our grasp of the incipient political conflict
becomes more secure. And then the subject of anti-
theatricalism comes up again, when Caesar remarks on
Cassius' philistine attitudes: 'He loves no plays, |
As thou dost, Antony; he hears no music' (I.2.202–3). This
time the undertone is sinister: if only Cassius were to
take more interest in aesthetic entertainments, Caesar
suggests, he would think less and consequently be less
prone to opposition. Inevitably our reaction will be
different, and more complex, than it was at the start of
the play: even if we are inclined to take against Cassius
for not loving plays, as we took against Flavius and
Marullus, we should hardly want to endorse Caesar's
view that theatregoing is an intellectual and political
soporific; and in any case we must be aware by now that
the subject is irrelevant to the issues at stake.

So the first scene draws us seductively into a mode of
political response which is subsequently disavowed: if
we have been gullible enough to translate our personal
dislike for the two tribunes into a negative assessment of
their political views, then the next scene's reminder of
the original basis for that dislike will serve to caution us
against such trivially reductive responses in future. The
point is reinforced later in the scene, when Casca reports,
'Marullus and Flavius, for pulling scarfs off Caesar's
images, are put to silence' (I.2.282–3). Many an editor

has glossed this line by quoting Shakespeare's source, Plutarch's *Lives of the Noble Grecians and Romans*, in which he read a straightforward assertion that the two tribunes were removed from office. But in writing his own version of the event, he introduced a sinister ambiguity: 'put to silence' can be played as one of the most chilling understatements in English drama. At one level, it doesn't matter whether the tribunes are silenced by impeachment or execution: either way, it gives strong support to the view of Caesar as a dangerous tyrant-in-waiting. But for an audience which has bristled against the characters in the previous scene, the possibility of their death induces a distinctive, uncomfortable feeling: the desire not to rejoice in the wrongful demise of people whom we have disliked. Nothing could be more effective in exorcizing our original crude reaction to the politics of opposition.

My point is not that we have been temporarily deluded into taking the wrong side, but that taking *any* side absolutely will result in an over-simplistic response to the action. We are given the opportunity of approaching events in a partisan way, so that such an approach can then be taken away from us. In that respect we are allowed to be different from the Roman mob: later on they cheer first for Brutus and then for Antony, changing their minds and allegiances without really understanding why; whereas, if we too have cause to reassess an initial judgement, it is because we can withdraw ourselves from judgement altogether and watch events with a historical detachment not available to the characters on stage. In other words, *Julius Caesar* is not so much a political play as a play about politics: not a play which advances a point of view but one which dramatizes the collision of multiple points of view with what Samuel Taylor

Coleridge called (in 1818, apropos of Shakespeare's later Roman tragedy *Coriolanus*) a 'philosophic impartiality'.

POLITICS AND HISTORY

The central issue in *Julius Caesar* is not one of policy but of power. The play isn't fundamentally concerned with a divergence of views on how the state should be governed: Caesar's apparently tyrannical behaviour is a side-issue, the more so when you remember that his opponents will prove just as ready to embrace murder as a political strategy. The nub of the matter is, rather, the question of who should govern, and by what right: Brutus and Cassius stand for senatorial rule, and the problem of Caesar is the encroachment of autocracy. The conflict is often expressed in terms of two different systems of government: republic versus monarchy. But those political concepts are so broad that we risk importing anachronistic considerations from the monarchies and republics of our own time, or of Shakespeare's. It is worth remembering how the play seeks to establish its own specifically Roman identity: as well as the alienation effect of passing contemporary reference, which establishes cultural distance, there is also the way the dialogue sets the scene with allusions to well-known geographical features of the city such as the Capitol or the River Tiber. There is no reason to suppose that events might be happening in a thinly disguised England, or in some generic state transfigurable to anywhere. In some ways it is more helpful to think about the play's politics in terms of an opposition between tradition and personality.

Tradition is important in Rome. The action takes place at a late – indeed, terminal – stage in the life of the

Roman Republic, and the past still exerts its influence. It is an important and distinctive part of the urban environment in the form of the statues which are repeatedly mentioned, and which were so uncommon in Elizabethan London where the play was first performed. There is 'old Brutus' statue' (I.3.146), for example, on which Cinna the conspirator sticks one of his seditious bills urging the play's Brutus to join the conspiracy. Caesar actually dies at the foot of a statue of his old rival, Pompey. Ancient Rome was known for such landmarks (in her *Tragedy of Mariam* (1604) the dramatist Elizabeth Cary even called it a 'statue-filled' city), but it is striking that *Julius Caesar* contains more references to statues than any other in the Shakespeare canon, including the three other Roman plays. There is evidently more to these statues than just local colour.

Statues are not just large pieces of stone carved to resemble human beings. They aren't just interesting features of the urban landscape. The statues in the play commemorate great men from the birth of the Republic to its most recent casualty; from Rome's liberator, Lucius Junius Brutus, ancestor of the play's Brutus, to Pompey the Great, the conqueror of the Eastern provinces who was murdered in Egypt four years before the action begins. They are a material focus for a community's memory of its heroic dead; and this makes them the physical correlative for the psychic domination of the past over many prominent Roman citizens.

For the conspirators, history is an important aspect of their sense of personal identity. Cassius is typical in his interest in what we would call genetic heredity – or, in his terminology, 'the breed of noble bloods' (I.2.150). Throughout the play characters will often proclaim their ancestry when they need to assert their own merit or

importance: one of Brutus' allies even dies in battle
declaring, 'I am the son of Marcus Cato, ho!' (V.4.4, 6).
They are figures who exist not just on their own account
but also as a continuation of famous forebears from
whom they derive their personal qualities. When Portia,
Brutus' wife, protests at his refusal to confide in her she
strikingly claims strength and the transcendence of what
were then considered to be female limitations by invoking
the males of her immediate family:

> I grant I am a woman; but withal
> A woman that Lord Brutus took to wife;
> I grant I am a woman; but withal
> A woman well reputed, Cato's daughter.
> Think you I am no stronger than my sex,
> Being so fathered, and so husbanded? (II.1.292–7)

Primarily she is emphasizing her credit, both in general
as 'A woman well reputed' and specifically as the woman
whom Brutus chose to marry; but when she names herself
Cato's daughter she appeals to heredity. Ultimately she
owes her reputation to the virtues she has inherited from
her great republican father.

The subject of heredity threads its way through the
early part of the action, defining and prescribing people's
behaviour whenever it is mentioned. Cassius tends to raise
it when he wants someone to join his conspiracy. Meeting
Casca in the night-time streets, for instance, he grumbles,

> Romans now
> Have thews and limbs like to their ancestors;
> But woe the while! our fathers' minds are dead,
> And we are governed with our mothers' spirits . . .
>   (I.3.80–83)

It's a sly piece of manipulation which gives Casca little option but to do as Cassius wishes: unless he demurs and actively conspires against Caesar he will be disowning his genetic past; in a patriarchal primogeniture culture preoccupied with biological legitimacy, taking after the female line is alarmingly close to outright bastardy. Brutus too uses heredity as a device to compel acquiescence, though he goes about it more directly. When the conspirators meet in his garden the night before the Ides of March, Cassius proposes that they should join in an oath of resolution, and Brutus overrules him with the same unanswerable argument:

> . . . every drop of blood
> That every Roman bears, and nobly bears,
> Is guilty of a several bastardy,
> If he do break the smallest particle
> Of any promise that hath passed from him. (II.1.136–40)

What Brutus is appealing to here is best summed up in the Latin word *Romanitas*. It's a difficult word to translate: it means a system of values, but as a word it associates those values with the accident of being born a Roman citizen – there is an interpenetration of genetics and ethics in the word itself that makes behaviour such as promise-breaking or submission to tyranny a mark not merely of dishonour but of bastardy. That is why heredity can be so powerful a spur to conspiracy.

The principle also works in more individual terms. In this connection it is worth thinking about the research process which lay behind Shakespeare's writing of the play. His main source was the *Life of Brutus* from *The Lives of the Noble Grecians and Romans* by the Greek historian Plutarch, which was translated into English in

1579 by Sir Thomas North (who used an intermediate French translation by Jacques Amyot). The opening sentence, one of the first things Shakespeare must have read when he started gathering his material, reads: 'Marcus Brutus came of that Junius Brutus, for whom the ancient Romans made his statue of brass to be set up in the Capitol, with the images of the kings, holding a naked sword in his hand, because he had valiantly put down the Tarquins from their kingdom of Rome' (T. J. B. Spencer (ed.), *Shakespeare's Plutarch*). It is no arbitrary whim that makes Cinna stick one of his seditious messages on that statue, or makes Cassius allude to the former Brutus when he first broaches the subject of Caesar's ambition: the latent message is that the descendant should follow in the ancestor's footsteps.

All this defines one reason why it's not particularly useful to think of the play in terms of modern concepts of republicanism. Republican Rome corresponds more to the classical definition of an aristocratic state, governed by a Senate: Lord Brutus and his fellow-conspirators are, in effect, noblemen. They are a privileged elite who mix socially as well as politically – early on Cassius invites Casca to dinner (I.2.285–7). Moreover, they have known each other all their lives. At each end of the play Brutus makes passing unsentimental reference to his schooldays: early on he remarks on the change in his future colleague in conspiracy, the dour and surly Casca, who had been such a quick-mettled boy at school (I.2.293); and later, defeated at Philippi, he tries unsuccessfully to persuade his old schoolfriend Volumnius to help him in a battle-field suicide (V.5.28). They are the sons of great men, educated together, marked out from childhood for government.

So in the conspirators' discourse, heredity is also a

metaphor for political power: it is another aspect of Roman life where the past passes smoothly into the future through the loins of great families. This republic is really a self-perpetuating oligarchy. It is true that there are constitutional checks and balances built in, like the Tribunes of the People, but we have already seen in the case of Flavius and Marullus how successful the establishment has been in sucking in such outsiders: in their attitude to the plebeians the two tribunes are if anything more patrician than the patricians themselves.

This helps to clarify one aspect of the conspirators' conflict with Caesar. Unlike them, he is a man with no ancestry, only a personal biography. The only inheritance associated with him is the one he leaves to the people of Rome in his will; the only blood-relation mentioned in the play is Octavius, his great-nephew, the future Emperor Augustus. Where his political enemies are defined by their links with Rome's great past, Caesar is a man whose only bonds are with futurity. So Caesar's claim to power comes not from any noble birth, but on his own account. Brutus may live by the republican deeds of his great forebear, but Caesar can point to his own career as Rome's greatest general.

In a sense, there *is* a great figure from the past prescribing Caesar's behaviour; but in his case it is not an ancestor like Cato or Junius Brutus. Rather it is Caesar's own younger self. One striking feature of Caesar's dialogue is how frequently he talks about himself in the third person: 'Caesar is turned to hear' (I.2.17), 'Caesar shall go forth' (II.2.48) and so on. It is as if he is turning his surname into a brand name, objectifying himself in order to foster the personality cult which underlies his power. The process has a physical counterpart in the proliferation of his statues around Rome, which are, tellingly, a

powerful focus for opposition: Marullus and Flavius met
their downfall for provocatively disrobing the statues of
their Lupercal decorations.

It is noticeable that Caesar's enemies never actually
refer to his statues *as* statues, though it's plainly what
they are. They always pointedly use the word 'images'
instead: 'let no images | Be hung with Caesar's trophies'
(I.1.68–9). The point is, of course, that Caesar's statues
are anomalous. Unlike Pompey and Lucius Junius Brutus,
whose statues are also mentioned in the play, Caesar is
a living politician: his statues are indeed 'images' in the
sense that they are re-presentations of an existing and
visible original. In a city which honours its dead by
carving them in stone, the propagation of similar monu-
ments to Caesar during his lifetime carries a sinister
political undertone. Cassius is a perceptive commentator
in his first conversation with Brutus, when he offers a
bitterly ironic stricture on the apparently unheroic times
which have, it seems, produced only one man worthy of
the immortality of stone:

> Age, thou art shamed!
> Rome, thou hast lost the breed of noble bloods!
> When went there by an age, since the great flood,
> But it was famed with more than with one man? (I.2.149–52)

It is as if Caesar is treating himself prematurely as a
historical figure, and then claiming power by association
with that figure in the same way that a republican aris-
tocrat might claim it from an ancestor.

When Mark Antony tells the plebeians that 'The evil
that men do lives after them, | The good is oft interrèd
with their bones' (III.2.76–7) he is being disingenuous
for political ends; but he has a point that men are not

always judged in the same way by their contemporaries as they are by history. That fact is Caesar's greatest political weakness. Again, Cassius articulates the problem effectively when he imagines Caesar himself as a gigantic statue:

> . . . he doth bestride the narrow world
> Like a Colossus, and we petty men
> Walk under his huge legs . . . (I.2.134–6)

In reality, as he goes on to stress, the actual man doesn't always live up to the greatness of the Colossus: Caesar's physical strength is limited, and he is not ague-proof. The play repeatedly underlines the point: we learn of Caesar's epilepsy, 'the falling sickness' (I.2.252), and of his deafness (I.2.212), an infirmity which Shakespeare evidently needed so much that he had to invent it. (It doesn't appear in Plutarch or any other classical source.) If Caesar's power depends on his really *being* the idealized figure of his propaganda, then the disparity between the two could prove politically fatal.

Caesar is clearly aware of the problem, for several times we see him striving to live up to his great reputation, using his own past self as a spur to present action in the same way as Cassius used Brutus' ancestor. Sometimes it works. When Calphurnia wants him to stay away from the Senate on the Ides of March and lie about it, he decides against doing so by remembering his military exploits: 'Have I in conquest stretched mine arm so far, | To be afeard to tell greybeards the truth?' (II.2.66–7). Sometimes, however, it is less effective. After he babbles out to Mark Antony the dangers of thin men like Cassius who dislike plays and think too much, Caesar's attempt to win back his dignity is transparent and almost pathetic:

'I rather tell thee what is to be feared | Than what I fear; for always I am Caesar' (I.2.210–11). It is the hasty retraction of a man who suddenly realizes that he has said too much, even to his closest, most politically supine confidant. Caesar can never escape his human limitations; and before long the conspirators will prove it thirty-three times with their daggers.

It must be said that, unlike the later Roman emperors, Caesar has never claimed to be immortal or a god, and he has never overtly denied his physical frailties. Indeed, his position seems secure even after he has had an epileptic fit in public, as Casca describes towards the end of the second scene. In that respect, Cassius' arguments are overstated and need to be treated with caution. His basic point is the egalitarian one that Caesar is a man like other men, and so can have no claim to govern his equals:

> I had as lief not be as live to be
> In awe of such a thing as I myself.
> I was born free as Caesar . . . (I.2.95–7)

It is on this basis that the conspirators proclaim themselves both publicly and privately as 'The men that gave their country liberty' (III.1.118) – that is, the liberty of not being subject to Caesar. Perhaps one may wonder whether most Roman citizens would be any better off under the aristocratic oligarchy of the Republic.

However, Caesar's personal fitness to rule is not the only issue, and liberty is not the conspirators' only watchword. One of their strongest political motives is a commitment to the established order, the order which Brutus' great ancestor helped to create centuries ago. The attitude is reflected in their respect and concern for older men, whom Caesar is apt to dismiss contemptuously as 'greybeards'. At one point, for example, it is proposed that old Cicero should be invited to join the plot:

> . . . his silver hairs
> Will purchase us a good opinion
> And buy men's voices to commend our deeds.
> It shall be said his judgement ruled our hands;
> Our youths and wildness shall no whit appear,
> But all be buried in his gravity. (II.1.144–9)

It's notable that, as Metellus Cimber expresses it there, Cicero will give the assassination political credibility not primarily because of who he is so much as simply because he is an old man: the speech betrays an instinctive belief in the rightness and authority of anything that has been around longer than Cimber has himself. In turn, Caesar, though technically an old man himself, is associated in Brutus' rhetoric with something young, a serpent's egg (II.1.32). As the conspirators are respectful of the old and established, so do they reject the new and progressive. However much they may discourse of 'liberty', there is quite another creed implicit in the cryptic note which Cinna throws through Brutus' window on the stormy, portentous night before the assassination: '*Brutus, thou sleep'st: awake, and see thyself.* | *Shall Rome, etc. Speak, strike, redress*' (II.1.46–7). The key word here is 'redress': by speaking, by striking, it is suggested, Brutus will redress matters, will restore the state to its former condition. These men are not just republican liberators opposing an incipient monarchy; they are also young conservatives, hostile to social and political change.

There are other ironies yet which complicate the

conspirators' self-image. We have already seen how the play occasionally and momentarily reminds the audience of its contemporary situation in order to foster a degree of detachment from the events. Perhaps the most famous, and certainly the most durable, example comes after the assassination, when the killers begin to congratulate themselves and, ironically in view of some of Cassius' strictures on Caesar, anticipate how they will go down in history:

CASSIUS
                How many ages hence
  Shall this our lofty scene be acted over,
  In states unborn, and accents yet unknown!
BRUTUS
  How many times shall Caesar bleed in sport,
  That now on Pompey's basis lies along,
  No worthier than the dust!
CASSIUS   So oft as that shall be,
  So often shall the knot of us be called
  The men that gave their country liberty. (III.1.111–18)

At that moment we are, of course, watching just such a dramatized re-enactment, performed not in the Latin which the historical Brutus and Cassius spoke but in what was to them an 'accent yet unknown', English, and in a 'state unborn', whether it be Shakespeare's own sixteenth-century England or wherever else it may be performed in our world of the twenty-first century. It is this moment more than any other which crystallizes the play's doubleness of perspective: the balance between our awareness of the characters as, simultaneously, both historical personages and living beings enacting their moral and political dilemmas before our eyes.

CAESAR, PAST AND PRESENT

One of the problems which Shakespeare must have encountered in writing *Julius Caesar* is, in a sense, the same problem faced by the modern director of any well-known Shakespeare play. It is that the story holds no surprises: a reasonably well-educated audience will already know what is going to happen. It is true that in any tragedy we will probably have a broad, generically induced awareness that the hero is going to die, but in this tragedy we know precisely what the sequence of events and their outcome will be: we know that Brutus will be persuaded to join the conspiracy against his friend, we know that Caesar will ignore advice and portent and go to the Senate on the Ides of March, and we know that there he will be stabbed to death. To the Elizabethans, the assassination of Julius Caesar in 44 BC was one of the great events of world history. The story had been recounted by many of the classical historians, some of whom were studied in the Elizabethan grammar schools, and it had been told by several English poets and play-wrights; in the later sixteenth century, in fact, Caesar was the single most dramatized historical figure on the English stage. In everything from full-length treatments to casual allusions the fall of Julius Caesar was a part of the common cultural knowledge of the sixteenth century, in the same way that *Hamlet* is part of the common cultural knowledge of the twenty-first.

We can see the difficulty this presented to an author planning to write his own version of the story, in a poem by one John Higgins that formed part of the 1587 edition of *A Mirror for Magistrates*. This was an anthology of poems retelling the lives and deaths of great men,

recounted by their own ghosts returned from the grave
to deliver an awful warning about the hazards of ambition and wrongdoing. Caesar's ghost starts to unfold his
tale like this:

> I Caius Julius Caesar, consul, had to name,
> That worthy Roman born, renowned with noble deeds.
> What need I here recite the lineage whence I came
> Or else my great exploits? Perdy, 'tis more than needs.
>   (Geoffrey Bullough, *Narrative and Dramatic Sources
>   of Shakespeare*, vol. V)

The poem is saved from an early ending in mid stanza
(which some readers might think preferable) only when
Caesar decides that he might as well jog memories
anyway, and proceeds with his life story. But what is
interesting about the poem is that initial momentary hesi-
tation: 'What need I here recite the lineage whence I
came . . . ?' It is as if the poet experiences a sudden
uneasy awareness that it is a labour of supererogation
to retell a tale that every schoolboy knows.

This is what Shakespeare brilliantly takes into account
in his play. One of the two crucial factors in the organ-
ization of the action is the likelihood that the audience
will already know the sequence of events. The other is
that the characters don't share that knowledge. We must
remember that history was once current affairs, that what
is now the past was once the future – and nobody in the
play, with the possible exception of the Soothsayer, can
know what that future is to be. The point is underlined
by the welter of portents and prophecies that flood the
first half: the Soothsayer's prediction, 'Beware the ides
of March' (I.2.18); strange sights in the streets of Rome;
strange dreams troubling Caesar's wife; a sacrificial

offering without a heart. We know that all this points to Caesar's death in the Capitol, but for the characters it is all alike ambiguous. The future is something they are struggling to create, each to his own specifications, and the meaning of the portents is correspondingly contested: as Cicero says, 'men may construe things after their fashion, | Clean from the purpose of the things them-selves' (I.3.34–5). Caesar rises on the morning of the Ides of March to the news that Calphurnia has dreamed of his statue spouting blood, but what this means, and indeed whether it means anything at all, is a matter of dispute: Calphurnia takes it as an intimation that blood will similarly gush from Caesar's body if he goes to the Senate, and urges him to heed the warning and stay at home; Decius Brutus, anxious that Caesar should go to meet that very fate, finds an alternative interpretation more palatable to his victim, and finally laughs it off as a triviality – '"Break up the Senate till another time, | When Caesar's wife shall meet with better dreams"' (II.2.98–9). The supernatural foreshadowings only shed their opacity once the Ides of March are not only come but gone; and retrospect is a point of view unavailable to the people on stage.

The effect of this juxtaposition of our knowledge with the characters' uncertainty is to make *Julius Caesar* not only a drama of politics but also, and simultaneously, a drama of the suspense that goes with historical hind-sight. In the great arc of the action that runs through the second act and into the third, almost every scene shows the characters taking decisions which move events ever closer to the outcome we know already: Caesar's death. Yet at each point there is a quality of wavering uncertainty: in this version of the story, nothing is ever a foregone conclusion, and the play repeatedly teases us with the possibility that this time history will be different. 'Shall no man else be touched but only Caesar?' (II.1.154). Brutus decides that Mark Antony shall be spared, but not before Cassius has spoken up for killing him along with Caesar. 'What mean you, Caesar? Think you to walk forth?' asks Calphurnia (II.2.8). Caesar ultimately decides to go to the Senate, but in the course of the scene he also decides not to, and has to be cajoled by Decius Brutus. When he gets there he is presented with Artemidorus' warning against the conspirators: 'O Caesar, read mine first; for mine's a suit | That touches Caesar nearer' (III.1.6–7). And, in the action which perhaps redounds most to his political credit, Caesar decides not to: 'What touches us ourself shall be last served' (III.1.8). The momentum of this section of the play comes in part from a series of historic bad decisions whose outcome ultimately destroys those who take them: Caesar is assassinated, and Mark Antony lives on to be the nemesis of his killers. It is like watching men unwittingly dig their own graves.

So, even as a part of us is engaged in the escalating political conflict, there must also be a detached sense of the futility of it all. When Brutus and Cassius applaud what they see as their own political heroism, welcome the return of liberty to Rome and think ahead to their immortal memory, they are giving events a misplaced finality, as if politics can now give way to history. When they make their exit, preparing to explain themselves before the people, control of the stage passes to Antony, and Octavius' servant arrives to herald the approach of the one major character who has yet to appear. The staging here confutes the conspirators by emphasizing that the play is not over as their behaviour seems to imply: we are only halfway through, and with Caesar dead it can now emerge that the historic act was also a political mistake.

Brutus may initially succeed in justifying the murder, before Antony is able to seize the initiative, but the crowd's ebullient reaction shows how little impact the conspirators have made on the terms of political debate. Instead of liberty and republicanism, we see a nascent personality cult for Brutus on the same terms as that for Caesar, statues and all:

FIRST PLEBEIAN
Bring him with triumph home unto his house.
SECOND PLEBEIAN
Give him a statue with his ancestors.
THIRD PLEBEIAN
Let him be Caesar. (III.2.49–51)

After Antony begins his work of turning the crowd, moreover, one of the first voices of doubt says, tellingly, 'I fear there will a worse come in his place' (III.2.112). The removal of Caesar is construed not in terms of the opportunity it affords to restore an old form of government or even devise a new, but simply as the creation of a vacancy which must be filled: another popular hero, another potential dictator; and that is not what the conspirators intended at all.

In Cassius' terms what the assassination proves, in a graphic and extreme way, is that Caesar is no god, that he has human limitations: like Shylock, if you prick him, does he not bleed? But its effect is, on the contrary, to release him from those limitations. Literally, it makes him a ghost, freed from the confines of his fleshly body and able to travel anywhere – even, as we see, to the very tent of Brutus at Sardis. Politically, it resolves the contradiction between the image and the actuality of

Caesar, by removing the actuality: in effect, it takes from Caesar his greatest political weakness. Caesar dead is paradoxically a stronger figure than Caesar living; and if he himself can no longer claim power on that account, he has a lieutenant, and he has an heir, who can. Connection with Caesar ennobles and empowers Mark Antony and Octavius; Caesar's assassins are damned by the same token.

TOMORROW BELONGS TO WHOM?

The second half of *Julius Caesar* can seem choppy and unstructured after the taut plot management of the first. From the conspirators' gathering in Brutus' orchard (II.1) to the lynching of Cinna the Poet (III.3) the action runs in unbroken sequence through the events of a single day, the Ides of March; but thereafter everything accelerates jerkily towards the play's conclusion at the battle of Philippi (which, historically, took place two years later in 42 BC). At the same time the political dimension becomes almost incidental: the focus shifts to the ups and downs in the personal relationship between Brutus and Cassius, and their attitude to the one significant public event in this part of the play, the battle, is consistently couched in terms of the likelihood of defeat rather than the opportunities that victory would bring. If the first half showed the conservative republicans making history in one transforming act, the second half deals with their inability to live in the future that ensues.

One way in which the political initiative is shown to be moving away from the conspirators is by a subtle shift of emphasis. Earlier on characters tended to be differentiated from the norm by reference to their age: figures

like silver-haired Cicero, for example, or Publius, the
elderly senator whom Cassius touchingly protects from
the crowd in the aftermath of the murder (III.1.92–3).
We have seen that in this conflict between tradition and
change older people tend to be valued and respected by
the republican faction. But as events move onwards the
focus shifts increasingly to people who are younger than
the norm, like Brutus' brother-in-law Cato and, as he is
insistently called in the dialogue, 'young Octavius'
(IV.3.92, 151, 166). There is an added emphasis too on
the fact that Brutus' servant Lucius is a boy, with a boy's
need for his sleep – 'I know young bloods look for a
time of rest', remarks Brutus (IV.3.260) with a consideration he doesn't offer his adult colleagues. (Uniquely
in this scene, moreover, the original stage directions,
often a useful guide to the way Shakespeare is thinking
about his characters, call the character '*Boy*' as well as
by name.)

'I have seen more days than you', Antony tells
Octavius (IV.1.18) when they first disagree, asserting his
seniority and, it is implied, his greater experience and
better judgement. Yet as the second half develops
everyone seems to have less time for the voice of matu-
rity – even Brutus and Cassius themselves. When a poet
presumes on his age to offer the quarrelling generals
some rhyming advice from Homer – 'Love, and be
friends, as two such men should be; | For I have seen
more years, I'm sure, than ye' (IV.3.129–30) – he gets
short shrift. The echo of Antony's words, spoken around
twelve minutes earlier, underlines how the action is
moving into a young man's world where years of life
do not necessarily confer authority. In the same scene,
when the two republican friends disagree over strategy,
it is Brutus' views' that are adopted; yet it is Cassius who

has been established as the 'elder' (IV.3.56) and more experienced soldier. Much the same thing happens in the opposite camp: in the next scene it is young Octavius and not Mark Antony who proves the better judge of the enemy's tactics, and who gets his way in the conduct of the battle.

It is apt that Cassius should die upon his birthday, the day that marks another advance in his age. He has already been called 'Old Cassius' (V.1.63) by Mark Antony, and we are now shown signs of the physical decrepitude of which he was earlier so critical in Caesar: 'My sight was ever thick', he admits (V.3.21). Yet it is to the point that this myopia is a chronic infirmity rather than a senile deterioration: 'ever' rather than newly thick sight. If he is now 'Old Cassius', he is also the same old Cassius, as puritanically antitheatrical as he was when Caesar wished him fatter and more contented: Antony's remark is provoked by Cassius' taunts of 'masquer' and 'reveller' (V.1.62). The republicans are pushed upwards into disregarded seniority by the emergence of even younger men, but they are also self-consistent to the point of inflexibility.

The point is first made at the very fulcrum of the play, in the contrast between Brutus and Antony as they address the Roman people after the assassination. Brutus fondly supposes that his measured prose speech, with its formal, balanced rhetorical patterning, can create a corresponding stability in his audience, bringing them firmly and securely round to his point of view. In that deluded confidence he leaves the Forum and hands the plebeians over to Antony's manipulation in a speech which, though written in verse, is less overtly structured and less concerned to inculcate a precise intellectual position. Antony can afford to undermine the rational approach with the emotive because, unlike Brutus, he is uncommitted to any particular political future: 'Now let it work. Mischief, thou art afoot, | Take thou what course thou wilt' (III.2.261–2). He creates chaos, dramatized not only in the terrifying irrationality with which the excited mob tears poor Cinna to pieces but also in the colder but no less murderous measures taken by the new triumvirate in the scene after that (IV.1). Antony can ride the unpredictability of the times, exploiting the temporary usefulness of Lepidus and casually bartering the life of nephew for brother to keep him happy. Brutus and Cassius, however, can only ride away, 'like madmen through the gates of Rome' (III.2.271), abandoning the city whose minds they have failed to win.

They do much the same when the battle goes against them at Philippi. For much of the play the two men have strikingly different attitudes to suicide. Cassius talks about it all the time as a possible response to adverse circumstances: he says he will kill himself if Caesar is crowned (I.3.89) and if the plot is discovered (III.1.20–22), and his quarrel with Brutus culminates in his offering his friend a dagger and his own breast to sheathe it in (IV.3.99–100). Self-destruction, he argues, is the last power left to the powerless:

> Cassius from bondage will deliver Cassius.
> Therein, ye gods, you make the weak most strong;
> Therein, ye gods, you tyrants do defeat. (I.3.90–92)

This is an aspect of his highly developed sense of *Romanitas* which achieves ultimate fulfilment at Philippi: Shakespeare tended to see suicide as a distinctive feature of the Roman sense of honour which, in a later tragedy set in Christian society, Macbeth dismisses as playing the Roman fool.

Brutus, however, initially considers suicide dishonourable, a failure of the dispassionate stoicism with
which, twice over, he bears the news of Portia's death.
He tells Cassius that he will meet defeat in battle,

> Even by the rule of that philosophy
> By which I did blame Cato for the death
> Which he did give himself – I know not how,
> But I do find it cowardly and vile,
> For fear of what might fall, so to prevent
> The time of life . . . (V.1.100–105)

If he cannot bring himself to extend quite the same
blame to Cato's daughter, whose death was also self-
inflicted, he only goes so far as to give her the excuse
of diminished responsibility caused by immoderate
grief: 'she fell distract, | And, her attendants absent,
swallowed fire' (IV.3.153–4). We have no way of
knowing whether Portia's insanity was a clinical reality
or just something construed after the event from the
fact of her suicide, an inference that allows Brutus, in
his own grief, to reconcile love and disapproval. (In
Plutarch it is an entirely rational, willed act with no
hint of madness.) The paradox is that suicide is itself
stoical, and the endurance of pain which stoicism entails
can often resemble distraction. There is a slightly
hysterical quality in Cassius' going out in a thunder-
storm with his doublet undone and inviting the lightning to strike him on the breast, or in Portia's wounding
herself in the thigh to prove to Brutus that she can keep
his secrets; but these are considered acts with a purpose
beyond self-mutilation. So too can suicide be: that is
the lesson Brutus learns at Philippi.

Killing themselves in defeat, then, is the conspirators'

final act of self-consistency, straightforwardly for Cassius as the exercise of what has always been his last resort, and for Brutus a noble death whose philosophical validity he has never till now understood:

> Our enemies have beat us to the pit.
> It is more worthy to leap in ourselves
> Than tarry till they push us. (V.5.23–5)

But it is also an act of despair, the ultimate replay of their leaving Rome in the hands of the riotous mob after persuasion had failed. Brutus calls dead Cassius 'The last of all the Romans' (V.3.99): he can imagine no future in which their political ideals and values, their definition of what it is to be a Roman, will have any place. Their part in history is finished: unable to grow into the new world their actions have brought about, they are yesterday's men, and all they can do is recognize the fact and opt out of a futurity which, the audience knows, has always belonged to the Caesars.

Martin Wiggins

The Play in Performance

The first recorded performance of *Julius Caesar* was seen by Thomas Platter at London's newest theatre, the Globe, on the afternoon of Tuesday 11 September 1599, when the play was probably no more than a few months old. (Platter gave the date as 21 September, and this is repeated in the standard reference books; but, like most mainland Europeans, he used the Gregorian calendar, whereas England still used the calendar introduced by Julius Caesar in 45 BC. For everyone else in the theatre 21 September was ten days into the future.) Platter, a Swiss medical student from a drama-minded family, enjoyed the performance and wrote up the visit in his journal, but he said little about the content of the play – the story was, after all, a familiar one. However, the scraps of information he did record, together with everything else we know about general staging practice at the Globe, allow us to deduce something about how *Julius Caesar* was originally designed as a piece for performance. Those conclusions are as relevant to performers in the twenty-first century as they were in the sixteenth.

One important thing Platter notes is that the production was staged by about fifteen actors; he may have been underestimating slightly, but the figure more or less matches the size of Shakespeare's company, the Lord

Chamberlain's Men. A corollary is that, as in most later productions, the minor roles must have been extensively doubled: the play contains a minimum of fifty distinct speaking parts, ranging from the principal characters to barely individuated soldiers and plebeians, but it is structured in a way that facilitates doubling. Except for Caesar, Cassius, Brutus, Antony and Lucius, no character appears in both the early and the later scenes, and the challenge of dividing the other roles among a small cast offers both opportunities and limitations.

For example, there are six minor conspirators in the first half of the play and twelve officers in Brutus' and Cassius' army in the second half. Directors rarely go so far as to conflate these roles, lengthening the stage-lives of Casca, Trebonius and the rest who would otherwise disappear after the assassination scene; but, given the arithmetic, might some or even all of them be doubled? If they are, and if the actors remain recognizable in their battlefield armour, then there will be a degree of human continuity in the republican ranks throughout the play. But conversely, if the doubling here is arbitrary and pragmatic, then it will leave open the option to imply that the other conspirators have met with the same fate as Cinna the Poet; and it will also enhance the sense of a second half full of new people emerging out of the welter of history for their brief moments of petty prominence.

A key emergent figure is Octavius, whose prominence will extend beyond the end of the play: he speaks the closing lines and is destined to become the sole ruler of the Roman world. The role can be doubled, but avoiding this has its advantages: the play gains a potent suggestion of the forward movement of history if, when he first appears in Act IV, scene 1, Octavius is not only a new character but also a new face. If production economy dictates that the actor takes another role early on, then, as with the conspirators, it needs to be decided whether or not the doubling should carry any artistic significance. If the audience is simply meant to affect not to notice, then most first-half roles are practical possibilities, except perhaps the plebeians and Cinna the Poet; sometimes Octavius has even, bizarrely, been doubled with one of his great-uncle's assassins. A more evocative option (albeit one that I have never seen attempted in production) might be to double him with Caesar. That would require an actor of some range, able to play both an old man and a young, and able to cope with two challenging costume changes: from a bloody corpse in Act III, scene 2 to a youth in Act IV, scene 1, and, between Act IV, scene 3 and Act V, scene 1, from ghost to general in about a minute's playing time. The effect would be to give greater centrality to the role of Caesar by effectively reincarnating him in the person of his only blood-relation in the cast, balancing the republican and Caesarian figures in a play that is otherwise apt to be dominated by the role of Brutus.

Many members of the large cast do not need to be individually distinctive, however: at one level they function almost as human scenery. The early performances at the Globe had no stage sets: this is why, in Act III, scene 1 and Act IV, scenes 2–3, the location can shift fluidly from outdoors to indoors without the characters leaving the stage. The action of the play took place in front of the permanent architecture of the playhouse, so all information about a scene's location and environment would be carried by the dialogue and the foreground visuals. In *Julius Caesar* part of the effect is created by the number of human bodies present at any particular moment: the action alternates between intimate sequences in which characters soliloquize or talk privately with one another, and public scenes in which the stage is crowded. It is never fuller than during Caesar's three principal scenes (I.2, II.2 and III.1), which contributes to our sense of his vast political importance (and perhaps also his charisma, depending on how the crowd is played), while the impression of things falling to pieces in the aftermath of the assassination comes in part from a progressive reduction in the numbers of visible cast members: in the second half's most populous scene (V.1) there are only seven named characters, plus soldiers and a messenger, compared with eleven, plus plebeians and Soothsayer, in Act I, scene 2, and thirteen, plus Soothsayer, in Act III, scene 1. This diminution is true even in the battle sequence: the stage is mainly held by twosomes and threesomes, and Brutus and Cassius ultimately go down to lonely deaths with only one other living character present.

The play can be very effective with its human scale inflated in production by the inclusion of a large, undifferentiated crowd: this intensifies the underlying threat of mob violence and, in Cinna the Poet's scene (III.3), adds to the sense of the plebeians as a many-headed monster which cannot be controlled because, unlike Mark Antony, Cinna can reason with only one of its heads at a time. Film versions, unconstrained by the limitations of theatre space and theatre budgets, can achieve this by simply engaging a cast of thousands: an especially notable example is Joseph L. Mankiewicz's 1953 film, with Marlon Brando as Antony, in which the overcrowded Forum scene (III.2) is all the more powerful when seen in a high-definition print on a cinema-sized screen. In the theatre the only comparable expedient is to co-opt

the audience of a promenade production, casting them
as the crowd; but this can detract from the more intimate
scenes, and may leave the promenaders in harm's way
during the battle. (When the Royal Shakespeare Company
took this approach in 1993 the milling audience was driven
back against the walls by yelling soldiers toting machine-
guns, leaving a central space clear for fighting.) However,
with Platter's fifteen-actor estimate in mind, there is also
a case for a relatively sparer production.

The most populated scene in the text as written (III.1)
begins with fourteen characters onstage. Some other
editions also call for supernumerary senators and citizens, but they aren't in the text as it was first published,
probably because the Lord Chamberlain's Men simply
didn't have anybody to spare at this point: this may be a
scene in which every adult male actor is on stage, with
only the three boy actors (playing Portia, Calphurnia and
Lucius) unemployed. This is supported by the technical
construction of this stretch of the action: anyone who
needs to change for doubling can do so while the boys
and Soothsayer hold the stage in Act II, scene 4, and in
Act III, scene 1 the non-aligned senators' early exit after
the assassination gives them plenty of time to get into
their next roles, probably as members of the mob in Act
III, scene 2. But what matters is how the numbers on
stage change the focus and impact of the murder. It is
the play's most public scene, but once Trebonius has
drawn away Mark Antony there are nevertheless only
eleven or twelve people onstage: Caesar, six assassins,
four other senators and perhaps the Soothsayer. With
more extras present cluttering the audience's sight-lines,
Caesar is struck down by an aggressively active minority;
but in the scene as Shakespeare seems to have written it,
he is one man overwhelmed by many.

One of the play's greatest challenges to its performers is the second half, when the action can all too easily fragment and lose focus. During countless performances of *Julius Caesar* over many years there was always a point, shortly after the interval, when my heart would sink at the knowledge that we were about to begin the quarrel scene (IV.2–3 in this edition). It is the longest single scene in the play, running for about twenty minutes uncut (which is around one-sixth of the play's typical running time), and it has the potential to be the most boring stretch of the action: even with accomplished actors playing Brutus and Cassius there can be something profoundly irritating about the spectacle of two grown men arguing petulantly over trivia while the movement of history passes them by. Yet it is also true that, from the seventeenth century onwards, the quarrel scene has been one of the most admired in the play; some Victorian actors even extracted it for performance on its own as a two-handed tour de force. The Royal Shakespeare Company recaptured that greatness when it staged the play in 2001: the collision between the nervy Cassius of Tim Pigott-Smith and Greg Hicks's ramrod Brutus was, unusually, the highlight of the production. Partly this was because the performances conveyed how much it mattered to the two men that their personal relations should have deteriorated so badly: in collaborating to assassinate Caesar they had invested so heavily in one another that the breakdown of their friendship was as catastrophic as the broader decline in their political and military fortunes. That interpretation of the scene was significantly abetted by a major structural choice: in this production the play was performed without an interval.

Much of the problem of the second half stems from our thinking of it *as* a 'second half'. In the modern theatre there are many factors which encourage the director of any play to schedule an interval, ranging from the quiet influence of tradition to a theatre bar's commercial imperative to sell interval drinks, to biological limitations like the capacity of the human bladder. In *Julius Caesar* there are also more specific pressures. One is the need to mop blood off the stage: the assassination scene requires at least enough blood for seven characters to cover their hands and forearms with it, and many a Forum scene has featured Brutus, Antony and the plebeians picking their way through the squelchy residue before the stagehands have a chance to clean up. A little later some productions need to change their scenery after the action leaves Rome, forcing a late interval after Act IV, scene 1. This can also be justified as a kind of punctuation marking the change of location; but directors thinking in these terms more often want to break the action after a high point of tension, and choose to end the first half on the murder of Cinna the Poet (III.3). At the Globe in 1599, however, the play was performed without interval from the first scene to the last: it was designed as a continous run of action rather than a two-part structure.

Wherever you choose to insert a mid-play interval into *Julius Caesar*, you do a disservice to everything that follows. An audience will always understand intellectually that the events of the later scenes wind out from the assassination's violent rupture of Rome's political status quo, but it is hard to *feel* that when coming back to the action after a break. The Ides of March sequence, running from Act II, scene 1 to Act III, scene 3, has an enormous forward momentum, each scene picking up where the last left off. The later scenes depend on that momentum to carry the audience through to the end of the play. From a standing start the quarrel scene can be tedious and the battle perfunctory; without an interval they are a powerful diminuendo from the play's early climax in Act III, scene 1.

To our eyes, the look of the play at the Globe in 1599 would have been 'Elizabethan': the dialogue tells us that Caesar wears a doublet in Act I, scene 2, and in Act II, scene 1 the conspirators muffle themselves up in voluminous cloaks and wide-brimmed hats which they can pull down over their ears. (Some modern productions have pointedly made them resemble the Gunpowder Plotters of 1605.) To contemporaries like Platter, however, the production would probably have looked 'Roman', for actors in Roman plays added some classical accoutrements to their sixteenth-century styles: Caesar's 'mantle' which ends up perforated with bloody gashes was probably a version of a toga. For a modern production the key question is, how Roman should Rome be? Full historical authenticity, not attempted in 1599, can have its drawbacks. The BBC's 1978 production, in accordance with the policy of the 'Complete Television Shakespeare' series, was set in a painstakingly researched recreation of 44 BC, but the austerity of late republican clothing made the play a visually drab experience. In the theatre the effect can be anonymizing: without the luxury of close-ups, a cast all dressed in similar white togas becomes hard to differentiate, and many designers seeking a Roman ambience have preferred the lusher clothing of the later imperial period, or a generic approximation of classical styles. Other productions have transplanted the action wholesale into a later period, which affects not only the play's look but its interpretation.

Of course, even a 'Roman' production can have contemporary implications; dictators have always feared and censored historians as well as agitators. Catherine the

Great's Russia, Hitler's Germany, Salazar's Portugal, Selassie's Ethiopia: the list of unsavoury authoritarian regimes to have cut or banned *Julius Caesar* testifies to the transferable power of its politics. Since the middle of the twentieth century productions have often located the action in a modern totalitarian state, making Caesar either Fascist leader or Communist commissar and the plebeians a baying mob of Brownshirts or jackbooted storm troopers. The risk here is of simplifying the action: such a Caesar can be too blatantly an object of hatred and disgust, with Brutus conversely sentimentalized as a democratic liberal, his declared ideals overstressed at the expense of the flaws in his reasoning. (Much of the interpretation of the role hangs on the soliloquy in Act II, scene 1 in which he proposes killing Caesar not because he *is* a tyrant but in case he might become one at some time in the future: what balance the actor strikes between the sincerity of his argument and its intellectual unsoundness will be crucial in defining levels of audience sympathy.) Modern resonances may also enhance the horror of collapsing social order after the assassination, but again the director needs to consider carefully how far such allusions will occlude issues of responsibility and historical causation. In the 1993 RSC production, for example, the civil war consciously echoed the chaos in the Balkans after the disintegration of Yugoslavia: it was powerful because it was real and contemporary, but that emotional impact made it easier to read the war merely as one of the nasty things that history periodically throws at humanity, and harder to engage with the already difficult issues of how such wars start and how much free citizens should tolerate in order to prevent them.

The last thing Platter saw at the Globe was not strictly part of the play proper: members of the cast danced

together in male and female costume. To modern
observers this may appear quaint or eccentric (as it did
in the new Globe's quatercentenary revival of *Julius
Caesar* in 1999), and its direct relevance to productions
today is limited to attempted antiquarian reconstructions
of the original staging. However, it tells us something
about how early audiences would have experienced the
play: not as an independent work but as the main feature
in an afternoon's programme of entertainment, perhaps
more like the modern cinema than the modern theatre.
That has a bearing on the wider issue of audience engagement. To follow tragedy with dancing seems to us slightly
improper, as if making light of the gravity of the
preceding action; but it also prevents an audience from
being sucked in by that gravity, and so, perhaps, plays a
part in re-establishing the sense of detachment and historical distance on which a measured political analysis ultimately depends. The change in our cultural sensibility
since the sixteenth century may prevent modern productions from ending in the same way as the Globe's did;
but they might find it worthwhile experimenting with
other staging devices which do the same job.

Martin Wiggins

Further Reading

All the other principal series of Shakespeare texts include reasonably up-to-date editions of *Julius Caesar*: the Oxford Shakespeare (edited by Arthur Humphreys, 1984), the New Cambridge Shakespeare (edited by Marvin Spevack, 1988) and the Arden Shakespeare (edited by David Daniell, 1998). The standard collection of source materials for Shakespeare's works is Geoffrey Bullough's *Narrative and Dramatic Sources of Shakespeare* (1957–75). *Julius Caesar* features in volume V: fourteen texts are reprinted complete or in extract, with a detailed introductory essay, providing a good overview of classical and Renaissance representations of Caesar in history and drama. The principal source, Sir Thomas North's translation of Plutarch's *Lives of the Noble Grecians and Romans*, is reproduced in *Shakespeare's Plutarch*, ed. T. J. B. Spencer (1964). David C. Green's *Julius Caesar and Its Source* (1979) is a careful account of how Shakespeare transformed Plutarch in writing the play.

A good starting point for the study of *Julius Caesar* as one of Shakespeare's 'Roman plays' is Alexander Leggatt's essay on the group in *Shakespeare: An Oxford Guide* (2003), edited by Stanley Wells and Lena Cowen Orlin; Leggatt supplements his account with a detailed reading of *Julius Caesar*. Useful longer works on the

subject include Robert Miola, *Shakespeare's Rome* (1983),
Vivian Thomas, *Shakespeare's Roman Worlds* (1989) and
chapter 5 of Ralph Berry's *Tragic Instance* (1999). Other
books exploring particular aspects of the play's creation
of a specifically Roman cultural setting are Jan H. Blits's
acute political analysis, *The End of the Ancient Republic*
(1982); Naomi Conn Liebler's *Shakespeare's Festive
Tragedy: The Ritual Foundations of Genre* (1995), which
covers the importance of communal ritual in the play;
and Geoffrey Miles's *Shakespeare and the Constant Romans*
(1996), which considers the action in terms of masculinity
and stoicism. Stoicism also features as an element of character psychology in A. D. Nuttall's reading of the play
in *A New Mimesis: Shakespeare and the Representation of
Reality* (1983). In addition, there is the issue of how far
the play transcends its cultural setting, and how far it is
a product of other intellectual traditions. In *Shakespeare's
Pagan World* (1974) J. L. Simmons explores the relevance of a Christian perspective in Shakespeare's treat-
ment of classical history, and John Roe reads the play's
politics in terms of one seminal sixteenth-century thinker
in his *Shakespeare and Machiavelli* (2002).

The play's construction as an artefact is the subject
of Adrien Bonjour's *The Structure of Julius Caesar* (1958),
which is also attentive to features of its language and
narrative, such as recurring imagery and the leitmotifs
of superstition, suicide and sleep. Another key study of
imagery is Maurice Charney's *Shakespeare's Roman Plays*
(1961). The play is also responsive to more avant-garde
modes of critical enquiry, of which a notable example is
René Girard's *A Theatre of Envy* (1991), which attends
to difficult issues of desire and sacrifice in appealingly
lucid prose.

A number of general and introductory studies of the

play, in various series, are entitled simply *Julius Caesar*.
Vivian Thomas, in the Harvester New Critical Introductions series (1992), pays particular attention to issues
of genre, source material and style. Anthony Davies
writes about the play's context and language in the
Cambridge Student Guides series (2002), and provides
a painless introduction to some of the more theoretical
approaches taken by modern criticism. A good, acces-
sible example of those approaches in action is Richard
Wilson's volume for Penguin Critical Studies (1992),
while Mary Hamer's contribution to the Writers and
Their Work series (1998) is a feminist analysis dealing
with the role and function of women in the play. There
are also a number of useful anthologies of critical writing:
Maurice Charney (ed.), *Discussions of Shakespeare's
Roman Plays* (1964); Leonard F. Dean (ed.), *Twentieth-
Century Interpretations of 'Julius Caesar'* (1968); Peter
Ure (ed.), *'Julius Caesar': A Casebook* (1969); Harold
Bloom (ed.), *William Shakespeare's 'Julius Caesar':
Modern Critical Interpretations* (1988); and Richard Wilson
(ed.), *New Casebooks: 'Julius Caesar'* (2002).

The standard account of the play's stage history is
John Ripley's *'Julius Caesar' on Stage in England and
America, 1599–1973* (1980). This may be usefully supplemented with Michael Dobson's study of the play's political applications after the Restoration, in Jean I. Marsden
(ed.), *The Appropriation of Shakespeare: Post-Renaissance
Reconstructions of the Works and the Myth* (1991). B. S.
Field's *Shakespeare's 'Julius Caesar': A Production Collection* (1980) offers a sequential commentary on the play
by theatre professionals, with reference to (and abun-
dant photographs from) a range of US productions. The
actor Corin Redgrave, whose experience of the play
extended from Octavius (1972) to Brutus (1986) to Caesar

in a production he also directed (1996), writes a compendious account in the Faber Actors on Shakespeare series, another volume entitled just *Julius Caesar* (2003). Two early adaptations of the play, staged at the Theatre Royal in 1680 and by J. P. Kemble in 1812, have been published in facsimile by the Cornmarket Press (1969 and 1970 respectively).

John W. Velz's *'The Tragedy of Julius Caesar': A Bibliography to Supplement the New Variorum Edition of 1913* (1977) offers a full list of writing on the play up to 1974. This may be supplemented with reference to chapter 14 of Stanley Wells (ed.), *Shakespeare: A Bibliographical Guide* (1990).

THE TRAGEDY OF
JULIUS CAESAR

The Characters in the Play

Julius CAESAR
CALPHURNIA, his wife

Marcus BRUTUS ⎫
Caius CASSIUS ⎪
CASCA ⎪
TREBONIUS ⎬ conspirators against Caesar
DECIUS Brutus ⎪
METELLUS Cimber ⎪
CINNA ⎪
Caius LIGARIUS ⎭

OCTAVIUS Caesar ⎫
Mark ANTONY ⎬ triumvirs after Caesar's death
LEPIDUS ⎭

CICERO ⎫
PUBLIUS ⎬ Senators
POPILIUS Lena ⎭

FLAVIUS ⎫
MARULLUS ⎬ Tribunes of the People

LUCILIUS
MESSALA
Young CATO
VOLUMNIUS
TITINIUS
VARRO   } followers of Brutus and Cassius
CLITUS
CLAUDIUS
DARDANIUS
Flavius
Labeo

PORTIA, Marcus Brutus's wife
ARTEMIDORUS
CINNA, a poet
PINDARUS, a servant of Cassius
LUCIUS   } servants of Brutus
STRATO

SOOTHSAYER
POET
COBBLER
CARPENTER
A SERVANT of Caesar
A SERVANT of Antony
A SERVANT of Octavius
The GHOST of Caesar
MESSENGER
SOLDIERS
PLEBEIANS
Senators
Attendants and others

*Enter Flavius, Marullus, and certain commoners
over the stage*

FLAVIUS

Hence! home, you idle creatures, get you home:
Is this a holiday? What, know you not,
Being mechanical, you ought not walk
Upon a labouring day without the sign
Of your profession? Speak, what trade art thou?

CARPENTER Why, sir, a carpenter.

MARULLUS

Where is thy leather apron, and thy rule?
What dost thou with thy best apparel on?
You, sir, what trade are you?

COBBLER Truly, sir, in respect of a fine workman, I   10
am but, as you would say, a cobbler.

MARULLUS But what trade art thou? Answer me directly.

COBBLER A trade, sir, that I hope I may use with a safe
conscience; which is, indeed, sir, a mender of bad soles.

FLAVIUS

What trade, thou knave? Thou naughty knave, what
trade?

COBBLER Nay, I beseech you, sir, be not out with me:
yet if you be out, sir, I can mend you.

MARULLUS

What meanest thou by that? Mend me, thou saucy
    fellow?

COBBLER Why, sir, cobble you.

FLAVIUS

20   Thou art a cobbler, art thou?

COBBLER Truly, sir, all that I live by is with the awl: I
    meddle with no tradesman's matters, nor women's mat-
    ters; but withal I am, indeed, sir, a surgeon to old shoes:
    when they are in great danger, I recover them. As proper
    men as ever trod upon neat's leather have gone upon
    my handiwork.

FLAVIUS

But wherefore art not in thy shop today?
Why dost thou lead these men about the streets?

COBBLER Truly, sir, to wear out their shoes to get myself
30   into more work. But indeed, sir, we make holiday to see
    Caesar, and to rejoice in his triumph.

MARULLUS

Wherefore rejoice? What conquest brings he home?
What tributaries follow him to Rome,
To grace in captive bonds his chariot wheels?
You blocks, you stones, you worse than senseless things!
O you hard hearts, you cruel men of Rome,
Knew you not Pompey? Many a time and oft
Have you climbed up to walls and battlements,
To towers and windows, yea, to chimney-tops,
40   Your infants in your arms, and there have sat
The livelong day, with patient expectation,
To see great Pompey pass the streets of Rome:
And when you saw his chariot but appear,
Have you not made an universal shout,
That Tiber trembled underneath her banks
To hear the replication of your sounds

Made in her concave shores?
And do you now put on your best attire?
And do you now cull out a holiday?
And do you now strew flowers in his way,   50
That comes in triumph over Pompey's blood?
Be gone!
Run to your houses, fall upon your knees,
Pray to the gods to intermit the plague
That needs must light on this ingratitude.

FLAVIUS

Go, go, good countrymen, and for this fault
Assemble all the poor men of your sort;
Draw them to Tiber banks, and weep your tears
Into the channel, till the lowest stream
Do kiss the most exalted shores of all.   60

Exeunt all the commoners

See where their basest mettle be not moved:
They vanish tongue-tied in their guiltiness.
Go you down that way towards the Capitol;
This way will I. Disrobe the images,
If you do find them decked with ceremonies.

MARULLUS

May we do so?
You know it is the feast of Lupercal.

FLAVIUS

It is no matter; let no images
Be hung with Caesar's trophies. I'll about,
And drive away the vulgar from the streets;   70
So do you too, where you perceive them thick.
These growing feathers plucked from Caesar's wing
Will make him fly an ordinary pitch,
Who else would soar above the view of men,
And keep us all in servile fearfulness.   *Exeunt*

I.2   *Enter Caesar; Antony, stripped for the course; Cal-*
               phurnia, Portia, Decius, Cicero, Brutus, Cassius,
               Casca, a Soothsayer, and a great crowd; after them
               Marullus and Flavius

CAESAR
   Calphurnia.
CASCA   Peace, ho! Caesar speaks.
CAESAR   Calphurnia.
CALPHURNIA Here, my lord.
CAESAR
   Stand you directly in Antonius' way
   When he doth run his course. Antonius.
ANTONY Caesar, my lord?
CAESAR
   Forget not, in your speed, Antonius,
   To touch Calphurnia; for our elders say,
   The barren, touchèd in this holy chase,
   Shake off their sterile curse.
ANTONY   I shall remember:
10 When Caesar says, 'Do this', it is performed.
CAESAR
   Set on, and leave no ceremony out.
SOOTHSAYER
   Caesar!
CAESAR
   Ha! Who calls?
CASCA
   Bid every noise be still; peace yet again!
CAESAR
   Who is it in the press that calls on me?
   I hear a tongue shriller than all the music
   Cry 'Caesar!' Speak. Caesar is turned to hear.
SOOTHSAYER
   Beware the ides of March.

CAESAR   What man is that?

BRUTUS

A soothsayer bids you beware the ides of March.

CAESAR

Set him before me; let me see his face.   20

CASSIUS

Fellow, come from the throng; look upon Caesar.

CAESAR

What sayst thou to me now? Speak once again.

SOOTHSAYER

Beware the ides of March.

CAESAR

He is a dreamer. Let us leave him. Pass.

Sennet. Exeunt
Brutus and Cassius remain

CASSIUS

Will you go see the order of the course?

BRUTUS

Not I.

CASSIUS

I pray you, do.

BRUTUS

I am not gamesome: I do lack some part
Of that quick spirit that is in Antony.
Let me not hinder, Cassius, your desires;   30
I'll leave you.

CASSIUS

Brutus, I do observe you now of late:
I have not from your eyes that gentleness
And show of love as I was wont to have.
You bear too stubborn and too strange a hand
Over your friend that loves you.

BRUTUS   Cassius,

Be not deceived: if I have veiled my look,

I turn the trouble of my countenance
Merely upon myself. Vexèd I am
40   Of late with passions of some difference,
Conceptions only proper to myself,
Which give some soil, perhaps, to my behaviours;
But let not therefore my good friends be grieved –
Among which number, Cassius, be you one –
Nor construe any further my neglect,
Than that poor Brutus, with himself at war,
Forgets the shows of love to other men.

CASSIUS
Then, Brutus, I have much mistook your passion,
By means whereof this breast of mine hath buried
50   Thoughts of great value, worthy cogitations.
Tell me, good Brutus, can you see your face?

BRUTUS
No, Cassius; for the eye sees not itself
But by reflection, by some other things.

CASSIUS
'Tis just;
And it is very much lamented, Brutus,
That you have no such mirrors as will turn
Your hidden worthiness into your eye,
That you might see your shadow. I have heard,
Where many of the best respect in Rome,
60   Except immortal Caesar, speaking of Brutus,
And groaning underneath this age's yoke,
Have wished that noble Brutus had his eyes.

BRUTUS
Into what dangers would you lead me, Cassius,
That you would have me seek into myself
For that which is not in me?

CASSIUS
Therefore, good Brutus, be prepared to hear;

And since you know you cannot see yourself
So well as by reflection, I, your glass,
Will modestly discover to yourself
That of yourself which you yet know not of.   70
And be not jealous on me, gentle Brutus:
Were I a common laughter, or did use
To stale with ordinary oaths my love
To every new protester; if you know
That I do fawn on men and hug them hard,
And after scandal them; or if you know
That I profess myself in banqueting
To all the rout, then hold me dangerous.

Flourish and shout

BRUTUS

What means this shouting? I do fear the people
Choose Caesar for their king.

CASSIUS   Ay, do you fear it?   80
Then must I think you would not have it so.

BRUTUS

I would not, Cassius; yet I love him well.
But wherefore do you hold me here so long?
What is it that you would impart to me?
If it be aught toward the general good,
Set honour in one eye, and death i'th'other,
And I will look on both indifferently;
For let the gods so speed me as I love
The name of honour more than I fear death.

CASSIUS

I know that virtue to be in you, Brutus,   90
As well as I do know your outward favour.
Well, honour is the subject of my story.
I cannot tell what you and other men
Think of this life; but for my single self,
I had as lief not be as live to be

In awe of such a thing as I myself.
I was born free as Caesar, so were you;
We both have fed as well, and we can both
Endure the winter's cold as well as he.
100 For once, upon a raw and gusty day,
The troubled Tiber chafing with her shores,
Caesar said to me, 'Dar'st thou, Cassius, now
Leap in with me into this angry flood,
And swim to yonder point?' Upon the word,
Accoutrèd as I was, I plungèd in
And bade him follow; so indeed he did.
The torrent roared, and we did buffet it
With lusty sinews, throwing it aside
And stemming it with hearts of controversy.
110 But ere we could arrive the point proposed,
Caesar cried, 'Help me, Cassius, or I sink!'
I, as Aeneas, our great ancestor,
Did from the flames of Troy upon his shoulder
The old Anchises bear, so from the waves of Tiber
Did I the tired Caesar. And this man
Is now become a god, and Cassius is
A wretched creature, and must bend his body
If Caesar carelessly but nod on him.
He had a fever when he was in Spain,
120 And when the fit was on him, I did mark
How he did shake; 'tis true, this god did shake;
His coward lips did from their colour fly,
And that same eye whose bend doth awe the world
Did lose his lustre; I did hear him groan;
Ay, and that tongue of his, that bade the Romans
Mark him and write his speeches in their books,
'Alas!' it cried, 'Give me some drink, Titinius',
As a sick girl. Ye gods, it doth amaze me
A man of such a feeble temper should

So get the start of the majestic world,   130
And bear the palm alone.
   Shout. Flourish

BRUTUS   Another general shout?
I do believe that these applauses are
For some new honours that are heaped on Caesar.

CASSIUS
Why, man, he doth bestride the narrow world
Like a Colossus, and we petty men
Walk under his huge legs, and peep about
To find ourselves dishonourable graves.
Men at some time are masters of their fates;
The fault, dear Brutus, is not in our stars,
But in ourselves, that we are underlings.   140
Brutus and Caesar. What should be in that 'Caesar'?
Why should that name be sounded more than yours?
Write them together, yours is as fair a name;
Sound them, it doth become the mouth as well;
Weigh them, it is as heavy; conjure with 'em,
'Brutus' will start a spirit as soon as 'Caesar'.
Now in the names of all the gods at once,
Upon what meat doth this our Caesar feed,
That he is grown so great? Age, thou art shamed!
Rome, thou hast lost the breed of noble bloods!   150
When went there by an age, since the great flood,
But it was famed with more than with one man?
When could they say, till now, that talked of Rome,
That her wide walls encompassed but one man?
Now is it Rome indeed, and room enough,
When there is in it but one only man.
O, you and I have heard our fathers say,
There was a Brutus once that would have brooked
Th'eternal devil to keep his state in Rome
As easily as a king.   160

BRUTUS
    That you do love me, I am nothing jealous;
    What you would work me to, I have some aim:
    How I have thought of this, and of these times,
    I shall recount hereafter. For this present,
    I would not – so with love I might entreat you –
    Be any further moved. What you have said
    I will consider; what you have to say
    I will with patience hear, and find a time
    Both meet to hear and answer such high things.
170   Till then, my noble friend, chew upon this:
    Brutus had rather be a villager
    Than to repute himself a son of Rome
    Under these hard conditions as this time
    Is like to lay upon us.
CASSIUS   I am glad
    That my weak words have struck but thus much show
    Of fire from Brutus.
     Enter Caesar and his train
BRUTUS
    The games are done and Caesar is returning.
CASSIUS
    As they pass by, pluck Casca by the sleeve,
    And he will, after his sour fashion, tell you
180   What hath proceeded worthy note today.
BRUTUS
    I will do so. But look you, Cassius,
    The angry spot doth glow on Caesar's brow,
    And all the rest look like a chidden train:
    Calphurnia's cheek is pale, and Cicero
    Looks with such ferret and such fiery eyes
    As we have seen him in the Capitol
    Being crossed in conference by some senators.

CASSIUS

    Casca will tell us what the matter is.

CAESAR

    Antonius.

ANTONY

    Caesar?   190

CAESAR

    Let me have men about me that are fat,
    Sleek-headed men, and such as sleep a-nights.
    Yond Cassius has a lean and hungry look;
    He thinks too much: such men are dangerous.

ANTONY

    Fear him not, Caesar; he's not dangerous;
    He is a noble Roman, and well given.

CAESAR

    Would he were fatter! But I fear him not;
    Yet if my name were liable to fear,
    I do not know the man I should avoid
    So soon as that spare Cassius. He reads much,   200
    He is a great observer, and he looks
    Quite through the deeds of men. He loves no plays,
    As thou dost, Antony; he hears no music;
    Seldom he smiles, and smiles in such a sort
    As if he mocked himself, and scorned his spirit
    That could be moved to smile at anything.
    Such men as he be never at heart's ease
    Whiles they behold a greater than themselves,
    And therefore are they very dangerous.
    I rather tell thee what is to be feared   210
    Than what I fear; for always I am Caesar.
    Come on my right hand, for this ear is deaf,
    And tell me truly what thou think'st of him.

                    Sennet. Exeunt Caesar and his train

CASCA

You pulled me by the cloak; would you speak with me?

BRUTUS

Ay, Casca, tell us what hath chanced today
That Caesar looks so sad.

CASCA Why, you were with him, were you not?

BRUTUS

I should not then ask Casca what had chanced.

CASCA Why, there was a crown offered him; and, being
220   offered him, he put it by with the back of his hand, thus;
and then the people fell a-shouting.

BRUTUS What was the second noise for?

CASCA Why, for that too.

CASSIUS They shouted thrice: what was the last cry for?

CASCA Why, for that too.

BRUTUS Was the crown offered him thrice?

CASCA Ay, marry, was't, and he put it by thrice, every
time gentler than other; and at every putting-by mine
honest neighbours shouted.

230 CASSIUS Who offered him the crown?

CASCA Why, Antony.

BRUTUS Tell us the manner of it, gentle Casca.

CASCA I can as well be hanged as tell the manner of it; it
was mere foolery; I did not mark it. I saw Mark Antony
offer him a crown; yet 'twas not a crown neither, 'twas
one of these coronets; and, as I told you, he put it by
once; but for all that, to my thinking, he would fain have
had it. Then he offered it to him again; then he put it by
again; but to my thinking, he was very loath to lay his
240   fingers off it. And then he offered it the third time; he
put it the third time by; and still as he refused it, the
rabblement hooted, and clapped their chopped hands,
and threw up their sweaty night-caps, and uttered such
a deal of stinking breath because Caesar refused the

crown, that it had, almost, choked Caesar; for he swooned, and fell down at it. And for mine own part, I durst not laugh, for fear of opening my lips and receiving the bad air.

CASSIUS

But soft, I pray you; what, did Caesar swoon?

CASCA He fell down in the market-place, and foamed at   250
mouth, and was speechless.

BRUTUS

'Tis very like; he hath the falling sickness.

CASSIUS

No, Caesar hath it not; but you, and I,
And honest Casca, we have the falling sickness.

CASCA I know not what you mean by that, but I am sure Caesar fell down. If the tag-rag people did not clap him and hiss him, according as he pleased and displeased them, as they use to do the players in the theatre, I am no true man.

BRUTUS

What said he when he came unto himself?   260

CASCA Marry, before he fell down, when he perceived the common herd was glad he refused the crown, he plucked me ope his doublet, and offered them his throat to cut. An I had been a man of any occupation, if I would not have taken him at a word, I would I might go to hell among the rogues. And so he fell. When he came to himself again, he said, if he had done or said anything amiss, he desired their worships to think it was his infirmity. Three or four wenches, where I stood, cried, 'Alas, good soul!' and forgave him with all their hearts;   270
but there's no heed to be taken of them; if Caesar had stabbed their mothers, they would have done no less.

BRUTUS

And after that, he came thus sad away?

CASCA Ay.

CASSIUS Did Cicero say anything?

CASCA Ay, he spoke Greek.

CASSIUS To what effect?

CASCA Nay, an I tell you that, I'll ne'er look you i'th'face
again. But those that understood him smiled at one another, and shook their heads; but for mine own part, it
was Greek to me. I could tell you more news too:
Marullus and Flavius, for pulling scarfs off Caesar's
images, are put to silence. Fare you well. There was more
foolery yet, if I could remember it.

CASSIUS Will you sup with me tonight, Casca?

CASCA No, I am promised forth.

CASSIUS Will you dine with me tomorrow?

CASCA Ay, if I be alive, and your mind hold, and your
dinner worth the eating.

CASSIUS Good; I will expect you.

CASCA Do so. Farewell, both.   *Exit*

BRUTUS

What a blunt fellow is this grown to be!
He was quick mettle when he went to school.

CASSIUS

So is he now in execution
Of any bold or noble enterprise,
However he puts on this tardy form.
This rudeness is a sauce to his good wit,
Which gives men stomach to disgest his words
With better appetite.

BRUTUS

And so it is. For this time I will leave you.
Tomorrow, if you please to speak with me,
I will come home to you; or if you will,
Come home to me, and I will wait for you.

CASSIUS

    I will do so: till then, think of the world.   *Exit Brutus*
    Well, Brutus, thou art noble; yet I see
    Thy honourable mettle may be wrought
    From that it is disposed: therefore it is meet
    That noble minds keep ever with their likes;
    For who so firm that cannot be seduced?
    Caesar doth bear me hard, but he loves Brutus.   310
    If I were Brutus now, and he were Cassius,
    He should not humour me. I will this night,
    In several hands, in at his windows throw,
    As if they came from several citizens,
    Writings, all tending to the great opinion
    That Rome holds of his name; wherein obscurely
    Caesar's ambition shall be glancèd at.
    And after this, let Caesar seat him sure,
    For we will shake him, or worse days endure.   *Exit*

    Thunder and lightning   I.3
    Enter Casca and Cicero, meeting

CICERO

    Good even, Casca: brought you Caesar home?
    Why are you breathless? and why stare you so?

CASCA

    Are not you moved, when all the sway of earth
    Shakes like a thing unfirm? O Cicero,
    I have seen tempests, when the scolding winds
    Have rived the knotty oaks, and I have seen
    Th'ambitious ocean swell and rage and foam,
    To be exalted with the threatening clouds;
    But never till tonight, never till now,
    Did I go through a tempest dropping fire.   10
    Either there is a civil strife in heaven,

Or else the world, too saucy with the gods,
Incenses them to send destruction.

CICERO

Why, saw you anything more wonderful?

CASCA

A common slave – you know him well by sight –
Held up his left hand, which did flame and burn
Like twenty torches joined; and yet his hand,
Not sensible of fire, remained unscorched.
Besides – I ha'not since put up my sword –
20   Against the Capitol I met a lion,
Who glazed upon me, and went surly by,
Without annoying me. And there were drawn
Upon a heap a hundred ghastly women,
Transformèd with their fear, who swore they saw
Men, all in fire, walk up and down the streets.
And yesterday the bird of night did sit,
Even at noon-day, upon the market-place,
Hooting and shrieking. When these prodigies
Do so conjointly meet, let not men say,
30   'These are their reasons, they are natural';
For I believe, they are portentous things
Unto the climate that they point upon.

CICERO

Indeed, it is a strange-disposèd time:
But men may construe things after their fashion,
Clean from the purpose of the things themselves.
Comes Caesar to the Capitol tomorrow?

CASCA

He doth; for he did bid Antonius
Send word to you he would be there tomorrow.

CICERO

Good night then, Casca: this disturbèd sky
40   Is not to walk in.

CASCA   Farewell, Cicero.   *Exit Cicero*
    Enter Cassius

CASSIUS
  Who's there?

CASCA   A Roman.

CASSIUS   Casca, by your voice.

CASCA
  Your ear is good. Cassius, what night is this!

CASSIUS
  A very pleasing night to honest men.

CASCA
  Who ever knew the heavens menace so?

CASSIUS
  Those that have known the earth so full of faults.
  For my part, I have walked about the streets,
  Submitting me unto the perilous night,
  And, thus unbracèd, Casca, as you see,
  Have bared my bosom to the thunder-stone;
  And when the cross blue lightning seemed to open   50
  The breast of heaven, I did present myself
  Even in the aim and very flash of it.

CASCA
  But wherefore did you so much tempt the heavens?
  It is the part of men to fear and tremble
  When the most mighty gods by tokens send
  Such dreadful heralds to astonish us.

CASSIUS
  You are dull, Casca, and those sparks of life
  That should be in a Roman you do want,
  Or else you use not. You look pale, and gaze,
  And put on fear, and cast yourself in wonder,   60
  To see the strange impatience of the heavens;
  But if you would consider the true cause
  Why all these fires, why all these gliding ghosts,

Why birds and beasts from quality and kind,
Why old men, fools, and children calculate,
Why all these things change from their ordinance,
Their natures, and pre-formèd faculties,
To monstrous quality, why, you shall find
That heaven hath infused them with these spirits
70   To make them instruments of fear and warning
Unto some monstrous state.
Now could I, Casca, name to thee a man
Most like this dreadful night,
That thunders, lightens, opens graves, and roars
As doth the lion in the Capitol;
A man no mightier than thyself, or me,
In personal action, yet prodigious grown,
And fearful, as these strange eruptions are.

CASCA
'Tis Caesar that you mean; is it not, Cassius?

CASSIUS
80   Let it be who it is: for Romans now
Have thews and limbs like to their ancestors;
But woe the while! our fathers' minds are dead,
And we are governed with our mothers' spirits:
Our yoke and sufferance show us womanish.

CASCA
Indeed, they say the senators tomorrow
Mean to establish Caesar as a king;
And he shall wear his crown by sea and land,
In every place save here in Italy.

CASSIUS
I know where I will wear this dagger then:
90   Cassius from bondage will deliver Cassius.
Therein, ye gods, you make the weak most strong;
Therein, ye gods, you tyrants do defeat.
Nor stony tower, nor walls of beaten brass,

Nor airless dungeon, nor strong links of iron,
Can be retentive to the strength of spirit;
But life, being weary of these worldly bars,
Never lacks power to dismiss itself.
If I know this, know all the world besides,
That part of tyranny that I do bear
I can shake off at pleasure.
    Thunder still

CASCA   So can I;   100
So every bondman in his own hand bears
The power to cancel his captivity.

CASSIUS
And why should Caesar be a tyrant then?
Poor man! I know he would not be a wolf,
But that he sees the Romans are but sheep.
He were no lion, were not Romans hinds.
Those that with haste will make a mighty fire
Begin it with weak straws. What trash is Rome,
What rubbish, and what offal, when it serves
For the base matter to illuminate   110
So vile a thing as Caesar! But, O grief,
Where hast thou led me? I perhaps speak this
Before a willing bondman; then I know
My answer must be made. But I am armed,
And dangers are to me indifferent.

CASCA
You speak to Casca, and to such a man
That is no fleering tell-tale. Hold, my hand;
Be factious for redress of all these griefs,
And I will set this foot of mine as far
As who goes farthest.

CASSIUS   There's a bargain made.   120
Now know you, Casca, I have moved already
Some certain of the noblest-minded Romans

To undergo with me an enterprise
Of honourable-dangerous consequence;
And I do know, by this they stay for me
In Pompey's Porch: for now, this fearful night,
There is no stir or walking in the streets;
And the complexion of the element
In favour's like the work we have in hand,
130   Most bloody, fiery, and most terrible.

    Enter Cinna

CASCA
Stand close awhile, for here comes one in haste.

CASSIUS
'Tis Cinna; I do know him by his gait;
He is a friend. Cinna, where haste you so?

CINNA
To find out you. Who's that? Metellus Cimber?

CASSIUS
No, it is Casca, one incorporate
To our attempts. Am I not stayed for, Cinna?

CINNA
I am glad on't. What a fearful night is this!
There's two or three of us have seen strange sights.

CASSIUS
Am I not stayed for? Tell me.

CINNA   Yes, you are.
140   O Cassius, if you could
But win the noble Brutus to our party –

CASSIUS
Be you content. Good Cinna, take this paper,
And look you lay it in the praetor's chair,
Where Brutus may but find it; and throw this
In at his window; set this up with wax
Upon old Brutus' statue. All this done,
Repair to Pompey's Porch, where you shall find us.

Is Decius Brutus and Trebonius there?

CINNA

All but Metellus Cimber; and he's gone
To seek you at your house. Well, I will hie,   150
And so bestow these papers as you bade me.

CASSIUS

That done, repair to Pompey's Theatre.   *Exit Cinna*
Come, Casca, you and I will yet ere day
See Brutus at his house: three parts of him
Is ours already, and the man entire
Upon the next encounter yields him ours.

CASCA

O, he sits high in all the people's hearts;
And that which would appear offence in us,
His countenance, like richest alchemy,
Will change to virtue and to worthiness.   160

CASSIUS

Him and his worth and our great need of him
You have right well conceited. Let us go,
For it is after midnight, and ere day
We will awake him, and be sure of him.   *Exeunt*

*

Enter Brutus in his orchard   II.I

BRUTUS

What, Lucius, ho!
I cannot, by the progress of the stars,
Give guess how near to day. Lucius, I say!
I would it were my fault to sleep so soundly.
When, Lucius, when? Awake, I say! What, Lucius!
    Enter Lucius

LUCIUS
  Called you, my lord?
BRUTUS
  Get me a taper in my study, Lucius;
  When it is lighted, come and call me here.
LUCIUS
  I will, my lord.   *Exit*
BRUTUS
10 It must be by his death; and for my part,
  I know no personal cause to spurn at him,
  But for the general. – He would be crowned.
  How that might change his nature, there's the question.
  It is the bright day that brings forth the adder,
  And that craves wary walking. Crown him! – that!
  And then, I grant, we put a sting in him
  That at his will he may do danger with.
  Th'abuse of greatness is when it disjoins
  Remorse from power; and, to speak truth of Caesar,
20 I have not known when his affections swayed
  More than his reason. But 'tis a common proof,
  That lowliness is young ambition's ladder,
  Whereto the climber-upward turns his face;
  But when he once attains the upmost round,
  He then unto the ladder turns his back,
  Looks in the clouds, scorning the base degrees
  By which he did ascend: so Caesar may;
  Then, lest he may, prevent. And, since the quarrel
  Will bear no colour for the thing he is,
30 Fashion it thus: that what he is, augmented,
  Would run to these and these extremities;
  And therefore think him as a serpent's egg
  Which, hatched, would, as his kind, grow mischievous,
  And kill him in the shell.

Enter Lucius

LUCIUS

The taper burneth in your closet, sir.
Searching the window for a flint, I found
This paper, thus sealed up; and I am sure
It did not lie there when I went to bed.

He gives him the letter

BRUTUS

Get you to bed again, it is not day.
Is not tomorrow, boy, the ides of March?   40

LUCIUS

I know not, sir.

BRUTUS

Look in the calendar and bring me word.

LUCIUS

I will, sir.   *Exit*

BRUTUS

The exhalations, whizzing in the air,
Give so much light that I may read by them.

He opens the letter and reads

Brutus, thou sleep'st: awake, and see thyself.
Shall Rome, etc. Speak, strike, redress.
'Brutus, thou sleep'st: awake.'
Such instigations have been often dropped
Where I have took them up.   50
'Shall Rome, etc.' Thus must I piece it out:
Shall Rome stand under one man's awe? What, Rome?
My ancestors did from the streets of Rome
The Tarquin drive, when he was called a king.
'Speak, strike, redress.' Am I entreated
To speak and strike? O Rome, I make thee promise,
If the redress will follow, thou receivest
Thy full petition at the hand of Brutus.

Enter Lucius

LUCIUS

Sir, March is wasted fifteen days.
    Knock within

BRUTUS

60   'Tis good. Go to the gate; somebody knocks.
                                          Exit Lucius

Since Cassius first did whet me against Caesar,
I have not slept.
Between the acting of a dreadful thing
And the first motion, all the interim is
Like a phantasma or a hideous dream:
The genius and the mortal instruments
Are then in council; and the state of man,
Like to a little kingdom, suffers then
The nature of an insurrection.
    Enter Lucius

LUCIUS

70   Sir, 'tis your brother Cassius at the door,
Who doth desire to see you.

BRUTUS   Is he alone?

LUCIUS

No, sir, there are more with him.

BRUTUS   Do you know them?

LUCIUS

No, sir, their hats are plucked about their ears,
And half their faces buried in their cloaks,
That by no means I may discover them
By any mark of favour.

BRUTUS   Let 'em enter.   *Exit Lucius*

They are the faction. O conspiracy,
Sham'st thou to show thy dangerous brow by night,
When evils are most free? O then, by day
80   Where wilt thou find a cavern dark enough

To mask thy monstrous visage? Seek none, conspiracy;
Hide it in smiles and affability:
For if thou path, thy native semblance on,
Not Erebus itself were dim enough
To hide thee from prevention.

Enter the conspirators: Cassius, Casca, Decius, Cinna,
Metellus, and Trebonius

CASSIUS
I think we are too bold upon your rest.
Good morrow, Brutus; do we trouble you?

BRUTUS
I have been up this hour, awake all night.
Know I these men that come along with you?

CASSIUS
Yes, every man of them; and no man here   90
But honours you; and every one doth wish
You had but that opinion of yourself
Which every noble Roman bears of you.
This is Trebonius.

BRUTUS   He is welcome hither.

CASSIUS
This, Decius Brutus.

BRUTUS   He is welcome too.

CASSIUS
This, Casca; this, Cinna; and this, Metellus Cimber.

BRUTUS
They are all welcome.
What watchful cares do interpose themselves
Betwixt your eyes and night?

CASSIUS
Shall I entreat a word?   100

They whisper apart

DECIUS
Here lies the east; doth not the day break here?

CASCA No.

CINNA

O pardon, sir, it doth; and yon grey lines
That fret the clouds are messengers of day.

CASCA

You shall confess that you are both deceived:
Here, as I point my sword, the sun arises,
Which is a great way growing on the south,
Weighing the youthful season of the year.
Some two months hence, up higher toward the north

110   He first presents his fire; and the high east
Stands, as the Capitol, directly here.

BRUTUS

Give me your hands all over, one by one.

CASSIUS

And let us swear our resolution.

BRUTUS

No, not an oath. If not the face of men,
The sufferance of our souls, the time's abuse –
If these be motives weak, break off betimes,
And every man hence to his idle bed;
So let high-sighted tyranny range on
Till each man drop by lottery. But if these,

120   As I am sure they do, bear fire enough
To kindle cowards and to steel with valour
The melting spirits of women, then, countrymen,
What need we any spur but our own cause
To prick us to redress? What other bond
Than secret Romans that have spoke the word,
And will not palter? And what other oath
Than honesty to honesty engaged
That this shall be, or we will fall for it?
Swear priests and cowards and men cautelous,

130   Old feeble carrions, and such suffering souls

That welcome wrongs; unto bad causes swear
Such creatures as men doubt; but do not stain
The even virtue of our enterprise,
Nor th'insuppressive mettle of our spirits,
To think that or our cause or our performance
Did need an oath; when every drop of blood
That every Roman bears, and nobly bears,
Is guilty of a several bastardy,
If he do break the smallest particle
Of any promise that hath passed from him.   140

CASSIUS
But what of Cicero? Shall we sound him?
I think he will stand very strong with us.

CASCA
Let us not leave him out.

CINNA   No, by no means.

METELLUS
O, let us have him, for his silver hairs
Will purchase us a good opinion
And buy men's voices to commend our deeds.
It shall be said his judgement ruled our hands;
Our youths and wildness shall no whit appear,
But all be buried in his gravity.

BRUTUS
O, name him not; let us not break with him,   150
For he will never follow anything
That other men begin.

CASSIUS   Then leave him out.

CASCA
Indeed he is not fit.

DECIUS
Shall no man else be touched but only Caesar?

CASSIUS
Decius, well urged. I think it is not meet

Mark Antony, so well beloved of Caesar,
Should outlive Caesar. We shall find of him
A shrewd contriver; and you know his means,
If he improve them, may well stretch so far
As to annoy us all; which to prevent,
Let Antony and Caesar fall together.

BRUTUS

Our course will seem too bloody, Caius Cassius,
To cut the head off and then hack the limbs,
Like wrath in death, and envy afterwards;
For Antony is but a limb of Caesar.
Let us be sacrificers, but not butchers, Caius.
We all stand up against the spirit of Caesar,
And in the spirit of men there is no blood.
O, that we then could come by Caesar's spirit,
And not dismember Caesar! But, alas,
Caesar must bleed for it. And, gentle friends,
Let's kill him boldly, but not wrathfully;
Let's carve him as a dish fit for the gods,
Not hew him as a carcass fit for hounds.
And let our hearts, as subtle masters do,
Stir up their servants to an act of rage,
And after seem to chide 'em. This shall make
Our purpose necessary, and not envious;
Which so appearing to the common eyes,
We shall be called purgers, not murderers.
And for Mark Antony, think not of him;
For he can do no more than Caesar's arm
When Caesar's head is off.

CASSIUS   Yet I fear him;
For in the ingrafted love he bears to Caesar –

BRUTUS

Alas, good Cassius, do not think of him.
If he love Caesar, all that he can do

Is to himself: take thought, and die for Caesar;
And that were much he should; for he is given
To sports, to wildness, and much company.

TREBONIUS

There is no fear in him; let him not die;   190
For he will live, and laugh at this hereafter.

A clock strikes

BRUTUS

Peace, count the clock.

CASSIUS   The clock hath stricken three.

TREBONIUS

'Tis time to part.

CASSIUS   But it is doubtful yet
Whether Caesar will come forth today or no;
For he is superstitious grown of late,
Quite from the main opinion he held once
Of fantasy, of dreams, and ceremonies.
It may be these apparent prodigies,
The unaccustomed terror of this night,
And the persuasion of his augurers   200
May hold him from the Capitol today.

DECIUS

Never fear that. If he be so resolved,
I can o'ersway him; for he loves to hear
That unicorns may be betrayed with trees,
And bears with glasses, elephants with holes,
Lions with toils, and men with flatterers.
But when I tell him he hates flatterers,
He says he does, being then most flatterèd.
Let me work;
For I can give his humour the true bent,   210
And I will bring him to the Capitol.

CASSIUS

Nay, we will all of us be there to fetch him.

BRUTUS

By the eighth hour; is that the uttermost?

CINNA

Be that the uttermost, and fail not then.

METELLUS

Caius Ligarius doth bear Caesar hard,
Who rated him for speaking well of Pompey;
I wonder none of you have thought of him.

BRUTUS

Now, good Metellus, go along by him;
He loves me well, and I have given him reasons.
220   Send him but hither, and I'll fashion him.

CASSIUS

The morning comes upon's; we'll leave you, Brutus.
And, friends, disperse yourselves; but all remember
What you have said, and show yourselves true Romans.

BRUTUS

Good gentlemen, look fresh and merrily;
Let not our looks put on our purposes,
But bear it as our Roman actors do,
With untired spirits and formal constancy.
And so good morrow to you every one.

Exeunt the conspirators

Brutus remains

Boy! Lucius! Fast asleep? It is no matter.
230   Enjoy the honey-heavy dew of slumber;
Thou hast no figures nor no fantasies,
Which busy care draws in the brains of men;
Therefore thou sleep'st so sound.

Enter Portia

PORTIA   Brutus, my lord.

BRUTUS

Portia! What mean you? Wherefore rise you now?
It is not for your health thus to commit

Your weak condition to the raw cold morning.

PORTIA

Nor for yours neither. Y' have ungently, Brutus,
Stole from my bed; and yesternight at supper
You suddenly arose and walked about,
Musing and sighing, with your arms across;   240
And when I asked you what the matter was,
You stared upon me with ungentle looks.
I urged you further; then you scratched your head,
And too impatiently stamped with your foot;
Yet I insisted, yet you answered not,
But with an angry wafture of your hand
Gave sign for me to leave you. So I did,
Fearing to strengthen that impatience
Which seemed too much enkindled, and withal
Hoping it was but an effect of humour,   250
Which sometime hath his hour with every man.
It will not let you eat, nor talk, nor sleep;
And could it work so much upon your shape,
As it hath much prevailed on your condition,
I should not know you Brutus. Dear my lord,
Make me acquainted with your cause of grief.

BRUTUS

I am not well in health, and that is all.

PORTIA

Brutus is wise, and were he not in health,
He would embrace the means to come by it.

BRUTUS

Why, so I do. Good Portia, go to bed.   260

PORTIA

Is Brutus sick? And is it physical
To walk unbracèd and suck up the humours
Of the dank morning? What, is Brutus sick?
And will he steal out of his wholesome bed

To dare the vile contagion of the night,
And tempt the rheumy and unpurgèd air,
To add unto his sickness? No, my Brutus;
You have some sick offence within your mind,
Which, by the right and virtue of my place,
270   I ought to know of; and, upon my knees,
I charm you, by my once commended beauty,
By all your vows of love, and that great vow
Which did incorporate and make us one,
That you unfold to me, your self, your half,
Why you are heavy, and what men tonight
Have had resort to you; for here have been
Some six or seven, who did hide their faces
Even from darkness.

BRUTUS   Kneel not, gentle Portia.

PORTIA

I should not need, if you were gentle Brutus.
280   Within the bond of marriage, tell me, Brutus,
Is it excepted I should know no secrets
That appertain to you? Am I your self
But, as it were, in sort or limitation,
To keep with you at meals, comfort your bed,
And talk to you sometimes? Dwell I but in the suburbs
Of your good pleasure? If it be no more,
Portia is Brutus' harlot, not his wife.

BRUTUS

You are my true and honourable wife,
As dear to me as are the ruddy drops
290   That visit my sad heart.

PORTIA

If this were true, then should I know this secret.
I grant I am a woman; but withal
A woman that Lord Brutus took to wife;
I grant I am a woman; but withal

A woman well reputed, Cato's daughter.
Think you I am no stronger than my sex,
Being so fathered, and so husbanded?
Tell me your counsels, I will not disclose 'em.
I have made strong proof of my constancy,
Giving myself a voluntary wound   300
Here, in the thigh; can I bear that with patience,
And not my husband's secrets?

BRUTUS   O ye gods,
Render me worthy of this noble wife!
    Knocking
Hark, hark! one knocks. Portia, go in awhile;
And by and by thy bosom shall partake
The secrets of my heart.
All my engagements I will construe to thee,
All the charactery of my sad brows.
Leave me with haste.   *Exit Portia*
    Enter Lucius and Ligarius
                        Lucius, who's that knocks?

LUCIUS
Here is a sick man that would speak with you.   310

BRUTUS
Caius Ligarius, that Metellus spake of.
Boy, stand aside. Caius Ligarius, how?

LIGARIUS
Vouchsafe good morrow from a feeble tongue.

BRUTUS
O, what a time have you chose out, brave Caius,
To wear a kerchief! Would you were not sick!

LIGARIUS
I am not sick if Brutus have in hand
Any exploit worthy the name of honour.

BRUTUS
Such an exploit have I in hand, Ligarius,

Had you a healthful ear to hear of it.

LIGARIUS

320   By all the gods that Romans bow before,
        I here discard my sickness.

He throws off the kerchief

                                Soul of Rome!
        Brave son, derived from honourable loins!
        Thou, like an exorcist, hast conjured up
        My mortifièd spirit. Now bid me run,
        And I will strive with things impossible,
        Yea, get the better of them. What's to do?

BRUTUS

        A piece of work that will make sick men whole.

LIGARIUS

        But are not some whole that we must make sick?

BRUTUS

        That must we also. What it is, my Caius,
330   I shall unfold to thee, as we are going
        To whom it must be done.

LIGARIUS   Set on your foot,
        And with a heart new-fired I follow you,
        To do I know not what; but it sufficeth
        That Brutus leads me on.

Thunder

BRUTUS   Follow me then.   *Exeunt*

II.2   *Thunder and lightning*
         Enter Julius Caesar in his night-gown

CAESAR

        Nor heaven nor earth have been at peace tonight;
        Thrice hath Calphurnia in her sleep cried out,
        'Help, ho! They murder Caesar!' Who's within?

Enter a Servant

SERVANT My lord?

CAESAR

Go bid the priests do present sacrifice,
And bring me their opinions of success.

SERVANT I will, my lord.   *Exit*

Enter Calphurnia

CALPHURNIA

What mean you, Caesar? Think you to walk forth?
You shall not stir out of your house today.

CAESAR

Caesar shall forth. The things that threatened me   10
Ne'er looked but on my back; when they shall see
The face of Caesar, they are vanishèd.

CALPHURNIA

Caesar, I never stood on ceremonies,
Yet now they fright me. There is one within,
Besides the things that we have heard and seen,
Recounts most horrid sights seen by the watch.
A lioness hath whelpèd in the streets,
And graves have yawned and yielded up their dead;
Fierce fiery warriors fought upon the clouds
In ranks and squadrons and right form of war,   20
Which drizzled blood upon the Capitol;
The noise of battle hurtled in the air,
Horses did neigh, and dying men did groan,
And ghosts did shriek and squeal about the streets.
O Caesar, these things are beyond all use,
And I do fear them.

CAESAR   What can be avoided
Whose end is purposed by the mighty gods?
Yet Caesar shall go forth; for these predictions
Are to the world in general as to Caesar.

CALPHURNIA

When beggars die, there are no comets seen;   30

The heavens themselves blaze forth the death of princes.

CAESAR

    Cowards die many times before their deaths;
    The valiant never taste of death but once.
    Of all the wonders that I yet have heard,
    It seems to me most strange that men should fear,
    Seeing that death, a necessary end,
    Will come when it will come.

      Enter a Servant

                         What say the augurers?

SERVANT

    They would not have you to stir forth today.
    Plucking the entrails of an offering forth,
40   They could not find a heart within the beast.

CAESAR

    The gods do this in shame of cowardice:
    Caesar should be a beast without a heart
    If he should stay at home today for fear.
    No, Caesar shall not. Danger knows full well
    That Caesar is more dangerous than he.
    We are two lions littered in one day,
    And I the elder and more terrible;
    And Caesar shall go forth.

CALPHURNIA   Alas, my lord,
    Your wisdom is consumed in confidence.
50   Do not go forth today: call it my fear
    That keeps you in the house, and not your own.
    We'll send Mark Antony to the Senate House,
    And he shall say you are not well today.
    Let me upon my knee prevail in this.

CAESAR

    Mark Antony shall say I am not well,
    And for thy humour I will stay at home.

      Enter Decius

Here's Decius Brutus; he shall tell them so.

DECIUS

Caesar, all hail! Good morrow, worthy Caesar;
I come to fetch you to the Senate House.

CAESAR

And you are come in very happy time   60
To bear my greeting to the senators,
And tell them that I will not come today:
Cannot, is false; and that I dare not, falser;
I will not come today. Tell them so, Decius.

CALPHURNIA

Say he is sick.

CAESAR   Shall Caesar send a lie?
Have I in conquest stretched mine arm so far,
To be afeard to tell greybeards the truth?
Decius, go tell them Caesar will not come.

DECIUS

Most mighty Caesar, let me know some cause,
Lest I be laughed at when I tell them so.   70

CAESAR

The cause is in my will: I will not come;
That is enough to satisfy the Senate.
But for your private satisfaction,
Because I love you, I will let you know:
Calphurnia here, my wife, stays me at home.
She dreamt tonight she saw my statue,
Which, like a fountain with an hundred spouts,
Did run pure blood; and many lusty Romans
Came smiling, and did bathe their hands in it.
And these does she apply for warnings and portents   80
And evils imminent; and on her knee
Hath begged that I will stay at home today.

DECIUS

This dream is all amiss interpreted;

It was a vision fair and fortunate:
Your statue spouting blood in many pipes,
In which so many smiling Romans bathed,
Signifies that from you great Rome shall suck
Reviving blood, and that great men shall press
For tinctures, stains, relics, and cognizance.

90   This by Calphurnia's dream is signified.

CAESAR
And this way have you well expounded it.

DECIUS
I have, when you have heard what I can say:
And know it now. The Senate have concluded
To give this day a crown to mighty Caesar.
If you shall send them word you will not come,
Their minds may change. Besides, it were a mock
Apt to be rendered, for some one to say,
'Break up the Senate till another time,
When Caesar's wife shall meet with better dreams.'

100   If Caesar hide himself, shall they not whisper,
'Lo, Caesar is afraid'?
Pardon me, Caesar, for my dear dear love
To your proceeding bids me tell you this,
And reason to my love is liable.

CAESAR
How foolish do your fears seem now, Calphurnia!
I am ashamèd I did yield to them.
Give me my robe, for I will go.
        Enter Brutus, Ligarius, Metellus, Casca, Trebonius,
        Cinna, and Publius
And look where Publius is come to fetch me.

PUBLIUS
Good morrow, Caesar.

CAESAR   Welcome, Publius.

110   What, Brutus, are you stirred so early too?

Good morrow, Casca. Caius Ligarius,
Caesar was ne'er so much your enemy
As that same ague which hath made you lean.
What is't o'clock?

BRUTUS   Caesar, 'tis strucken eight.

CAESAR

I thank you for your pains and courtesy.

Enter Antony

See! Antony, that revels long a-nights,
Is notwithstanding up. Good morrow, Antony.

ANTONY

So to most noble Caesar.

CAESAR   Bid them prepare within.

I am to blame to be thus waited for.
Now, Cinna; now, Metellus; what, Trebonius;   120
I have an hour's talk in store for you;
Remember that you call on me today;
Be near me, that I may remember you.

TREBONIUS

Caesar, I will. (*Aside*) And so near will I be
That your best friends shall wish I had been further.

CAESAR

Good friends, go in, and taste some wine with me;
And we, like friends, will straightway go together.

BRUTUS (*aside*)

That every like is not the same, O Caesar,
The heart of Brutus earns to think upon.   *Exeunt*

Enter Artemidorus reading a paper   II.3

ARTEMIDORUS *Caesar, beware of Brutus; take heed of*
    Cassius; come not near Casca; have an eye to Cinna; trust
    not Trebonius; mark well Metellus Cimber; Decius Brutus

loves thee not; thou hast wronged Caius Ligarius. There is
but one mind in all these men, and it is bent against Caesar.
If thou beest not immortal, look about you: security gives
way to conspiracy. The mighty gods defend thee!

                  Thy lover,

                        Artemidorus.

10   Here will I stand till Caesar pass along,
And as a suitor will I give him this.
My heart laments that virtue cannot live
Out of the teeth of emulation.
If thou read this, O Caesar, thou mayst live;
If not, the Fates with traitors do contrive.   *Exit*

II.4   *Enter Portia and Lucius*

PORTIA
I prithee, boy, run to the Senate House.
Stay not to answer me, but get thee gone.
Why dost thou stay?

LUCIUS   To know my errand, madam.

PORTIA
I would have had thee there and here again
Ere I can tell thee what thou shouldst do there.
O constancy, be strong upon my side;
Set a huge mountain 'tween my heart and tongue!
I have a man's mind, but a woman's might.
How hard it is for women to keep counsel!
10   Art thou here yet?

LUCIUS   Madam, what should I do?
Run to the Capitol and nothing else?
And so return to you, and nothing else?

PORTIA
Yes, bring me word, boy, if thy lord look well,
For he went sickly forth; and take good note

What Caesar doth, what suitors press to him.
Hark, boy, what noise is that?

LUCIUS

I hear none, madam.

PORTIA   Prithee, listen well.
I heard a bustling rumour like a fray,
And the wind brings it from the Capitol.

LUCIUS

Sooth, madam, I hear nothing.   20

   Enter the Soothsayer

PORTIA

Come hither fellow. Which way hast thou been?

SOOTHSAYER

At mine own house, good lady.

PORTIA

What is't o'clock?

SOOTHSAYER   About the ninth hour, lady.

PORTIA

Is Caesar yet gone to the Capitol?

SOOTHSAYER

Madam, not yet; I go to take my stand,
To see him pass on to the Capitol.

PORTIA

Thou hast some suit to Caesar, hast thou not?

SOOTHSAYER

That I have, lady, if it will please Caesar
To be so good to Caesar as to hear me:
I shall beseech him to befriend himself.   30

PORTIA

Why, know'st thou any harm's intended towards him?

SOOTHSAYER

None that I know will be, much that I fear may chance.
Good morrow to you. Here the street is narrow;
The throng that follows Caesar at the heels,

Of senators, of praetors, common suitors,
Will crowd a feeble man almost to death;
I'll get me to a place more void, and there
Speak to great Caesar as he comes along.   *Exit*

PORTIA

I must go in. Ay me, how weak a thing
40   The heart of woman is! O Brutus,
The heavens speed thee in thine enterprise!
(*Aside*) Sure, the boy heard me. (*To Lucius*) Brutus hath
   a suit
That Caesar will not grant. (*Aside*) O, I grow faint.
Run, Lucius, and commend me to my lord;
Say I am merry; come to me again,
And bring me word what he doth say to thee.   *Exeunt*

*

III.1   *Flourish*
          Enter Caesar, Brutus, Cassius, Casca, Decius,
          Metellus, Trebonius, Cinna, Antony, Lepidus,
          Popilius, Artemidorus, Publius, and the Soothsayer

CAESAR (*to the Soothsayer*)

The ides of March are come.

SOOTHSAYER

Ay, Caesar, but not gone.

ARTEMIDORUS

Hail, Caesar! Read this schedule.

DECIUS

Trebonius doth desire you to o'er-read,
At your best leisure, this his humble suit.

ARTEMIDORUS

O Caesar, read mine first; for mine's a suit
That touches Caesar nearer. Read it, great Caesar.

CAESAR
   What touches us ourself shall be last served.
ARTEMIDORUS
   Delay not, Caesar. Read it instantly.
CAESAR
   What, is the fellow mad?
PUBLIUS   Sirrah, give place.   10
CASSIUS
   What, urge you your petitions in the street?
   Come to the Capitol.
      Caesar enters the Capitol, the rest following
POPILIUS
   I wish your enterprise today may thrive.
CASSIUS
   What enterprise, Popilius?
POPILIUS   Fare you well.
      He goes to speak to Caesar
BRUTUS
   What said Popilius Lena?
CASSIUS
   He wished today our enterprise might thrive.
   I fear our purpose is discoverèd.
BRUTUS
   Look how he makes to Caesar: mark him.
CASSIUS
   Casca, be sudden, for we fear prevention.
   Brutus, what shall be done? If this be known,   20
   Cassius or Caesar never shall turn back,
   For I will slay myself.
BRUTUS   Cassius, be constant:
   Popilius Lena speaks not of our purposes;
   For look, he smiles, and Caesar doth not change.
CASSIUS
   Trebonius knows his time; for look you, Brutus,

He draws Mark Antony out of the way.
                                        Exeunt Antony and Trebonius

DECIUS

Where is Metellus Cimber? Let him go,
And presently prefer his suit to Caesar.

BRUTUS

He is addressed. Press near and second him.

CINNA

30   Casca, you are the first that rears your hand.

CAESAR

Are we all ready? What is now amiss
That Caesar and his senate must redress?

METELLUS (*kneeling*)

Most high, most mighty, and most puissant Caesar,
Metellus Cimber throws before thy seat
An humble heart —

CAESAR   I must prevent thee, Cimber;
These couchings, and these lowly courtesies
Might fire the blood of ordinary men,
And turn pre-ordinance and first decree
Into the law of children. Be not fond,
40   To think that Caesar bears such rebel blood
That will be thawed from the true quality
With that which melteth fools — I mean sweet words,
Low-crookèd curtsies and base spaniel fawning.
Thy brother by decree is banishèd:
If thou dost bend and pray and fawn for him,
I spurn thee like a cur out of my way.
Know, Caesar doth not wrong, nor without cause
Will he be satisfied.

METELLUS

Is there no voice more worthy than my own,
50   To sound more sweetly in great Caesar's ear
For the repealing of my banished brother?

BRUTUS
　I kiss thy hand, but not in flattery, Caesar,
　Desiring thee that Publius Cimber may
　Have an immediate freedom of repeal.
CAESAR What, Brutus?
CASSIUS (*kneeling*)   Pardon, Caesar; Caesar, pardon;
　As low as to thy foot doth Cassius fall,
　To beg enfranchisement for Publius Cimber.
CAESAR
　I could be well moved, if I were as you;
　If I could pray to move, prayers would move me;
　But I am constant as the northern star,   60
　Of whose true-fixed and resting quality
　There is no fellow in the firmament.
　The skies are painted with unnumbered sparks,
　They are all fire, and every one doth shine;
　But there's but one in all doth hold his place.
　So in the world: 'tis furnished well with men,
　And men are flesh and blood, and apprehensive;
　Yet in the number I do know but one
　That unassailable holds on his rank,
　Unshaked of motion; and that I am he,   70
　Let me a little show it, even in this:
　That I was constant Cimber should be banished,
　And constant do remain to keep him so.
CINNA
　O Caesar —
CAESAR   Hence! Wilt thou lift up Olympus?
DECIUS
　Great Caesar —
CAESAR   Doth not Brutus bootless kneel?
CASCA
　Speak hands for me!
　　They stab Caesar

CAESAR
   Et tu, Brute? – Then fall Caesar!   *He dies*
CINNA
   Liberty! Freedom! Tyranny is dead!
   Run hence, proclaim, cry it about the streets.
CASSIUS
80   Some to the common pulpits, and cry out,
   'Liberty, freedom, and enfranchisement!'
BRUTUS
   People and senators, be not affrighted.
   Fly not; stand still; ambition's debt is paid.
CASCA
   Go to the pulpit, Brutus.
DECIUS   And Cassius too.
BRUTUS
   Where's Publius?
CINNA
   Here, quite confounded with this mutiny.
METELLUS
   Stand fast together, lest some friend of Caesar's
   Should chance –
BRUTUS
   Talk not of standing. Publius, good cheer;
90   There is no harm intended to your person,
   Nor to no Roman else. So tell them, Publius.
CASSIUS
   And leave us, Publius, lest that the people,
   Rushing on us, should do your age some mischief.
BRUTUS
   Do so; and let no man abide this deed
   But we the doers.
     Enter Trebonius
CASSIUS
   Where is Antony?

TREBONIUS   Fled to his house amazed.
  Men, wives, and children stare, cry out, and run,
  As it were doomsday.
BRUTUS   Fates, we will know your pleasures.
  That we shall die, we know; 'tis but the time
  And drawing days out, that men stand upon.   100
CASCA
  Why, he that cuts off twenty years of life
  Cuts off so many years of fearing death.
BRUTUS
  Grant that, and then is death a benefit:
  So are we Caesar's friends, that have abridged
  His time of fearing death. Stoop, Romans, stoop,
  And let us bathe our hands in Caesar's blood
  Up to the elbows, and besmear our swords;
  Then walk we forth, even to the market-place,
  And waving our red weapons o'er our heads,
  Let's all cry, 'Peace, freedom, and liberty!'   110
CASSIUS
  Stoop then, and wash. How many ages hence
  Shall this our lofty scene be acted over,
  In states unborn, and accents yet unknown!
BRUTUS
  How many times shall Caesar bleed in sport,
  That now on Pompey's basis lies along,
  No worthier than the dust!
CASSIUS   So oft as that shall be,
  So often shall the knot of us be called
  The men that gave their country liberty.
DECIUS
  What, shall we forth?
CASSIUS   Ay, every man away.
  Brutus shall lead, and we will grace his heels   120
  With the most boldest and best hearts of Rome.

Enter a Servant

BRUTUS

Soft, who comes here? A friend of Antony's.

SERVANT (*kneeling*)

Thus, Brutus, did my master bid me kneel;
Thus did Mark Antony bid me fall down;
And, being prostrate, thus he bade me say:
Brutus is noble, wise, valiant, and honest;
Caesar was mighty, bold, royal, and loving:
Say I love Brutus, and I honour him;
Say I feared Caesar, honoured him, and loved him.

130   If Brutus will vouchsafe that Antony
May safely come to him, and be resolved
How Caesar hath deserved to lie in death,
Mark Antony shall not love Caesar dead
So well as Brutus living; but will follow
The fortunes and affairs of noble Brutus
Thorough the hazards of this untrod state,
With all true faith. So says my master Antony.

BRUTUS

Thy master is a wise and valiant Roman;
I never thought him worse.

140   Tell him, so please him come unto this place,
He shall be satisfied; and, by my honour,
Depart untouched.

SERVANT   I'll fetch him presently.

Exit Servant

BRUTUS

I know that we shall have him well to friend.

CASSIUS

I wish we may: but yet have I a mind
That fears him much; and my misgiving still
Falls shrewdly to the purpose.

Enter Antony

BRUTUS

    But here comes Antony. Welcome, Mark Antony.

ANTONY

    O mighty Caesar! Dost thou lie so low?
    Are all thy conquests, glories, triumphs, spoils
    Shrunk to this little measure? Fare thee well.   150
    I know not, gentlemen, what you intend,
    Who else must be let blood, who else is rank:
    If I myself, there is no hour so fit
    As Caesar's death's hour; nor no instrument
    Of half that worth as those your swords, made rich
    With the most noble blood of all this world.
    I do beseech ye, if you bear me hard,
    Now, whilst your purpled hands do reek and smoke,
    Fulfil your pleasure. Live a thousand years,
    I shall not find myself so apt to die;   160
    No place will please me so, no mean of death,
    As here by Caesar, and by you cut off,
    The choice and master spirits of this age.

BRUTUS

    O Antony, beg not your death of us.
    Though now we must appear bloody and cruel,
    As by our hands and this our present act
    You see we do, yet see you but our hands
    And this the bleeding business they have done.
    Our hearts you see not; they are pitiful;
    And pity to the general wrong of Rome –   170
    As fire drives out fire, so pity, pity –
    Hath done this deed on Caesar. For your part,
    To you our swords have leaden points, Mark Antony;
    Our arms in strength of malice, and our hearts
    Of brothers' temper, do receive you in
    With all kind love, good thoughts, and reverence.

CASSIUS
> Your voice shall be as strong as any man's
> In the disposing of new dignities.

BRUTUS
> Only be patient till we have appeased
180
> The multitude, beside themselves with fear,
> And then we will deliver you the cause
> Why I, that did love Caesar when I struck him,
> Have thus proceeded.

ANTONY   I doubt not of your wisdom.
> Let each man render me his bloody hand.
> First, Marcus Brutus, will I shake with you;
> Next, Caius Cassius, do I take your hand;
> Now, Decius Brutus, yours; now yours, Metellus;
> Yours, Cinna; and, my valiant Casca, yours;
> Though last, not least in love, yours, good Trebonius.
190
> Gentlemen all – alas, what shall I say?
> My credit now stands on such slippery ground,
> That one of two bad ways you must conceit me,
> Either a coward, or a flatterer.
> That I did love thee, Caesar, O, 'tis true!
> If then thy spirit look upon us now,
> Shall it not grieve thee dearer than thy death,
> To see thy Antony making his peace,
> Shaking the bloody fingers of thy foes,
> Most noble, in the presence of thy corse?
200
> Had I as many eyes as thou hast wounds,
> Weeping as fast as they stream forth thy blood,
> It would become me better than to close
> In terms of friendship with thine enemies.
> Pardon me, Julius! Here wast thou bayed, brave hart;
> Here didst thou fall; and here thy hunters stand,
> Signed in thy spoil, and crimsoned in thy lethe.
> O world, thou wast the forest to this hart;

And this indeed, O world, the heart of thee.
How like a deer, strucken by many princes,
Dost thou here lie!   210

CASSIUS
Mark Antony –

ANTONY   Pardon me, Caius Cassius;
The enemies of Caesar shall say this;
Then, in a friend, it is cold modesty.

CASSIUS
I blame you not for praising Caesar so;
But what compact mean you to have with us?
Will you be pricked in number of our friends,
Or shall we on, and not depend on you?

ANTONY
Therefore I took your hands, but was indeed
Swayed from the point by looking down on Caesar.
Friends am I with you all, and love you all,   220
Upon this hope, that you shall give me reasons
Why, and wherein, Caesar was dangerous.

BRUTUS
Or else were this a savage spectacle.
Our reasons are so full of good regard,
That were you, Antony, the son of Caesar,
You should be satisfied.

ANTONY   That's all I seek,
And am moreover suitor that I may
Produce his body to the market-place,
And in the pulpit, as becomes a friend,
Speak in the order of his funeral.   230

BRUTUS
You shall, Mark Antony.

CASSIUS   Brutus, a word with you.
(*Aside to Brutus*) You know not what you do; do not
    consent

That Antony speak in his funeral.
Know you how much the people may be moved
By that which he will utter?

BRUTUS (*aside to Cassius*)   By your pardon:
I will myself into the pulpit first,
And show the reason of our Caesar's death.
What Antony shall speak, I will protest
He speaks by leave and by permission;
240   And that we are contented Caesar shall
Have all true rites and lawful ceremonies,
It shall advantage more than do us wrong.

CASSIUS (*aside to Brutus*)
I know not what may fall; I like it not.

BRUTUS
Mark Antony, here take you Caesar's body.
You shall not in your funeral speech blame us,
But speak all good you can devise of Caesar,
And say you do't by our permission;
Else shall you not have any hand at all
About his funeral. And you shall speak
250   In the same pulpit whereto I am going,
After my speech is ended.

ANTONY   Be it so;
I do desire no more.

BRUTUS
Prepare the body, then, and follow us.   *Exeunt*
        Antony remains

ANTONY
O, pardon me, thou bleeding piece of earth,
That I am meek and gentle with these butchers.
Thou art the ruins of the noblest man
That ever livèd in the tide of times.
Woe to the hand that shed this costly blood!
Over thy wounds now do I prophesy –

Which like dumb mouths do ope their ruby lips,   260
To beg the voice and utterance of my tongue –
A curse shall light upon the limbs of men;
Domestic fury and fierce civil strife
Shall cumber all the parts of Italy;
Blood and destruction shall be so in use,
And dreadful objects so familiar,
That mothers shall but smile when they behold
Their infants quartered with the hands of war,
All pity choked with custom of fell deeds;
And Caesar's spirit, ranging for revenge,   270
With Ate by his side, come hot from hell,
Shall in these confines with a monarch's voice
Cry havoc and let slip the dogs of war,
That this foul deed shall smell above the earth
With carrion men, groaning for burial.
    Enter Octavius' Servant
You serve Octavius Caesar, do you not?

SERVANT
    I do, Mark Antony.

ANTONY
    Caesar did write for him to come to Rome.

SERVANT
    He did receive his letters, and is coming,
    And bid me say to you by word of mouth –   280
    O Caesar!

ANTONY
    Thy heart is big; get thee apart and weep.
    Passion, I see, is catching, for mine eyes,
    Seeing those beads of sorrow stand in thine,
    Began to water. Is thy master coming?

SERVANT
    He lies tonight within seven leagues of Rome.

ANTONY
    Post back with speed, and tell him what hath chanced.
    Here is a mourning Rome, a dangerous Rome,
    No Rome of safety for Octavius yet.
290   Hie hence, and tell him so. Yet stay awhile;
    Thou shalt not back till I have borne this corse
    Into the market-place; there shall I try,
    In my oration, how the people take
    The cruel issue of these bloody men;
    According to the which, thou shalt discourse
    To young Octavius of the state of things.
    Lend me your hand.   *Exeunt*

III.2   *Enter Brutus and later goes into the pulpit, and*
           Cassius, with the Plebeians

PLEBEIANS
    We will be satisfied: let us be satisfied.
BRUTUS
    Then follow me, and give me audience, friends.
    Cassius, go you into the other street,
    And part the numbers.
    Those that will hear me speak, let 'em stay here;
    Those that will follow Cassius, go with him;
    And public reasons shall be renderèd
    Of Caesar's death.
FIRST PLEBEIAN   I will hear Brutus speak.
SECOND PLEBEIAN
    I will hear Cassius, and compare their reasons,
10   When severally we hear them renderèd.
             Exit Cassius, with some of the Plebeians
THIRD PLEBEIAN
    The noble Brutus is ascended. Silence!

BRUTUS
Be patient till the last.
Romans, countrymen, and lovers, hear me for my cause,
and be silent, that you may hear. Believe me for mine
honour, and have respect to mine honour, that you may
believe. Censure me in your wisdom, and awake your
senses, that you may the better judge. If there be any in
this assembly, any dear friend of Caesar's, to him I say
that Brutus' love to Caesar was no less than his. If then
that friend demand why Brutus rose against Caesar, this   20
is my answer: not that I loved Caesar less, but that I
loved Rome more. Had you rather Caesar were living,
and die all slaves, than that Caesar were dead, to live
all free men? As Caesar loved me, I weep for him; as
he was fortunate, I rejoice at it; as he was valiant, I
honour him; but, as he was ambitious, I slew him.
There is tears for his love; joy for his fortune; honour
for his valour; and death for his ambition. Who is here
so base that would be a bondman? If any, speak; for
him have I offended. Who is here so rude that would   30
not be a Roman? If any, speak; for him have I offended. Who is here so vile that will not love his country?
If any, speak; for him have I offended. I pause for a
reply.
ALL None, Brutus, none.
BRUTUS Then none have I offended. I have done no more
to Caesar than you shall do to Brutus. The question of
his death is enrolled in the Capitol; his glory not extenu-
ated, wherein he was worthy; nor his offences enforced,
for which he suffered death.   40
    Enter Mark Antony and others, with Caesar's body
Here comes his body, mourned by Mark Antony, who,
though he had no hand in his death, shall receive the
benefit of his dying, a place in the commonwealth, as

which of you shall not? With this I depart, that, as I
slew my best lover for the good of Rome, I have the
same dagger for myself, when it shall please my country
to need my death.

ALL Live, Brutus! live! live!

FIRST PLEBEIAN
  Bring him with triumph home unto his house.

SECOND PLEBEIAN

50 Give him a statue with his ancestors.

THIRD PLEBEIAN
  Let him be Caesar.

FOURTH PLEBEIAN   Caesar's better parts
  Shall be crowned in Brutus.

FIRST PLEBEIAN
  We'll bring him to his house with shouts and clamours.

BRUTUS
  My countrymen —

SECOND PLEBEIAN   Peace! Silence! Brutus speaks.

FIRST PLEBEIAN Peace, ho!

BRUTUS
  Good countrymen, let me depart alone,
  And, for my sake, stay here with Antony.
  Do grace to Caesar's corpse, and grace his speech
  Tending to Caesar's glories, which Mark Antony,
60 By our permission, is allowed to make.
  I do entreat you, not a man depart,
  Save I alone, till Antony have spoke.   *Exit*

FIRST PLEBEIAN
  Stay, ho! and let us hear Mark Antony.

THIRD PLEBEIAN
  Let him go up into the public chair;
  We'll hear him. Noble Antony, go up.

ANTONY
  For Brutus' sake, I am beholding to you.

FOURTH PLEBEIAN
    What does he say of Brutus?
THIRD PLEBEIAN   He says, for Brutus' sake
    He finds himself beholding to us all.
FOURTH PLEBEIAN
    'Twere best he speak no harm of Brutus here!
FIRST PLEBEIAN
    This Caesar was a tyrant.
THIRD PLEBEIAN   Nay, that's certain.   70
    We are blest that Rome is rid of him.
SECOND PLEBEIAN
    Peace! let us hear what Antony can say.
ANTONY
    You gentle Romans –
SECOND PLEBEIAN   Peace, ho! let us hear him.
ANTONY
    Friends, Romans, countrymen, lend me your ears;
    I come to bury Caesar, not to praise him.
    The evil that men do lives after them,
    The good is oft interrèd with their bones;
    So let it be with Caesar. The noble Brutus
    Hath told you Caesar was ambitious.
    If it were so, it was a grievous fault,   80
    And grievously hath Caesar answered it.
    Here, under leave of Brutus and the rest –
    For Brutus is an honourable man;
    So are they all, all honourable men –
    Come I to speak in Caesar's funeral.
    He was my friend, faithful and just to me;
    But Brutus says he was ambitious,
    And Brutus is an honourable man.
    He hath brought many captives home to Rome,
    Whose ransoms did the general coffers fill: 90
    Did this in Caesar seem ambitious?

When that the poor have cried, Caesar hath wept;
Ambition should be made of sterner stuff:
Yet Brutus says he was ambitious,
And Brutus is an honourable man.
You all did see that on the Lupercal
I thrice presented him a kingly crown,
Which he did thrice refuse. Was this ambition?
Yet Brutus says he was ambitious,
And sure he is an honourable man.
I speak not to disprove what Brutus spoke,
But here I am to speak what I do know.
You all did love him once, not without cause;
What cause withholds you then to mourn for him?
O judgement! thou art fled to brutish beasts,
And men have lost their reason. Bear with me;
My heart is in the coffin there with Caesar,
And I must pause till it come back to me.

FIRST PLEBEIAN
Methinks there is much reason in his sayings.

SECOND PLEBEIAN
If thou consider rightly of the matter,
Caesar has had great wrong.

THIRD PLEBEIAN   Has he, masters?
I fear there will a worse come in his place.

FOURTH PLEBEIAN
Marked ye his words? He would not take the crown;
Therefore 'tis certain he was not ambitious.

FIRST PLEBEIAN
If it be found so, some will dear abide it.

SECOND PLEBEIAN
Poor soul! His eyes are red as fire with weeping.

THIRD PLEBEIAN
There's not a nobler man in Rome than Antony.

FOURTH PLEBEIAN

Now mark him; he begins again to speak.

ANTONY

But yesterday the word of Caesar might
Have stood against the world; now lies he there,   120
And none so poor to do him reverence.
O masters! If I were disposed to stir
Your hearts and minds to mutiny and rage,
I should do Brutus wrong, and Cassius wrong,
Who, you all know, are honourable men.
I will not do them wrong; I rather choose
To wrong the dead, to wrong myself and you,
Than I will wrong such honourable men.
But here's a parchment with the seal of Caesar;
I found it in his closet; 'tis his will.   130
Let but the commons hear this testament,
Which, pardon me, I do not mean to read,
And they would go and kiss dead Caesar's wounds,
And dip their napkins in his sacred blood,
Yea, beg a hair of him for memory,
And, dying, mention it within their wills,
Bequeathing it as a rich legacy
Unto their issue.

FOURTH PLEBEIAN

We'll hear the will. Read it, Mark Antony.

ALL

The will, the will! We will hear Caesar's will!   140

ANTONY

Have patience, gentle friends; I must not read it.
It is not meet you know how Caesar loved you.
You are not wood, you are not stones, but men;
And being men, hearing the will of Caesar,
It will inflame you, it will make you mad.
'Tis good you know not that you are his heirs;

For if you should, O, what would come of it?

FOURTH PLEBEIAN
Read the will! We'll hear it, Antony!
You shall read us the will, Caesar's will!

ANTONY
150   Will you be patient? Will you stay awhile?
I have o'ershot myself to tell you of it.
I fear I wrong the honourable men
Whose daggers have stabbed Caesar; I do fear it.

FOURTH PLEBEIAN They were traitors. Honourable men!
ALL The will! The testament!
SECOND PLEBEIAN They were villains, murderers! The
will! Read the will!

ANTONY
You will compel me then to read the will?
Then make a ring about the corpse of Caesar,
160   And let me show you him that made the will.
Shall I descend? And will you give me leave?

ALL Come down.

Antony comes down from the pulpit

SECOND PLEBEIAN
Descend.

THIRD PLEBEIAN
You shall have leave.

FOURTH PLEBEIAN
A ring! Stand round.

FIRST PLEBEIAN
Stand from the hearse! Stand from the body!

SECOND PLEBEIAN
Room for Antony, most noble Antony!

ANTONY
Nay, press not so upon me; stand far off.

ALL Stand back! Room! Bear back!

ANTONY

    If you have tears, prepare to shed them now.   170
    You all do know this mantle. I remember
    The first time ever Caesar put it on;
    'Twas on a summer's evening in his tent,
    That day he overcame the Nervii.
    Look, in this place ran Cassius' dagger through;
    See what a rent the envious Casca made;
    Through this, the well-belovèd Brutus stabbed,
    And as he plucked his cursèd steel away,
    Mark how the blood of Caesar followed it,
    As rushing out of doors, to be resolved   180
    If Brutus so unkindly knocked or no;
    For Brutus, as you know, was Caesar's angel.
    Judge, O you gods, how dearly Caesar loved him!
    This was the most unkindest cut of all;
    For when the noble Caesar saw him stab,
    Ingratitude, more strong than traitors' arms,
    Quite vanquished him: then burst his mighty heart;
    And in his mantle muffling up his face,
    Even at the base of Pompey's statue,
    Which all the while ran blood, great Caesar fell.   190
    O, what a fall was there, my countrymen!
    Then I, and you, and all of us fell down,
    Whilst bloody treason flourished over us.
    O, now you weep, and I perceive you feel
    The dint of pity. These are gracious drops.
    Kind souls, what weep you when you but behold
    Our Caesar's vesture wounded? Look you here,
    Here is himself, marred, as you see, with traitors.

    Antony plucks off the mantle

FIRST PLEBEIAN O piteous spectacle!
SECOND PLEBEIAN O noble Caesar!   200
THIRD PLEBEIAN O woeful day!

FOURTH PLEBEIAN O traitors! villains!

FIRST PLEBEIAN O most bloody sight!

SECOND PLEBEIAN We will be revenged.

ALL Revenge! About! Seek! Burn! Fire! Kill! Slay! Let
not a traitor live.

ANTONY Stay, countrymen.

FIRST PLEBEIAN Peace there! Hear the noble Antony!

SECOND PLEBEIAN We'll hear him, we'll follow him,
210 we'll die with him.

ANTONY

    Good friends, sweet friends, let me not stir you up
    To such a sudden flood of mutiny.
    They that have done this deed are honourable.
    What private griefs they have, alas, I know not,
    That made them do it. They are wise and honourable,
    And will, no doubt, with reasons answer you.
    I come not, friends, to steal away your hearts;
    I am no orator, as Brutus is,
    But, as you know me all, a plain blunt man,
220 That love my friend; and that they know full well
    That gave me public leave to speak of him.
    For I have neither wit, nor words, nor worth,
    Action, nor utterance, nor the power of speech
    To stir men's blood; I only speak right on.
    I tell you that which you yourselves do know,
    Show you sweet Caesar's wounds, poor poor dumb
        mouths,
    And bid them speak for me. But were I Brutus,
    And Brutus Antony, there were an Antony
    Would ruffle up your spirits, and put a tongue
230 In every wound of Caesar that should move
    The stones of Rome to rise and mutiny.

ALL

    We'll mutiny.

FIRST PLEBEIAN We'll burn the house of Brutus.

THIRD PLEBEIAN
  Away then! Come, seek the conspirators.

ANTONY
  Yet hear me, countrymen; yet hear me speak.

ALL Peace, ho! Hear Antony, most noble Antony!

ANTONY
  Why, friends, you go to do you know not what.
  Wherein hath Caesar thus deserved your loves?
  Alas, you know not! I must tell you then:
  You have forgot the will I told you of.

ALL
  Most true. The will! Let's stay and hear the will.   240

ANTONY.
  Here is the will, and under Caesar's seal.
  To every Roman citizen he gives,
  To every several man, seventy-five drachmas.

SECOND PLEBEIAN
  Most noble Caesar! We'll revenge his death.

THIRD PLEBEIAN O royal Caesar!

ANTONY Hear me with patience.

ALL Peace, ho!

ANTONY
  Moreover, he hath left you all his walks,
  His private arbours, and new-planted orchards,
  On this side Tiber; he hath left them you,   250
  And to your heirs for ever: common pleasures,
  To walk abroad and recreate yourselves.
  Here was a Caesar! When comes such another?

FIRST PLEBEIAN
  Never, never! Come, away, away!
  We'll burn his body in the holy place,
  And with the brands fire the traitors' houses.
  Take up the body.

SECOND PLEBEIAN Go fetch fire.

THIRD PLEBEIAN Pluck down benches.

260 FOURTH PLEBEIAN Pluck down forms, windows, anything.

Exeunt Plebeians with the body

ANTONY

Now let it work. Mischief, thou art afoot,

Take thou what course thou wilt.

Enter Servant

How now, fellow?

SERVANT

Sir, Octavius is already come to Rome.

ANTONY Where is he?

SERVANT

He and Lepidus are at Caesar's house.

ANTONY

And thither will I straight to visit him.

He comes upon a wish. Fortune is merry,

And in this mood will give us anything.

SERVANT

270 I heard him say Brutus and Cassius

Are rid like madmen through the gates of Rome.

ANTONY

Belike they had some notice of the people,

How I had moved them. Bring me to Octavius.

Exeunt

III.3   *Enter Cinna the Poet, and after him the Plebeians*

CINNA

I dreamt tonight that I did feast with Caesar,

And things unluckily charge my fantasy;

I have no will to wander forth of doors,

Yet something leads me forth.

The Plebeians surround him

FIRST PLEBEIAN What is your name?

SECOND PLEBEIAN Whither are you going?

THIRD PLEBEIAN Where do you dwell?

FOURTH PLEBEIAN Are you a married man or a bachelor?

SECOND PLEBEIAN Answer every man directly.

FIRST PLEBEIAN Ay, and briefly.   10

FOURTH PLEBEIAN Ay, and wisely.

THIRD PLEBEIAN Ay, and truly, you were best.

CINNA What is my name? Whither am I going? Where
do I dwell? Am I a married man or a bachelor? Then to
answer every man directly and briefly, wisely and truly;
wisely I say, I am a bachelor.

SECOND PLEBEIAN That's as much as to say they are
fools that marry. You'll bear me a bang for that, I fear.
Proceed, directly.

CINNA Directly, I am going to Caesar's funeral.   20

FIRST PLEBEIAN As a friend or an enemy?

CINNA As a friend.

SECOND PLEBEIAN That matter is answered directly.

FOURTH PLEBEIAN For your dwelling, briefly.

CINNA Briefly, I dwell by the Capitol.

THIRD PLEBEIAN Your name, sir, truly.

CINNA Truly, my name is Cinna.

FIRST PLEBEIAN Tear him to pieces! He's a conspirator.

CINNA I am Cinna the poet, I am Cinna the poet.

FOURTH PLEBEIAN Tear him for his bad verses, tear him   30
for his bad verses!

CINNA I am not Cinna the conspirator.

FOURTH PLEBEIAN It is no matter, his name's Cinna;
pluck but his name out of his heart, and turn him going.

THIRD PLEBEIAN Tear him, tear him!

They attack Cinna

Come, brands, ho, firebrands! To Brutus', to Cassius';

burn all! Some to Decius' house, and some to Casca's;
some to Ligarius'. Away, go!

Exeunt all the Plebeians with Cinna's body

*

IV.1   *Enter Antony, Octavius, and Lepidus*

ANTONY

These many then shall die; their names are pricked.

OCTAVIUS

Your brother too must die; consent you, Lepidus?

LEPIDUS

I do consent.

OCTAVIUS   Prick him down, Antony.

LEPIDUS

Upon condition Publius shall not live,
Who is your sister's son, Mark Antony.

ANTONY

He shall not live. Look, with a spot I damn him.
But, Lepidus, go you to Caesar's house;
Fetch the will hither, and we shall determine
How to cut off some charge in legacies.

LEPIDUS

10   What, shall I find you here?

OCTAVIUS

Or here or at the Capitol.   *Exit Lepidus*

ANTONY

This is a slight unmeritable man,
Meet to be sent on errands. Is it fit,
The three-fold world divided, he should stand
One of the three to share it?

OCTAVIUS   So you thought him,
And took his voice who should be pricked to die

In our black sentence and proscription.

ANTONY

Octavius, I have seen more days than you;
And though we lay these honours on this man,
To ease ourselves of divers slanderous loads,   20
He shall but bear them as the ass bears gold,
To groan and sweat under the business,
Either led or driven, as we point the way;
And having brought our treasure where we will,
Then take we down his load, and turn him off,
Like to the empty ass, to shake his ears
And graze in commons.

OCTAVIUS   You may do your will;
But he's a tried and valiant soldier.

ANTONY

So is my horse, Octavius, and for that
I do appoint him store of provender.   30
It is a creature that I teach to fight,
To wind, to stop, to run directly on,
His corporal motion governed by my spirit.
And, in some taste, is Lepidus but so:
He must be taught, and trained, and bid go forth:
A barren-spirited fellow; one that feeds
On objects, arts, and imitations,
Which, out of use and staled by other men,
Begins his fashion. Do not talk of him
But as a property. And now, Octavius,   40
Listen great things. Brutus and Cassius
Are levying powers; we must straight make head.
Therefore let our alliance be combined,
Our best friends made, our means stretched;
And let us presently go sit in council,
How covert matters may be best disclosed,
And open perils surest answerèd.

OCTAVIUS

　　Let us do so; for we are at the stake,

　　And bayed about with many enemies;

50　　And some that smile have in their hearts, I fear,

　　Millions of mischiefs.   *Exeunt*

IV.2　　　*Drum*

　　　　Enter Brutus, Lucilius, Lucius, and the army. Titinius

　　　　and Pindarus meet them

BRUTUS Stand, ho!

LUCILIUS Give the word, ho! and stand!

BRUTUS

　　What now, Lucilius, is Cassius near?

LUCILIUS

　　He is at hand, and Pindarus is come

　　To do you salutation from his master.

BRUTUS

　　He greets me well. Your master, Pindarus,

　　In his own change, or by ill officers,

　　Hath given me some worthy cause to wish

　　Things done undone; but if he be at hand

10　　I shall be satisfied.

PINDARUS　　　　　I do not doubt

　　But that my noble master will appear

　　Such as he is, full of regard and honour.

BRUTUS

　　He is not doubted. A word, Lucilius;

　　　Brutus and Lucilius draw apart

　　How he received you, let me be resolved.

LUCILIUS

　　With courtesy and with respect enough,

　　But not with such familiar instances,

　　Nor with such free and friendly conference,

As he hath used of old.

BRUTUS   Thou hast described
A hot friend cooling. Ever note, Lucilius,
When love begins to sicken and decay,   20
It useth an enforcèd ceremony.
There are no tricks in plain and simple faith;
But hollow men, like horses hot at hand,
Make gallant show and promise of their mettle;
    Low march within
But when they should endure the bloody spur,
They fall their crests, and like deceitful jades
Sink in the trial. Comes his army on?

LUCILIUS
They mean this night in Sardis to be quartered;
The greater part, the horse in general,
Are come with Cassius.
    Enter Cassius and his powers
                        Hark! he is arrived.   30
March gently on to meet him.

CASSIUS Stand, ho!

BRUTUS Stand, ho! Speak the word along.

FIRST SOLDIER Stand!

SECOND SOLDIER Stand!

THIRD SOLDIER Stand!

CASSIUS
Most noble brother, you have done me wrong.

BRUTUS
Judge me, you gods; wrong I mine enemies?
And if not so, how should I wrong a brother?

CASSIUS
Brutus, this sober form of yours hides wrongs;   40
And when you do them –

BRUTUS   Cassius, be content.
Speak your griefs softly; I do know you well.

Before the eyes of both our armies here,
Which should perceive nothing but love from us,
Let us not wrangle. Bid them move away;
Then in my tent, Cassius, enlarge your griefs,
And I will give you audience.

CASSIUS   Pindarus,
Bid our commanders lead their charges off
A little from this ground.

BRUTUS
50   Lucius, do you the like, and let no man
Come to our tent till we have done our conference.
Lucilius and Titinius guard our door.

Exeunt all except Brutus and Cassius

IV.3   CASSIUS
That you have wronged me doth appear in this:
You have condemned and noted Lucius Pella
For taking bribes here of the Sardians;
Wherein my letters, praying on his side,
Because I knew the man, was slighted off.

BRUTUS
You wronged yourself to write in such a case.

CASSIUS
In such a time as this it is not meet
That every nice offence should bear his comment.

BRUTUS
Let me tell you, Cassius, you yourself
10   Are much condemned to have an itching palm,
To sell and mart your offices for gold
To undeservers.

CASSIUS   I an itching palm!
You know that you are Brutus that speaks this,
Or, by the gods, this speech were else your last.

BRUTUS
     The name of Cassius honours this corruption,
     And chastisement doth therefore hide his head.
CASSIUS
     Chastisement!
BRUTUS
     Remember March, the ides of March remember.
     Did not great Julius bleed for justice' sake?
     What villain touched his body, that did stab,   20
     And not for justice? What, shall one of us,
     That struck the foremost man of all this world
     But for supporting robbers, shall we now
     Contaminate our fingers with base bribes,
     And sell the mighty space of our large honours
     For so much trash as may be graspèd thus?
     I had rather be a dog, and bay the moon,
     Than such a Roman.
CASSIUS   Brutus, bait not me;
     I'll not endure it. You forget yourself,
     To hedge me in. I am a soldier, I,   30
     Older in practice, abler than yourself
     To make conditions.
BRUTUS   Go to! You are not, Cassius.
CASSIUS I am.
BRUTUS I say you are not.
CASSIUS
     Urge me no more, I shall forget myself;
     Have mind upon your health; tempt me no further.
BRUTUS Away, slight man!
CASSIUS
     Is't possible?
BRUTUS   Hear me, for I will speak.
     Must I give way and room to your rash choler?
     Shall I be frighted when a madman stares?   40

CASSIUS

    O ye gods, ye gods! Must I endure all this?

BRUTUS

    All this? Ay, more: fret till your proud heart break;
    Go show your slaves how choleric you are,
    And make your bondmen tremble. Must I budge?
    Must I observe you? Must I stand and crouch
    Under your testy humour? By the gods,
    You shall disgest the venom of your spleen,
    Though it do split you; for, from this day forth,
    I'll use you for my mirth, yea, for my laughter,
50   When you are waspish.

CASSIUS   Is it come to this?

BRUTUS

    You say you are a better soldier:
    Let it appear so; make your vaunting true,
    And it shall please me well. For mine own part,
    I shall be glad to learn of noble men.

CASSIUS

    You wrong me every way; you wrong me, Brutus.
    I said an elder soldier, not a better;
    Did I say better?

BRUTUS   If you did, I care not.

CASSIUS

    When Caesar lived, he durst not thus have moved me.

BRUTUS

    Peace, peace! You durst not so have tempted him.

60 CASSIUS I durst not?

BRUTUS No.

CASSIUS

    What, durst not tempt him?

BRUTUS   For your life you durst not.

CASSIUS

    Do not presume too much upon my love;

I may do that I shall be sorry for.

BRUTUS
You have done that you should be sorry for.
There is no terror, Cassius, in your threats;
For I am armed so strong in honesty
That they pass by me as the idle wind,
Which I respect not. I did send to you
For certain sums of gold, which you denied me;   70
For I can raise no money by vile means;
By heaven, I had rather coin my heart,
And drop my blood for drachmas, than to wring
From the hard hands of peasants their vile trash
By any indirection. I did send
To you for gold to pay my legions.
Which you denied me; was that done like Cassius?
Should I have answered Caius Cassius so?
When Marcus Brutus grows so covetous,
To lock such rascal counters from his friends,   80
Be ready, gods, with all your thunderbolts,
Dash him to pieces!

CASSIUS   I denied you not.

BRUTUS
You did.

CASSIUS   I did not. He was but a fool
That brought my answer back. Brutus hath rived my
        heart;
A friend should bear his friend's infirmities;
But Brutus makes mine greater than they are.

BRUTUS
I do not, till you practise them on me.

CASSIUS
You love me not.

BRUTUS   I do not like your faults.

CASSIUS
    A friendly eye could never see such faults.

BRUTUS
90   A flatterer's would not, though they do appear
    As huge as high Olympus.

CASSIUS
    Come, Antony, and young Octavius, come,
    Revenge yourselves alone on Cassius,
    For Cassius is aweary of the world;
    Hated by one he loves; braved by his brother;
    Checked like a bondman; all his faults observed,
    Set in a notebook, learned, and conned by rote,
    To cast into my teeth. O, I could weep
    My spirit from mine eyes! There is my dagger,
100   And here my naked breast; within, a heart
    Dearer than Pluto's mine, richer than gold:
    If that thou be'st a Roman, take it forth.
    I, that denied thee gold, will give my heart:
    Strike, as thou didst at Caesar; for I know,
    When thou didst hate him worst, thou lovedst him better
    Than ever thou lovedst Cassius.

BRUTUS   Sheathe your dagger.
    Be angry when you will, it shall have scope;
    Do what you will, dishonour shall be humour.
    O Cassius, you are yokèd with a lamb
110   That carries anger as the flint bears fire,
    Who, much enforcèd, shows a hasty spark,
    And straight is cold again.

CASSIUS   Hath Cassius lived
    To be but mirth and laughter to his Brutus,
    When grief and blood ill-tempered vexeth him?

BRUTUS
    When I spoke that, I was ill-tempered too.

CASSIUS

   Do you confess so much? Give me your hand.

BRUTUS

   And my heart too.

CASSIUS   O Brutus!

BRUTUS   What's the matter?

CASSIUS

   Have not you love enough to bear with me,
   When that rash humour which my mother gave me
   Makes me forgetful?

BRUTUS   Yes, Cassius; and from henceforth,   120
   When you are over-earnest with your Brutus,
   He'll think your mother chides, and leave you so.

   Enter a Poet followed by Lucius; Titinius and Lucilius
   attempting to restrain him

POET

   Let me go in to see the Generals.
   There is some grudge between 'em; 'tis not meet
   They be alone.

LUCILIUS   You shall not come to them.

POET

   Nothing but death shall stay me.

CASSIUS

   How now? What's the matter?

POET

   For shame, you Generals! What do you mean?
   Love, and be friends, as two such men should be;
   For I have seen more years, I'm sure, than ye.   130

CASSIUS

   Ha, ha! How vilely doth this cynic rhyme!

BRUTUS

   Get you hence, sirrah! Saucy fellow, hence!

CASSIUS

   Bear with him, Brutus; 'tis his fashion.

BRUTUS

    I'll know his humour, when he knows his time.

    What should the wars do with these jigging fools?

    Companion, hence!

CASSIUS   Away, away, be gone!   *Exit Poet*

BRUTUS

    Lucilius and Titinius, bid the commanders

    Prepare to lodge their companies tonight.

CASSIUS

    And come yourselves, and bring Messala with you

140   Immediately to us.   *Exeunt Lucilius and Titinius*

BRUTUS   Lucius, a bowl of wine.   *Exit Lucius*

CASSIUS

    I did not think you could have been so angry.

BRUTUS

    O Cassius, I am sick of many griefs.

CASSIUS

    Of your philosophy you make no use,

    If you give place to accidental evils.

BRUTUS

    No man bears sorrow better. Portia is dead.

CASSIUS Ha? Portia?

BRUTUS She is dead.

CASSIUS

    How 'scaped I killing, when I crossed you so?

    O insupportable and touching loss!

150   Upon what sickness?

BRUTUS   Impatient of my absence,

    And grief that young Octavius with Mark Antony

    Have made themselves so strong; for with her death

    That tidings came. With this she fell distract,

    And, her attendants absent, swallowed fire.

CASSIUS

    And died so?

BRUTUS   Even so.

CASSIUS   O ye immortal gods!
    Enter Boy (Lucius) with wine and tapers

BRUTUS
    Speak no more of her. Give me a bowl of wine.
    In this I bury all unkindness, Cassius.
      He drinks

CASSIUS
    My heart is thirsty for that noble pledge.
    Fill, Lucius, till the wine o'erswell the cup;
    I cannot drink too much of Brutus' love.   *Exit Lucius*   160
      Cassius drinks
      Enter Titinius and Messala

BRUTUS
    Come in, Titinius. Welcome, good Messala.
    Now sit we close about this taper here,
    And call in question our necessities.

CASSIUS
    Portia, art thou gone?

BRUTUS   No more, I pray you.
    Messala, I have here receivèd letters,
    That young Octavius and Mark Antony
    Come down upon us with a mighty power,
    Bending their expedition toward Philippi.

MESSALA
    Myself have letters of the self-same tenor.

BRUTUS
    With what addition?   170

MESSALA
    That by proscription and bills of outlawry
    Octavius, Antony, and Lepidus
    Have put to death an hundred senators.

BRUTUS
    Therein our letters do not well agree.

Mine speak of seventy senators that died
By their proscriptions, Cicero being one.

CASSIUS

Cicero one?

MESSALA   Cicero is dead,
And by that order of proscription.
Had you your letters from your wife, my lord?

180 BRUTUS No, Messala.

MESSALA

Nor nothing in your letters writ of her?

BRUTUS

Nothing, Messala.

MESSALA   That, methinks, is strange.

BRUTUS

Why ask you? Hear you aught of her in yours?

MESSALA

No, my lord.

BRUTUS

Now, as you are a Roman, tell me true.

MESSALA

Then like a Roman bear the truth I tell;
For certain she is dead, and by strange manner.

BRUTUS

Why, farewell, Portia. We must die, Messala.
With meditating that she must die once,

190 I have the patience to endure it now.

MESSALA

Even so great men great losses should endure.

CASSIUS

I have as much of this in art as you,
But yet my nature could not bear it so.

BRUTUS

Well, to our work alive. What do you think
Of marching to Philippi presently?

CASSIUS

   I do not think it good.

BRUTUS   Your reason?

CASSIUS   This it is:

   'Tis better that the enemy seek us;

   So shall he waste his means, weary his soldiers,

   Doing himself offence, whilst we, lying still,

   Are full of rest, defence, and nimbleness.   200

BRUTUS

   Good reasons must of force give place to better.

   The people 'twixt Philippi and this ground

   Do stand but in a forced affection;

   For they have grudged us contribution.

   The enemy, marching along by them,

   By them shall make a fuller number up,

   Come on refreshed, new-added, and encouraged;

   From which advantage shall we cut him off,

   If at Philippi we do face him there,

   These people at our back.

CASSIUS   Hear me, good brother –   210

BRUTUS

   Under your pardon. You must note beside

   That we have tried the utmost of our friends,

   Our legions are brim-full, our cause is ripe.

   The enemy increaseth every day;

   We, at the height, are ready to decline.

   There is a tide in the affairs of men,

   Which, taken at the flood, leads on to fortune;

   Omitted, all the voyage of their life

   Is bound in shallows and in miseries.

   On such a full sea are we now afloat,   220

   And we must take the current when it serves,

   Or lose our ventures.

CASSIUS   Then, with your will, go on;

We'll along ourselves, and meet them at Philippi.

BRUTUS

The deep of night is crept upon our talk,
And nature must obey necessity,
Which we will niggard with a little rest.
There is no more to say?

CASSIUS   No more. Good night.
Early tomorrow will we rise, and hence.

BRUTUS

Lucius!

Enter Lucius

My gown.   *Exit Lucius*

Farewell, good Messala.
230   Good night, Titinius. Noble, noble Cassius,
Good night, and good repose.

CASSIUS   O my dear brother,
This was an ill beginning of the night;
Never come such division 'tween our souls!
Let it not, Brutus.

Enter Lucius, with the gown

BRUTUS   Everything is well.

CASSIUS

Good night, my lord.

BRUTUS   Good night, good brother.

TITINIUS *and* MESSALA

Good night, Lord Brutus.

BRUTUS   Farewell, every one.

Exeunt Cassius, Titinius, and Messala

Give me the gown. Where is thy instrument?

LUCIUS

Here in the tent.

BRUTUS   What, thou speak'st drowsily?
Poor knave, I blame thee not; thou art o'erwatched.
240   Call Claudius and some other of my men;

I'll have them sleep on cushions in my tent.

LUCIUS Varro and Claudius!

Enter Varro and Claudius

VARRO Calls my lord?

BRUTUS

I pray you, sirs, lie in my tent and sleep;
It may be I shall raise you by and by
On business to my brother Cassius.

VARRO

So please you, we will stand and watch your pleasure.

BRUTUS

I will not have it so; lie down, good sirs.
It may be I shall otherwise bethink me.

Varro and Claudius lie down

Look, Lucius, here's the book I sought for so;   250
I put it in the pocket of my gown.

LUCIUS

I was sure your lordship did not give it me.

BRUTUS

Bear with me, good boy, I am much forgetful.
Canst thou hold up thy heavy eyes awhile,
And touch thy instrument a strain or two?

LUCIUS

Ay, my lord, an't please you.

BRUTUS   It does, my boy.
I trouble thee too much, but thou art willing.

LUCIUS

It is my duty, sir.

BRUTUS

I should not urge thy duty past thy might;
I know young bloods look for a time of rest.   260

LUCIUS

I have slept, my lord, already.

BRUTUS

It was well done, and thou shalt sleep again;
I will not hold thee long. If I do live,
I will be good to thee.
    Music, and a song
    Lucius falls asleep
This is a sleepy tune; O murderous slumber,
Layest thou thy leaden mace upon my boy,
That plays thee music? Gentle knave, good night;
I will not do thee so much wrong to wake thee.
If thou dost nod, thou break'st thy instrument;
270   I'll take it from thee; and, good boy, good night.
Let me see, let me see; is not the leaf turned down
Where I left reading? Here it is, I think.
    He sits and reads
    Enter the Ghost of Caesar
How ill this taper burns! Ha! Who comes here?
I think it is the weakness of mine eyes
That shapes this monstrous apparition.
It comes upon me. Art thou any thing?
Art thou some god, some angel, or some devil,
That mak'st my blood cold, and my hair to stare?
Speak to me what thou art.

GHOST

280   Thy evil spirit, Brutus.

BRUTUS   Why com'st thou?

GHOST

To tell thee thou shalt see me at Philippi.

BRUTUS Well; then I shall see thee again?

GHOST Ay, at Philippi.

BRUTUS

Why, I will see thee at Philippi then.   *Exit Ghost*
Now I have taken heart, thou vanishest.
Ill spirit, I would hold more talk with thee.

Boy! Lucius! Varro! Claudius! Sirs, awake!
Claudius!

LUCIUS

The strings, my lord, are false.

BRUTUS

He thinks he still is at his instrument.   290
Lucius, awake!

LUCIUS

My lord?

BRUTUS

Didst thou dream, Lucius, that thou so criedst out?

LUCIUS

My lord, I do not know that I did cry.

BRUTUS

Yes, that thou didst. Didst thou see anything?

LUCIUS

Nothing, my lord.

BRUTUS

Sleep again, Lucius. Sirrah Claudius!
Fellow thou, awake!

VARRO   My lord?

CLAUDIUS   My lord?

BRUTUS

Why did you so cry out, sirs, in your sleep?

VARRO *and* CLAUDIUS

Did we, my lord?

BRUTUS   Ay; saw you anything?   300

VARRO

No, my lord, I saw nothing.

CLAUDIUS   Nor I, my lord.

BRUTUS

Go, and commend me to my brother Cassius.
Bid him set on his powers betimes before,

And we will follow.

VARRO *and* CLAUDIUS It shall be done, my lord.

Exeunt

*

V.I   *Enter Octavius, Antony, and their army*

OCTAVIUS

Now, Antony, our hopes are answerèd:
You said the enemy would not come down,
But keep the hills and upper regions.
It proves not so; their battles are at hand;
They mean to warn us at Philippi here,
Answering before we do demand of them.

ANTONY

Tut, I am in their bosoms, and I know
Wherefore they do it. They could be content
To visit other places, and come down
With fearful bravery, thinking by this face
To fasten in our thoughts that they have courage;
But 'tis not so.

Enter a Messenger

MESSENGER   Prepare you, Generals;
The enemy comes on in gallant show.
Their bloody sign of battle is hung out,
And something to be done immediately.

ANTONY

Octavius, lead your battle softly on
Upon the left hand of the even field.

OCTAVIUS

Upon the right hand I. Keep thou the left.

ANTONY

Why do you cross me in this exigent?

OCTAVIUS
 I do not cross you; but I will do so.   20
   March
   Drum
   Enter Brutus, Cassius, and their army; Lucilius,
   Titinius, Messala, and others
BRUTUS
 They stand, and would have parley.
CASSIUS
 Stand fast, Titinius; we must out and talk.
OCTAVIUS
 Mark Antony, shall we give sign of battle?
ANTONY
 No, Caesar, we will answer on their charge.
 Make forth; the Generals would have some words.
OCTAVIUS
 Stir not until the signal.
BRUTUS
 Words before blows: is it so, countrymen?
OCTAVIUS
 Not that we love words better, as you do.
BRUTUS
 Good words are better than bad strokes, Octavius.
ANTONY
 In your bad strokes, Brutus, you give good words;   30
 Witness the hole you made in Caesar's heart,
 Crying, 'Long live! Hail, Caesar!'
CASSIUS   Antony,
 The posture of your blows are yet unknown;
 But for your words, they rob the Hybla bees,
 And leave them honeyless.
ANTONY   Not stingless too.
BRUTUS
 O yes, and soundless too;

For you have stolen their buzzing, Antony,
And very wisely threat before you sting.

ANTONY

Villains! You did not so, when your vile daggers
40   Hacked one another in the sides of Caesar:
You showed your teeth like apes, and fawned like hounds,
And bowed like bondmen, kissing Caesar's feet;
Whilst damnèd Casca, like a cur, behind
Struck Caesar on the neck. O you flatterers!

CASSIUS

Flatterers? Now, Brutus, thank yourself:
This tongue had not offended so today,
If Cassius might have ruled.

OCTAVIUS

Come, come, the cause. If arguing make us sweat,
The proof of it will turn to redder drops.
50   Look,
I draw a sword against conspirators.
When think you that the sword goes up again?
Never till Caesar's three and thirty wounds
Be well avenged; or till another Caesar
Have added slaughter to the sword of traitors.

BRUTUS

Caesar, thou canst not die by traitors' hands,
Unless thou bring'st them with thee.

OCTAVIUS   So I hope.
I was not born to die on Brutus' sword.

BRUTUS

O, if thou wert the noblest of thy strain,
60   Young man, thou couldst not die more honourable.

CASSIUS

A peevish schoolboy, worthless of such honour,
Joined with a masquer and a reveller.

ANTONY
  Old Cassius, still!
OCTAVIUS   Come, Antony; away!
  Defiance, traitors, hurl we in your teeth.
  If you dare fight today, come to the field;
  If not, when you have stomachs.
                    Exeunt Octavius, Antony, and army
CASSIUS
  Why now, blow wind, swell billow, and swim bark!
  The storm is up, and all is on the hazard.
BRUTUS
  Ho, Lucilius, hark, a word with you.
LUCILIUS   My lord?
      Lucilius stands forth, and talks with Brutus apart
CASSIUS
  Messala.
MESSALA What says my General?
      Messala stands forth
CASSIUS   Messala,   70
  This is my birthday; as this very day
  Was Cassius born. Give me thy hand, Messala:
  Be thou my witness that against my will —
  As Pompey was — am I compelled to set
  Upon one battle all our liberties.
  You know that I held Epicurus strong,
  And his opinion; now I change my mind,
  And partly credit things that do presage.
  Coming from Sardis, on our former ensign
  Two mighty eagles fell, and there they perched,   80
  Gorging and feeding from our soldiers' hands,
  Who to Philippi here consorted us.
  This morning are they fled away and gone,
  And in their steads do ravens, crows, and kites
  Fly o'er our heads and downward look on us,

As we were sickly prey; their shadows seem
A canopy most fatal, under which
Our army lies, ready to give up the ghost.

MESSALA

Believe not so.

CASSIUS   I but believe it partly,
90   For I am fresh of spirit, and resolved
To meet all perils very constantly.

BRUTUS

Even so, Lucilius.

Brutus rejoins Cassius

CASSIUS   Now, most noble Brutus,
The gods today stand friendly, that we may,
Lovers in peace, lead on our days to age!
But since the affairs of men rests still incertain,
Let's reason with the worst that may befall.
If we do lose this battle, then is this
The very last time we shall speak together;
What are you then determinèd to do?

BRUTUS

100   Even by the rule of that philosophy
By which I did blame Cato for the death
Which he did give himself – I know not how,
But I do find it cowardly and vile,
For fear of what might fall, so to prevent
The time of life – arming myself with patience
To stay the providence of some high powers
That govern us below.

CASSIUS   Then, if we lose this battle,
You are contented to be led in triumph
Thorough the streets of Rome?

BRUTUS

110   No, Cassius, no; think not, thou noble Roman,
That ever Brutus will go bound to Rome;

He bears too great a mind. But this same day
Must end that work the ides of March begun;
And whether we shall meet again I know not.
Therefore our everlasting farewell take:
For ever, and for ever, farewell, Cassius.
If we do meet again, why, we shall smile;
If not, why then this parting was well made.

CASSIUS
For ever, and for ever, farewell, Brutus.
If we do meet again, we'll smile indeed;   120
If not, 'tis true this parting was well made.

BRUTUS
Why then, lead on. O, that a man might know
The end of this day's business ere it come!
But it sufficeth that the day will end,
And then the end is known. Come, ho! Away! *Exeunt*

Alarum   V.2
Enter Brutus and Messala

BRUTUS
Ride, ride, Messala, ride, and give these bills
Unto the legions on the other side.
    Loud alarum
Let them set on at once; for I perceive
But cold demeanour in Octavius' wing,
And sudden push gives them the overthrow.
Ride, ride, Messala; let them all come down. *Exeunt*

Alarums   V.3
Enter Cassius and Titinius

CASSIUS
O, look, Titinius, look, the villains fly.

Myself have to mine own turned enemy:
This Ensign here of mine was turning back;
I slew the coward, and did take it from him.

TITINIUS

O Cassius, Brutus gave the word too early,
Who, having some advantage on Octavius,
Took it too eagerly; his soldiers fell to spoil,
Whilst we by Antony are all enclosed.

Enter Pindarus

PINDARUS

Fly further off, my lord, fly further off!

10   Mark Antony is in your tents, my lord.
Fly therefore, noble Cassius, fly far off!

CASSIUS

This hill is far enough. Look, look, Titinius!
Are those my tents where I perceive the fire?

TITINIUS

They are, my lord.

CASSIUS   Titinius, if thou lov'st me,
Mount thou my horse, and hide thy spurs in him,
Till he have brought thee up to yonder troops
And here again, that I may rest assured
Whether yond troops are friend or enemy.

TITINIUS

I will be here again, even with a thought.   *Exit*

CASSIUS

20   Go, Pindarus, get higher on that hill;
My sight was ever thick. Regard Titinius,
And tell me what thou not'st about the field.

Pindarus ascends

This day I breathèd first. Time is come round,
And where I did begin, there shall I end.
My life is run his compass. (*To Pindarus*) Sirrah, what
     news?

PINDARUS (*above*)
  O my lord!
CASSIUS
  What news?
PINDARUS
  Titinius is enclosèd round about
  With horsemen, that make to him on the spur,
  Yet he spurs on. Now they are almost on him.   30
  Now, Titinius! Now some light. O, he lights too!
  He's ta'en!
    Shout
            And hark! They shout for joy.
CASSIUS
  Come down; behold no more.
  O, coward that I am, to live so long,
  To see my best friend ta'en before my face!
    Enter Pindarus from above
  Come hither, sirrah.
  In Parthia did I take thee prisoner;
  And then I swore thee, saving of thy life,
  That whatsoever I did bid thee do,
  Thou shouldst attempt it. Come now, keep thine oath;   40
  Now be a freeman; and with this good sword,
  That ran through Caesar's bowels, search this bosom.
  Stand not to answer. Here, take thou the hilts,
  And when my face is covered, as 'tis now,
  Guide thou the sword. — Caesar, thou art revenged,
  Even with the sword that killed thee.   *He dies*
PINDARUS
  So, I am free; yet would not so have been,
  Durst I have done my will. O Cassius!
  Far from this country Pindarus shall run,
  Where never Roman shall take note of him.   *Exit*   50
    Enter Titinius and Messala

MESSALA

    It is but change, Titinius; for Octavius
    Is overthrown by noble Brutus' power,
    As Cassius' legions are by Antony.

TITINIUS

    These tidings will well comfort Cassius.

MESSALA

    Where did you leave him?

TITINIUS   All disconsolate,
    With Pindarus his bondman, on this hill.

MESSALA

    Is not that he that lies upon the ground?

TITINIUS

    He lies not like the living. O my heart!

MESSALA

    Is not that he?

TITINIUS   No, this was he, Messala,
60   But Cassius is no more. O setting sun,
    As in thy red rays thou dost sink to night,
    So in his red blood Cassius' day is set.
    The sun of Rome is set. Our day is gone;
    Clouds, dews, and dangers come; our deeds are done.
    Mistrust of my success hath done this deed.

MESSALA

    Mistrust of good success hath done this deed.
    O hateful Error, Melancholy's child,
    Why dost thou show to the apt thoughts of men
    The things that are not? O Error, soon conceived,
70   Thou never com'st unto a happy birth,
    But kill'st the mother that engendered thee.

TITINIUS

    What, Pindarus! Where art thou, Pindarus?

MESSALA

    Seek him, Titinius, whilst I go to meet

The noble Brutus, thrusting this report
Into his ears. I may say 'thrusting' it;
For piercing steel and darts envenomèd
Shall be as welcome to the ears of Brutus
As tidings of this sight.

TITINIUS   Hie you, Messala,
And I will seek for Pindarus the while.   *Exit Messala*
Why didst thou send me forth, brave Cassius?   80
Did I not meet thy friends, and did not they
Put on my brows this wreath of victory,
And bid me give it thee? Didst thou not hear their shouts?
Alas, thou hast misconstrued everything!
But hold thee, take this garland on thy brow;
Thy Brutus bid me give it thee, and I
Will do his bidding. Brutus, come apace,
And see how I regarded Caius Cassius.
By your leave, gods. This is a Roman's part;
Come, Cassius' sword, and find Titinius' heart.   90

                                        He dies

   Alarum
   Enter Brutus, Messala, Young Cato, Strato,
   Volumnius, Labeo, Flavius, and Lucilius

BRUTUS
Where, where, Messala, doth his body lie?

MESSALA
Lo, yonder, and Titinius mourning it.

BRUTUS
Titinius' face is upward.

CATO   He is slain.

BRUTUS
O Julius Caesar, thou art mighty yet!
Thy spirit walks abroad, and turns our swords
In our own proper entrails.

   Low alarums

CATO   Brave Titinius,
    Look where he have not crowned dead Cassius.
BRUTUS
    Are yet two Romans living such as these?
    The last of all the Romans, fare thee well!
100   It is impossible that ever Rome
    Should breed thy fellow. Friends, I owe more tears
    To this dead man than you shall see me pay.
    I shall find time, Cassius, I shall find time.
    Come therefore, and to Thasos send his body.
    His funerals shall not be in our camp,
    Lest it discomfort us. Lucilius, come;
    And come, young Cato; let us to the field.
    Labeo and Flavius, set our battles on.
    'Tis three o'clock; and, Romans, yet ere night
110   We shall try fortune in a second fight.   *Exeunt*

V.4   *Alarum*
    Enter Brutus, Messala, Young Cato, Lucilius, and
    Flavius
BRUTUS
    Yet countrymen, O, yet hold up your heads!
        Exit, followed by Messala and Flavius
CATO
    What bastard doth not? Who will go with me?
    I will proclaim my name about the field.
    I am the son of Marcus Cato, ho!
    A foe to tyrants, and my country's friend.
    I am the son of Marcus Cato, ho!
    Enter soldiers, and fight
LUCILIUS
    And I am Brutus, Marcus Brutus, I!
    Brutus, my country's friend; know me for Brutus!

Young Cato is slain

O young and noble Cato, art thou down?

Why, now thou diest as bravely as Titinius,   10

And mayst be honoured, being Cato's son.

FIRST SOLDIER

Yield, or thou diest.

LUCILIUS   Only I yield to die.

There is so much that thou wilt kill me straight:

Kill Brutus, and be honoured in his death.

FIRST SOLDIER We must not. A noble prisoner!

Enter Antony

SECOND SOLDIER

Room, ho! Tell Antony, Brutus is ta'en.

FIRST SOLDIER

I'll tell the news. Here comes the General.

Brutus is ta'en, Brutus is ta'en, my lord.

ANTONY Where is he?

LUCILIUS

Safe, Antony; Brutus is safe enough.   20

I dare assure thee that no enemy

Shall ever take alive the noble Brutus;

The gods defend him from so great a shame!

When you do find him, or alive or dead,

He will be found like Brutus, like himself.

ANTONY

This is not Brutus, friend; but, I assure you,

A prize no less in worth. Keep this man safe;

Give him all kindness. I had rather have

Such men my friends than enemies. Go on,

And see where Brutus be alive or dead;   30

And bring us word unto Octavius' tent

How every thing is chanced.   *Exeunt*

V.5   *Enter Brutus, Dardanius, Clitus, Strato, and Volumnius*

BRUTUS

Come, poor remains of friends, rest on this rock.

CLITUS

Statilius showed the torch-light; but, my lord,
He came not back; he is or ta'en or slain.

BRUTUS

Sit thee down, Clitus. Slaying is the word;
It is a deed in fashion. Hark thee, Clitus.
      He whispers

CLITUS

What, I, my lord? No, not for all the world.

BRUTUS

Peace then. No words.

CLITUS   I'll rather kill myself.

BRUTUS

Hark thee, Dardanius.
      He whispers

DARDANIUS   Shall I do such a deed?

CLITUS O Dardanius!

10 DARDANIUS O Clitus!

CLITUS

What ill request did Brutus make to thee?

DARDANIUS

To kill him, Clitus. Look, he meditates.

CLITUS

Now is that noble vessel full of grief,
That it runs over even at his eyes.

BRUTUS

Come hither, good Volumnius; list a word.

VOLUMNIUS

What says my lord?

BRUTUS   Why, this, Volumnius:
The ghost of Caesar hath appeared to me

Two several times by night: at Sardis once,
And this last night, here in Philippi fields.
I know my hour is come.

VOLUMNIUS   Not so, my lord.   20

BRUTUS

Nay, I am sure it is, Volumnius.
Thou seest the world, Volumnius, how it goes:
Our enemies have beat us to the pit.

    Low alarums

It is more worthy to leap in ourselves
Than tarry till they push us. Good Volumnius,
Thou know'st that we two went to school together;
Even for that our love of old, I prithee
Hold thou my sword-hilts whilst I run on it.

VOLUMNIUS

That's not an office for a friend, my lord.

    Alarum still

CLITUS

Fly, fly, my lord, there is no tarrying here.   30

BRUTUS

Farewell to you; and you; and you, Volumnius.
Strato, thou hast been all this while asleep;
Farewell to thee too, Strato. Countrymen,
My heart doth joy that yet in all my life
I found no man but he was true to me.
I shall have glory by this losing day
More than Octavius and Mark Antony
By this vile conquest shall attain unto.
So fare you well at once; for Brutus' tongue
Hath almost ended his life's history.   40
Night hangs upon mine eyes; my bones would rest,
That have but laboured to attain this hour.

    Alarum
    Cry within, 'Fly, fly, fly!'

CLITUS
    Fly, my lord, fly!
BRUTUS   Hence! I will follow.
                    Exeunt Clitus, Dardanius, and Volumnius
    I prithee, Strato, stay thou by thy lord.
    Thou art a fellow of a good respect;
    Thy life hath had some smatch of honour in it.
    Hold then my sword, and turn away thy face,
    While I do run upon it. Wilt thou, Strato?
STRATO
    Give me your hand first. Fare you well, my lord.
BRUTUS
50   Farewell, good Strato. – Caesar, now be still;
    I killed not thee with half so good a will.   *He dies*
        Alarum
        Retreat
        Enter Antony, Octavius, Messala, Lucilius, and the
        army
OCTAVIUS
    What man is that?
MESSALA
    My master's man. Strato, where is thy master?
STRATO
    Free from the bondage you are in, Messala.
    The conquerors can but make a fire of him;
    For Brutus only overcame himself,
    And no man else hath honour by his death.
LUCILIUS
    So Brutus should be found. I thank thee, Brutus,
    That thou hast proved Lucilius' saying true.
OCTAVIUS
60   All that served Brutus, I will entertain them.
    Fellow, wilt thou bestow thy time with me?

STRATO

Ay, if Messala will prefer me to you.

OCTAVIUS

Do so, good Messala.

MESSALA

How died my master, Strato?

STRATO

I held the sword, and he did run on it.

MESSALA

Octavius, then take him to follow thee,

That did the latest service to my master.

ANTONY

This was the noblest Roman of them all.

All the conspirators save only he

Did that they did in envy of great Caesar;   70

He only, in a general honest thought

And common good to all, made one of them.

His life was gentle, and the elements

So mixed in him, that Nature might stand up

And say to all the world, 'This was a man!'

OCTAVIUS

According to his virtue let us use him,

With all respect and rites of burial.

Within my tent his bones tonight shall lie,

Most like a soldier, ordered honourably.

So call the field to rest, and let's away,   80

To part the glories of this happy day.   *Exeunt all*

An Account of the Text

The Tragedy of Julius Caesar was first printed in the Folio edition (F) of Shakespeare's plays of 1623. The copy the printers used was probably a transcript of some kind rather than Shakespeare's own manuscript, as there is an absence of typical Shakespeare spellings such as appear in other texts printed from authorial copy. The manuscript may well have been one that had been used as a prompt book, because some of the stage directions appear to be theatrical in character. The Folio text is the only early printed version of the play which has any authority; the texts found in the later Folios of 1632, 1664 and 1685, and in the six seventeenth-century Quarto editions, are all ultimately based on the first printing.

In general the text is a good one, the only errors being a few typographical misprints, occasional mispunctuation, some mislineation due to the requirements of spacing on the Folio page, some wrong assignment of speeches and some verbal corruptions. The origin of most of the readings that are obviously or probably incorrect is susceptible of satisfactory explanation.

But there is some evidence that the play underwent a certain amount of revision between its composition and its first appearance in print. Two passages convincingly support this hypothesis. The first is at III.1.47–8, which reads:

Know, Caesar doth not wrong, nor without cause
Will he be satisfied.

This was apparently not the original and acted version of the lines, for Ben Jonson, in his *Timber: Or Discoveries Made Upon Men and Matters* (1640), notes about Shakespeare:

Many times he fell into those things, could not escape laughter: as when he said in the person of Caesar, one speaking to him, *Caesar thou dost me wrong*; he replied, *Caesar did never wrong, but with just cause*; and such like, which were ridiculous.

In *The Staple of News* (1625) also, Jonson makes fun of the same lines:

EXPECTATION I can do that too, if I have cause.
PROLOGUE Cry you mercy, *you never did wrong, but with just cause.*

It would seem probable, therefore, that the Folio text represents an adjustment of the original lines made by Shakespeare or his theatre company in response to Jonson's criticism.

The second passage occurs in IV.3.145–93, where there are two contradictory accounts of Portia's death. The first of these, at lines 145–56, shows Brutus in part accounting for his loss of temper with the intruding poet by informing Cassius of his grief at having heard the news that Portia has committed suicide, and thus reinforces our impression of Brutus as a very human though publicly dedicated man. In the second account, at lines 179–93, Brutus denies he has had word from Rome concerning his wife, and on being informed of her death by Messala, accepts the news with a display of superhuman fortitude:

Why, farewell, Portia. We must die, Messala.
With meditating that she must die once,
I have the patience to endure it now . . .
Well, to our work alive.

Although some critics have defended the presence of these two passages, it is generally believed that the version at lines 145–56 was a later addition intended to replace the exchange at lines 179–93, which was imperfectly deleted in the manuscript from which the Folio text was printed. If lines 179–93 are omitted, the scene runs quite smoothly with Brutus' line 'Well, to our work alive' referring to Cicero's death, which is announced by Messala in lines 177–8, instead of to Portia's.

Other pieces of evidence of revision or cutting, which have been adduced by various scholars, and which carry less conviction than those already mentioned, are: the appearance of Publius at Caesar's house in II.2 in place of Cassius who declares, at II.1.212, that he intends to join the other conspirators in bringing Caesar to the Capitol; and some inconsistencies seen in the behaviour of Casca, which have led to the contention that he is a 'ragbag' character formed from the conflating of previously separate roles.

COLLATIONS

l

Below are listed departures in the present text of *Julius Caesar* from that of the first Folio, whose reading is given on the right of the square bracket. Most of these emendations were first made by eighteenth-century editors of the play. Those found in one of the three seventeenth-century reprints of the Folio (F2, F3 and F4) are indicated.

I.1

22 tradesman's] Tradesmans
women's] womens

37 Pompey? Many a time and oft] Pompey many a time and oft?

39 windows, yea,] Windowes? Yea,

I.2

127 'Alas!'] *It is not clear from* F1 *whether* Alas *is part of Caesar's reported speech, or Cassius' comment on it.*

154 walls] Walkes

165 not – so with] not so (with

242 hooted] howted

246 swooned] swoonded

249 swoon] swound

252 like; he] like he

I.3

    28 Hooting] Howting

  129 In favour's like] Is Fauors, like

II.1

    15 Crown him! – that!] Crowne him that

    23 climber-upward] Climber upward

    40 ides] first

    52 What, Rome?] What Rome?

    67 of man] (F2); of a man

    83 path, thy] path thy

  246 wafture] wafter

  295 reputed, Cato's] reputed: Cato's

  330 going] going,

II.2

    19 fought] fight

    23 did neigh] (F2); do neigh

    46 are] heare

III.1

    39 law] lane

  113 states] (F2); state

  115 lies] (F2); lye

  209 strucken] stroken

  283 catching, for] (F2); catching from

III.2

  105 art] (F2); are

  111 Has he, masters?] Ha's hee Masters?

  158 will?] Will:

204–6 SECOND PLEBEIAN We will be revenged. | ALL
        Revenge! . . . live.] 2. We will be reueng'd: Reueng |
        About . . . slay, | Let . . . liue.

  222 wit] (F2); writ

IV.2

    13 Lucilius;] Lucillius

    14 you,] you:

    50 Lucius] Lucilius

    52 Lucilius] Let Lucius

IV.3

  4–5 letters, praying . . . man, was] Letters, praying . . .
      man was

227 say?] say.
229 *Enter Lucius*] *In* F1 *this follows* hence (*line 228 of this edition*)

V.I

41 teeth] (F3); teethes
69 *Lucilius stands forth, and talks with Brutus apart*] *Lucillius and Messala stand forth. In* F1 *this follows* with you (*line 69 of this edition*)
109 Rome?] Rome.

V.3

97 have not crowned] *Some copies of* F1 *have:* haue crown'd
101 more tears] mo teares *Some copies of* F1 *have:* no teares
104 Thasos] Tharsus

V.4

7–8 LUCILIUS] F1 *has no speech-prefix*
9 O] *Luc.* O
17 the news] thee news

V.5

23 *Low alarums*] *Some copies of* F1 *have:* Loud Alarums
33 to thee too, Strato. Countrymen] to thee, to Strato, Countrymen:
40 life's] liues
71 He only,] (F2); He, onely

2

Below are listed instances where the present text of *Julius Caesar* preserves readings of the first Folio (modernized according to the principles of this edition) that have often, with some plausibility, been amended. Emendations found in some editions of the play are given after the square bracket.

I.I

15 FLAVIUS] MARULLUS
22 tradesman's] (F1 Tradesmans); tradesmen's; trade, – man's; trades, man's
women's] (F1 womens); woman's

23 withal I] with all. I; with awl. I
61 where] whe're; whe'r; whether

I.2

72 laughter] laugher; lover; talker
87 both] death
123 bend] beam
159 eternal] infernal
187 senators] senator
242 hooted] (F1 howted); shouted
246 swooned] (F1 swoonded); swounded
252 like; he] (F1 like he); like, he

I.3

21 glazed] gazed; glared
65 old men, fools] old men fool
129 In favour's like] (F1 Is Fauors, like); Is favoured
   like; Is feav'rous like; It favours like

II.1

15 Crown him! – that!] (F1 Crowne him that); Crown
   him? – that –
83 path, thy] (F1 path thy); march, thy; put thy; pass
   thy; hath thy
114 not the face] that the face; that the fate; not the
   faiths; not the faith
255 know you Brutus] know you, Brutus
279 gentle Brutus] gentle, Brutus
295 reputed, Cato's] (F1 reputed: Cato's); reputed Cato's

II.2

19 fought] (F1 fight); did fight
46 are] (F1 heare); were
81 And] Of
129 earns] yearns

III.1

21 or] on
39 law] (F1 lane); line; play; lune
101 CASCA] CASSIUS
105–10 Stoop . . . liberty!] *Some editors give these lines to
   Casca*
114 BRUTUS] CASCA
116 CASSIUS] BRUTUS

174 in strength of malice] exempt from malice; no
strength of malice; in strength of amity; in strength
of welcome; forspent of malice; in strength of
friendship; in strength of manhood; unfraught of
malice

206 lethe] death

209 strucken] (F1 stroken); stricken

258 hand] hands

262 limbs] line; loins; lives; times; minds; kind; tombs;
souls; heads; bonds

285 Began] Begin

III.2

71 blest] most blest

111 Has he, masters?] (F1 Ha's hee Masters?); Has he,
my master?; Has he not, masters?; That he has,
masters.; That has he, masters.

250 this] that

III.3

2 unluckily] unlucky; unlikely

IV.1

37 objects, arts] abject orts; abjects, orts; abject arts

44 our means stretched] and our best means stretched
out; our means stretched to the utmost; our means,
our plans stretched out; our choicest means stretched
out; all our means stretched

IV.3

4–5 letters, praying . . . man, was] (F1 Letters, praying
. . . man was); letter, praying . . . man, was; letter
(praying . . . man) was; letters, praying . . . man,
were

13 speaks] speak

27 bay] bait

28 bait] bay

54 noble] able

108 humour] honour

109 lamb] man; temper; heart

207 new-added] (F1 new added); new aided; new-
hearted

V.1

    105 time] term
    106 some] those

V.3

    97 where] whether; whe'r; if
    99 The last] Thou last
    104 Thasos] (F1 Tharsus); Thassos

V.4

    7–8 LUCILIUS] (F1 *has no speech-prefix*); BRUTUS
    30 where] whe'r; whether; if

3

In the present edition of *Julius Caesar* some of the stage directions
printed in the first Folio have been expanded. Also directions for
stage action clearly required by the text have been added. The
following list records in square brackets the more important additional directions, and those words introduced into the directions
of the Folio.

I.2

    o *Enter . . . Antony,* [*stripped*] *for the course, . . .* [*and a
    great crowd*]

I.3

    o *Enter Casca and Cicero* [*, meeting*]

II.1

    60 [*Exit Lucius*]
    76 [*Exit Lucius*]
    100 *They whisper* [*apart*]
    191 [*A*] *clock strikes*
    228 *Exeunt* [*the conspirators*]
    303 *Knock*[*ing*]
    321 [*He throws off the kerchief*]

II.2

    124 TREBONIUS Caesar, I will. [(*Aside*)] And so near . . .

II.3

    o *Enter Artemidorus* [*reading a paper*]

III.1

    o *Enter Caesar . . .* [*Popilius,*] *. . .*

12 [*Caesar enters the Capitol, the rest following*]
14 [*He goes to speak to Caesar*]
26 [*Exeunt Antony and Trebonius*]

III.2

0 *Enter Brutus and* [*later*] *goes into the pulpit* . . .
10 [*Exit Cassius, with some of the Plebeians*]
40 *Enter Mark Antony* [*and others*], . . .
162 [*Antony comes down from the pulpit*]
198 [*Antony plucks off the mantle*]
261 *Exeunt Plebeians* [*with the body*] (F1: *Exit Plebeians*)

III.3

4 [*The Plebeians surround him*]
35 [*They attack Cinna*]
38 *Exeunt all the Plebeians* [*with Cinna's body*]

IV.2

0 *Enter Brutus, Lucilius,* [*Lucius,*] . . .
13 [*Brutus and Lucilius draw apart*]
52 *Exeunt* [*all except Brutus and Cassius*] (F1: *Manet Brutus and Cassius*)

IV.3

122 *Enter a Poet* [*followed by Lucius; Titinius and Lucilius attempting to restrain him*]
140 [*Exeunt Lucilius and Titinius*]
    [*Exit Lucius*]
155 *Enter Boy* [(*Lucius*)]
160 [*Exit Lucius*] [*Cassius drinks*]
229 [*Exit Lucius*]
236 *Exeunt* [*Cassius, Titinius, and Messala*]
249 [*Varro and Claudius lie down*]
264 [*Lucius falls asleep*]
272 [*He sits and reads*]
284 [*Exit Ghost*]

V.1

20 *Enter Brutus* . . . [*Lucilius, Titinius, Messala, and others*]
69 [*Lucilius stands forth, and talks with Brutus apart*]
70 [*Messala stands forth*]
92 [*Brutus rejoins Cassius*]

V.3

    22 [*Pindarus ascends*]
    25 [(*To Pindarus*)]
    35 *Enter Pindarus* [*from above*]
    46 [*He dies*]
    50 [*Exit*]
    79 [*Exit Messala*]
    90 *Enter Brutus . . . Volumnius,* [*Labeo, Flavius,*] *. . .*

V.4

    0 *Enter Brutus, Messala,* [*Young*] *Cato . . .*
    1 [*Exit, followed by Messala and Flavius*]
    8 [*Young Cato is slain*]

V.5

    5 [*He whispers*]
    8 [*He whispers*]
    43 [*Exeunt Clitus, Dardanius, and Volumnius*]

Commentary

The act and scene divisions are those of Peter Alexander's edition of the *Complete Works* (1951). References to North's Plutarch are to *Shakespeare's Plutarch*, ed. T. J. B. Spencer (1964).

THE CHARACTERS IN THE PLAY

There is a good deal of inconsistency in the form of some of these names in the Folio text (F), and many of them differ from both the Roman forms and those used by North. For example, the Folio has *Murellus* or *Murrellus*, *Antonio*, *Flavio*, *Labio*, *Octavio*, *Varrus* and *Claudio*. Most previous editors of the play have changed these so that they conform to North's usage. However, they have also inconsistently retained the Folio's *Portia*, *Lena* and *Dardanius*, rather than replaced them with North's Porcia, Laena and Dardanus. Although editorial consistency is desirable, it is probably impractical in this case, owing to the number of reference and critical works keyed to the practice of earlier editions. I have, therefore, followed the well-established 'tradition' of inconsistency.

Both Calphurnia and Calpurnia are used by North, and many previous editors have favoured the latter form. As the Folio is consistent in its use of the former, I have retained it in this text.

There are two characters, Labeo and Flavius, who appear in V.3 and 4 but do not speak.

I.I

    0 *Flavius, Marullus*: In Plutarch these are Tribunes of
the People; but Shakespeare makes them also partisans
of Pompey, which is their main function in this scene,
so that they may display an antagonism to Caesar and
his ambitions which prepares the audience for the later
enmity of Brutus and Cassius.

    over the stage: This is probably an indication for the
crowd to enter first and swarm about the stage prior
to the entrance of the Tribunes.

    3 *Being mechanical*: Belonging to the artisan class.

  4–5 *without the sign | Of your profession*: No particular sign
is referred to here; Flavius merely means 'not having
tools and not wearing working clothes'; see 7–8.

   10 *in respect of*: In comparison with.

   11 *cobbler*: The pun is on (1) 'shoe-mender', (2) 'bungler',
'botcher'. This character is probably derived from
Plutarch's phrase 'cobblers, tapsters, or suchlike base
mechanical people' (*Brutus*).

   12 *directly*: Straightforwardly, without quibbling.

   14 *soles*: The pun is on (1) 'bottoms of shoes', (2) 'souls'.

   15 *What trade . . . what trade*: Many editors give this
speech to Marullus on the grounds that Flavius is the
more conciliatory of the two. Shakespeare is obviously
distributing the speeches to keep both actors occupied;
and the cobbler finds no difficulty in speaking to both
in the following lines.

    naughty: Worthless, rascally.

   16 *be not out with me*: Do not be angry with me. The pun
is with *out* at 17 meaning 'out at heels, with worn shoes'.

   17 *mend*: The pun is on (1) 'repair' (shoes), (2) 'reform'
(souls).

   19 *cobble you*: Mend your shoes. This makes clear to
Marullus the cobbler's trade which is still in doubt for
him owing to the punning at 10–17.

  21–3 *Truly, sir . . . old shoes*: The cobbler continues his
punning with the play on *awl* and *all*, and also on
meddle meaning 'to interfere' and 'to have sexual relations'. This passage may contain an allusion to Thomas

Dekker's play *The Shoemakers' Holiday*, which was acted in 1599 and in which the hero, Simon Eyre, claims not to interfere with concerns which lie outside the practice of his trade as cobbler.

24 *recover*: The pun is on (1) 're-sole', 'patch', (2) 'restore to health'.

24–5 *As proper men as ever trod upon neat's leather*: A proverbial expression meaning 'as handsome men as ever walked in shoes made of cowhide'.

31 *triumph*: This was a procession celebrating a military victory. Caesar defeated Gnaeus and Sextus, the sons of Pompey the Great, at Munda in Spain on 17 March 45 BC; and his triumph took place at the beginning of October the same year.

32–4 *Wherefore rejoice? . . . wheels*: Shakespeare based these lines on a passage in Plutarch's *Caesar*:

> But the Triumph he made into Rome . . . did as much offend the Romans, and more, than anything that ever he had done before; because he had not overcome captains that were strangers, nor barbarous kings, but had destroyed the sons of the noblest man in Rome, whom fortune had overthrown. And, because he had plucked up his race by the roots, men did not think it meet for him to triumph so for the calamities of his country.

33 *tributaries*: Captives who will pay tribute.

34 *grace*: Pay honour to.
   captive bonds: Fetters.

35 *senseless*: Without feelings.

37 *Pompey*: Pompey the Great, defeated by Caesar in 48 BC, and later assassinated.

42 *pass the streets*: Pass through the streets.

46 *replication*: Reverberation.

47 *concave shores*: Hollowed-out or overhanging banks (which create an echo).

49 *cull out a holiday*: Pick out a working day and turn it into a holiday. The verb was probably suggested by association with *flowers* at 50; which idea Shakespeare

took from Plutarch's remark 'there were some that cast
flowers . . . as they commonly use to do unto any man
when he hath obtained victory' (*Caesar*).

51 *Pompey's blood*: The term is used with the double
meaning (1) 'Pompey's sons', (2) 'the spilt blood of
Pompey in his sons'.

54 *intermit*: Withhold, suspend. Marullus indicates that a
plague is almost the inevitable punishment for the citizens' actions.

59–60 *till the lowest stream . . . of all*: So that the river level
even at its lowest ebb may rise to the highest banks.

61 *where*: Whether.
mettle: Temperament, disposition.

64–5 *Disrobe the images . . . with ceremonies*: Plutarch notes
in *Brutus*:

Caesar's flatterers . . . beside many other exceeding and
unspeakable honours they daily devised for him, in the night-
time they did put diadems upon the heads of his images,
supposing thereby to allure the common people to call him
King, instead of Dictator.

65 *ceremonies*: Symbols of rule.

67 *the feast of Lupercal*: This feast of expiation and purifi-
cation was held in honour of Lupercus, the god of
shepherds, on 15 February. Shakespeare combines this
with the day of Caesar's triumph (see note to 31) for
dramatic effect; the two events are dealt with separately by Plutarch.

68–71 *let no images . . . thick*: This is based on Plutarch's
Caesar: 'Those [diadems] the two Tribunes, Flavius
and Marullus, went and pulled down; and furthermore,
meeting with them that first saluted Caesar as king,
they committed them to prison.'

68 *images*: Statues.

69 *trophies*: Ornaments (such as the scarfs mentioned by
Casca at I.2.282, or the 'diadems' and laurel crown of
Plutarch's account).
about: Go about.

70 *the vulgar*: The common people.

72–3 *These growing feathers . . . fly an ordinary pitch*: The metaphor here is from falconry: Flavius sees their actions as stripping Caesar of some of his power, even as a falcon with plucked wings would have a lower *pitch*, which is the height soared to before diving.

74 *above the view of men*: Beyond human sight. This is the first of many references to Caesar as superman, many of them, as here, coming from his enemies; cf. I.2.60, 115–16.

I.2

0 *Antony, stripped for the course*: Plutarch in his *Caesar* describes the *holy chase* thus:

. . . that day there are divers noblemen's sons, young men . . . which run naked through the city, striking in sport them they meet in their way with leather thongs, hair and all on, to make them give place. . . . Antonius, who was Consul at that time, was one of them that ran this holy course.

6–9 *Forget not . . . curse*: Plutarch makes no mention of Calphurnia's sterility, but states the general Roman belief:

And many noblewomen and gentlewomen also go of purpose to stand in their way, and do put forth their hands to be stricken . . . persuading themselves that, being with child, they shall have good delivery, and also, being barren, that it will make them to conceive with child. (*Caesar*)

11 *Set on*: Proceed.

15 *press*: Crowd.

17 *Caesar is turned to hear*: Caesar's use of the third person here indicates his arrogance, and reflects his practice in his writings. If 212 indicates that Caesar is deaf (see note) then the phrase here may be taken literally.

18 *Beware the ides of March*: This is based on Plutarch's *Caesar*: 'there was a certain soothsayer that had given

Caesar warning long time afore, to take heed of the
day of the Ides of March . . . for on that day he should
be in great danger.' The *ides* means the halfway point
in the month; in March, the 15th.

19 *A soothsayer bids you beware the ides of March*: The
repetition is dramatically effective in fixing the remark
in the audience's mind; but it is also ironical in that it
is Brutus' first utterance in the play.

24 *Pass*: Advance.
    Sennet: A flourish of trumpets indicating a ceremonial
    exit.

25 *the order of the course*: The progress of the race.

28–9 *I am not gamesome . . . that quick spirit that is in Antony*:
Brutus is probably hinting, by quibbles, at his disapproval of the scene he has just witnessed; with *gamesome* meaning (1) 'sport-loving', (2) 'frivolous'; and
quick meaning (1) 'speedy in running', (2) 'lively in
disposition', (3) 'prompt (to comply with Caesar's
whims)'.

33–4 *I have not from your eyes . . . wont to have*: Shakespeare
changes his source here in making Brutus' worries
about Caesar's ambitions the reason for his coldness
to Cassius. In Plutarch the hostility between them
developed by virtue of Caesar's granting Brutus a prae-
torship for which Cassius was a rival candidate, an
action which was also 'the first cause of Cassius' malice
against Caesar'.

33 *gentleness*: Well-bred courtesy.

34 *show*: Manifestation.
    wont: Accustomed.

35 *too strange a hand*: The metaphor is from horsemanship.
    strange: Hostile.

37–9 *if I have veiled . . . upon myself*: If my face has worn
a troubled look, the expression has been directed only
towards myself not to the beholder of it. Portia makes
the same point about Brutus' recent behaviour at
II.1.242.

39 *Merely*: Entirely, solely.

40 *passions of some difference*: Conflicting emotions. This

is the crux of Brutus' dilemma: the tension between
his affection for Caesar and his own political ideals.
See also 46.

41 *Conceptions only proper to myself*. Thoughts pertaining
only to me.

42 *soil*: Blemish, taint.

45 *Nor construe any further my neglect*: Do not make
anything more of my neglect of you. The accent is
on the first syllable in *construe*.

48 *passion*: Feelings.

50 *worthy*: Important.

54 *just*: True.

55–62 *And it is very much . . . his eyes*: This is based on
Plutarch's account in *Brutus*:

> Cassius being bold, and taking hold of this word, 'Why,'
> quoth he, 'what Roman is he alive that will suffer thee to die
> for the liberty? What, knowest thou not that thou art Brutus?
> . . . The noblest men and best citizens . . . specially require,
> as a due debt unto them, the taking away of the tyranny,
> being fully bent to suffer any extremity for thy sake, so that
> thou wilt show thyself to be the man thou art taken for, and
> that they hope thou art.'

56 *turn*: Reflect.

58 *shadow*: Image.

59 *of the best respect*: Of the people held in highest estimation.

60 *immortal Caesar*: Cassius' first reference to Caesar is
highly sarcastic, but ironically it is from him that we
receive the most colourfully, and therefore most memo-
rably, phrased evidence of how Caesar was viewed by
the majority of Romans; cf. 134–7.

62 *had his eyes*: There are two possible meanings here: (1)
'were using his eyes properly' (to see Caesar's
tyranny), (2) 'had the speaker's eyes' (saw Caesar as
the speaker did).

66 *Therefore*: This may mean 'so far as that is concerned',
or, as many editors have suggested, that Cassius is

merely sidestepping Brutus' doubts in order to proceed with his own line of thought.

68 *glass*: Mirror.

69 *modestly discover*: Make known without exaggeration.

71 *jealous on*: Suspicious of.

72 *laughter*: The F reading has been retained with the meaning 'an object of laughter'; cf. Brutus' lines at IV.3.49. The two most common emendations are 'laugher' meaning 'jester', and 'loffer' meaning 'lover'.

73–4 *To stale with ordinary oaths . . . protester*: To make stale, or cheapen, my affection to every new acquaintance who makes a declaration of friendship for me, by using commonplace oaths. There is perhaps the sense of 'tavern oaths' in the use of *ordinary*.

76 *after scandal them*: Later libel them.

77 *profess myself*: Declare friendship.

78 *all the rout*: The whole common rabble.

Flourish and shout: The noises offstage in this scene are used by Shakespeare to keep the audience in mind of the presence of Caesar and the Roman people. Notice his use here of the close juxtaposition of Cassius' despising reference to the crowd and the behaviour of the people to whom Caesar is at this moment pandering.

85–9 *If it be . . . death*: This is a much discussed passage of which several explanations have been given. The difficulty is caused chiefly by (1) whether *indifferently* means 'with indifference' or 'impartially', and (2) what Brutus means by *honour*. I take the meaning to be: 'In matters concerning the public welfare, my honour demands that if death is the alternative to its exercise then I will die. For let the Fates make me prosper only in proportion to the degree to which I put my honour above my personal safety.' The relevant passage in Plutarch's *Brutus* is: '"For myself then," said Brutus, "I mean not to hold my peace, but to withstand it, and rather die than lose my liberty."'

91 *outward favour*: External features.

92 *Well, honour is the subject of my story*: Cassius seizes

upon Brutus' use of the word *honour* and takes it to mean 'reputation', 'status in the city'.

95-6 *I had as lief ... as I myself*: This and the following lines are based on Plutarch's hint: 'Cassius being a choleric man and hating Caesar privately, more than he did the tyranny openly, he incensed Brutus against him' (*Brutus*).

95 *I had as lief not be*: I would just as soon be dead. There is the possibility of a quibble on *lief* and *life*.

99-128 *Endure the winter's ... sick girl*: Plutarch gives the opposite impression of Caesar:

... yet therefore [he] yielded not to the disease of his body, to make it a cloak to cherish him withal, but, contrarily, took the pains of war as a medicine to cure his sick body, fighting always with his disease, travelling continually, living soberly, and commonly lying abroad in the field. (*Caesar*)

100-115 *For once, upon a raw and gusty day ... Caesar*: This swimming match and its outcome is Shakespeare's own invention; both Plutarch and Suetonius, in his *Life of Caesar* included in his book *Lives of the Twelve Caesars*, make special mention of Caesar's prowess as a swimmer.

101 *chafing with her shores*: Resenting the constraint constituted by the banks of the river.

109 *hearts of controversy*: Hearts eager for competition with the waves and with each other.

112-14 *as Aeneas, our great ancestor ... old Anchises bear*: According to Virgil's *Aeneid*, II.721ff., Aeneas was the progenitor of the Roman nation who rescued his father, Anchises, from the city of Troy after it had been burned by the Greeks.

117 *bend his body*: Make an obeisance.

119-24 *He had a fever ... groan*: This is based on Plutarch's account of Caesar's health: 'he was lean, white, and soft skinned, and often subject to headache, and otherwhile to the falling sickness (the which took him the first time as it is reported, in Corduba, a city of Spain)' (*Caesar*).

122 *His coward lips did from their colour fly*: Shakespeare evokes the comparison of a soldier deserting his flag, to vivify the simple evidence of cowardice.

123 *bend*: Direction, inclination (of a look or glance).

124 *his*: Its.

125–6 *Ay, and that tongue of his ... in their books*: Shakespeare here makes specific the general remark of Plutarch's *Caesar*:

It is reported that Caesar had an excellent natural gift to speak well before the people; and, besides that rare gift, he was excellently well studied, so that doubtless he was counted the second man for eloquence in his time.

126 *books*: Writing tablets.

127 *Alas*: It is possible that this is not part of Caesar's reported words, but Cassius being sarcastic.
Titinius: According to Plutarch he was 'one of Cassius' chiefest friends', for which see IV.2 and V.3.

128 *amaze*: Stupefy.

129 *temper*: Temperament, disposition, constitution.

130 *get the start of*: A metaphor from racing: 'outstrip and carry off the prize' – 'bear the palm'.

131 *Shout. Flourish*: Just as the first offstage noise at 78 was timed to appear in conjunction with Cassius' remarks about the *rout*, and thus stimulate Brutus' fears about Caesar's power over the mob, so here the stage direction is associated with the crowning of Caesar.

135 *Colossus*: Shakespeare probably had in mind the most famous giant statue of antiquity: the hundred-foot image of Apollo at Rhodes, which was one of the seven wonders of the world, and in some accounts was said to straddle the harbour.

137 *dishonourable graves*: The graves of bondmen.

138 *Men at some time are masters of their fates*: Brutus echoes this sentiment at IV.3.216–19.

139 *our stars*: The reference is to the basic astrological belief that a man's character and behaviour are

governed by the relative positions of the planets at the time of his birth.

142 *be sounded more*: Resound more famously.

145 *conjure with 'em*: Conjure (up spirits) with them.

146 *start*: Raise up.

150 *the breed*: The art of breeding.

bloods: The quibble is on (1) 'stock', (2) 'disposition', 'spirit', 'temper'. Cassius may purposely be alluding here to Brutus' lineage of which he is so conscious.

151 *great flood*: The reference is to the inundation of the earth by Zeus, when only Deucalion, King of Phthia, and his wife, Pyrrha, were saved.

152 *famed with*: Celebrated for.

154 *walls*: The verb *encompassed* demands the emendation. While the adjective *wide* appears to justify the F reading *walkes*, it can also mean 'extensive, extending over a large space or region'.

155 *Rome indeed, and room enough*: This is a pun, as the words were apparently pronounced identically in Elizabethan English.

158 *a Brutus once*: Cf.:

Marcus Brutus came of that Junius Brutus for whom the ancient Romans made his statue of brass to be set up in the Capitol with the images of the kings, holding a naked sword in his hand, because he had valiantly put down the Tarquins from their kingdom of Rome. (Plutarch's *Brutus*)

brooked: Tolerated.

159 *eternal*: Here used to express extreme abhorrence, probably by confusion with 'infernal'; or perhaps the connotation is 'eternally damned'.

to keep his state: To maintain his court.

161–9 *That you . . . things*: This is Brutus' characteristic mode of speech, composed of balanced and antithetical phrases, the best example of which is his funeral oration in III.2. The whole speech is really an answer to Cassius at 71; he almost ignores Cassius' personal animosity towards Caesar.

161 *nothing jealous*: Not at all uncertain.

162 *work*: Persuade.

   aim: Guess, conjecture, idea.

164 *present*: Moment.

165 *so with love I might entreat you*: If I may ask you as a friend.

166 *moved*: Urged.

169 *meet*: Suitable, fitting.

   high things: Important affairs.

170 *chew upon*: Ponder, consider.

173 *these*: Such.

178 *pluck Casca by the sleeve*: This is an anachronism; togas had no sleeves.

180 *worthy note*: Worthy of notice.

185 *ferret*: Fiery, blood-shot (with anger or resentment).

187 *conference*: Debate, argument.

191–4 *Let me have . . . dangerous*: Shakespeare here conflates two incidents given by Plutarch:

> Caesar also had Cassius in great jealousy and suspected him much. Whereupon he said on a time to his friends: 'What will Cassius do, think ye? I like not his pale looks.' Another time, when Caesar's friends complained unto him of Antonius and Dolabella, that they pretended some mischief towards him, he answered them again: 'As for those fat men and smooth-combed heads,' quoth he, 'I never reckon of them. But these pale-visaged and carrion lean people, I fear them most' – meaning Brutus and Cassius. (*Caesar*; see also *Brutus*)

196 *well given*: Well disposed. Shakespeare takes the phrase from Plutarch, who notes that Cassius was 'Brutus' familiar friend, but not so well given and conditioned as he'.

198 *my name*: This is a periphrasis typical of the arrogance of both the public and the private Caesar.

201–2 *he looks . . . deeds of men*: He looks behind men's actions to determine their motives.

202–3 *He loves no plays . . . Antony*: According to Plutarch,

Antony 'himself passed away the time in hearing of foolish plays' (*Antonius*).

203 *he hears no music*: There lies behind this idea the Platonic belief that the man in whose nature the elements are harmoniously blended loves music naturally; on the contrary

> The man that hath no music in himself,
> Nor is not moved with concord of sweet sounds,
> Is fit for treasons, stratagems, and spoils . . .
> Let no such man be trusted.
> (*The Merchant of Venice*, V.1.83–5, 88)

204 *sort*: Way, manner.

210–11 *I rather tell thee . . . always I am Caesar*: Plutarch in his *Caesar* gave Shakespeare the hint for this when he relates how Cornelius Balbus prevented Caesar from rising before the Senate: 'What, do you not remember that you are Caesar, and will you not let them reverence you and do their duties?'

212–13 *Come on my right hand, for this ear is deaf . . . think'st of him*: There is no foundation for Caesar's deafness in Plutarch; and these lines have been used as evidence of Shakespeare's stressing Caesar's physical defects, and of his juxtaposing them with arrogant claims to semi-divinity. However, it has been pointed out that Shakespeare may here be using merely a common proverbial expression which is explained by a contemporary as 'It is the same that we use to speak proverbially, when we hear a thing that liketh us not, saying thus "I cannot hear in that side."'

216 *sad*: Serious, grave. The phrase is derived from Plutarch's account of Caesar's return to Rome from Alba: 'he went his way heavy and sorrowful' (*Caesar*).

219 *there was a crown offered him*: Plutarch gives two accounts of Antony's offering Caesar the crown in his *Caesar* and in *Antonius*; it is the latter that Shakespeare follows the more closely in Casca's narration in this scene.

220 *put it by*: Pushed it aside.

227 *marry*: Indeed (originally an oath meaning 'by the Virgin Mary').

228 *gentler than other*: Less violently than on the previous occasion (hence more reluctantly).

236 *coronets*: This is Shakespeare's Tudor version of the symbolic 'laurel crown . . . having a royal band or diadem wreathed about it' of Plutarch.

237 *fain*: Willingly.

241 *still*: Each time.

241–2 *the rabblement hooted, and clapped their chopped hands*: Shakespeare brings together details from Plutarch's two accounts: 'But when Caesar refused it again the second time . . . all the whole people shouted' (*Caesar*); and 'as oft also as Caesar refused it, all the people together clapped their hands' (*Antonius*).

242 *hooted*: There is no need for the emendation 'shouted', as the word is in keeping with the rest of Casca's description of the mob, showing his contempt for their behaviour.

chopped: Roughened by manual labour.

246 *swooned*: Fainted. Shakespeare based this incident on Plutarch's account of Caesar's return from Alba in *Caesar*:

> . . . it is reported that afterwards . . . he imputed it to his disease, saying that their wits are not perfect which have his disease of the falling evil, when standing on their feet they speak to the common people, but are soon troubled with a trembling of their body and a sudden dimness and giddiness.

249 *soft*: Slowly.

252 *like; he*: F has no stop between these two words, and consequently implies that Brutus is uncertain that Caesar is epileptic. This is untenable in view of the fact that the two men were close friends, and that Caesar's illness was common knowledge in Rome.

like: Likely.

253–4 *No, Caesar hath it not . . . the falling sickness*: Cassius

deliberately misunderstands Brutus' term, and takes it
to mean that they have fallen under Caesar's sway –
that is, that they are bondmen.

256 *tag-rag people*: Rabble.

262–4 *he plucked me ope his doublet, and offered them his throat
to cut*: After Caesar had offended the Senate, Plutarch
reports that 'Caesar . . . departed home to his house,
and tearing open his doublet collar, making his neck
bare, he cried aloud to his friends that his throat was
ready to offer to any man that would come and cut it'
(*Caesar*).

263 *plucked me ope*: Opened.

  doublet: A short jacket. The anachronism comes from
North's Elizabethan rendering of Amyot's French
word '*robe*'.

264 *An*: If.

  a man of any occupation: This could mean either (1) 'a
tradesman' (to whom the offer was made), or (2) 'a
man of action'.

266–9 *When he came to himself . . . his infirmity*: See note to
246.

271–2 *Caesar had stabbed their mothers*: A bawdy joke is probably intended here.

278 *an*: If.

280–81 *it was Greek to me*: I could not understand it. However,
Plutarch notes in his account of Caesar's murder that
Casca, after striking the first blow, cried out 'in Greek
to his brother: "Brother, help me"' (*Caesar*).

281–3 *I could tell you . . . put to silence*: See I.1.63–9. In Plutarch
the laurel crown offered by Antony 'was afterwards
put upon the head of one of Caesar's statues or images,
the which one of the Tribunes plucked off . . . Howbeit
Caesar did turn them out of their offices for it'
(*Antonius*; see also *Caesar*). Shakespeare makes the
incident more sinisterly ambiguous; see the Introduction, pp. xxxii–xxxiii.

286 *am promised forth*: Have promised to dine elsewhere.

287 *dine*: Lunch.

288 *hold*: Does not change.

292 *blunt*: Abrupt, unpolished in manner.

293 *quick mettle*: Of lively disposition.

294–5 *So is he now . . . noble enterprise*: Cassius deliberately mistakes Brutus' meaning (as at 253–4), and takes *mettle* to mean 'courage'.

296 *However*: In spite of the fact that.
     tardy form: Pretence of slow-wittedness, affectation of dullness.

297 *rudeness*: Rough manner.
     good wit: Intelligence. Cassius' images grow naturally out of the lunch invitation he has just issued to Casca.

298 *disgest*: Digest.

304 *world*: The present state of affairs.

305–17 *Well, Brutus . . . glancèd at*: This soliloquy illustrates well the difference between Brutus and Cassius. While the former is concerned primarily with the abstract principles of protecting Rome from possible tyranny, the latter is chiefly occupied with making the assassination of Caesar a reality. Thus Cassius can view their duologue with a detachment impossible for the uncalculating and personally involved Brutus.

306 *honourable mettle*: Upstanding spirit.

306–7 *wrought . . . disposed*: Twisted out of its natural inclination. The metaphor comes from alchemy and is based on the 'mettle'/'metal' quibble; *noble* metals (like gold) could not be *wrought*.

307 *meet*: Fitting.

310 *bear me hard*: Feel ill-will towards me.

311–12 *If I were Brutus now . . . not humour me*: It has been suggested that *He* at 312 refers to Caesar rather than Brutus; and that Cassius is expressing the fear that Brutus has been corrupted by Caesar's favour. However, this makes the lines unnecessarily complicated. They obviously mean 'if I were Brutus and he were I, he would not be able to influence me as I have just been moulding him'.

313 *In several hands*: In different kinds of handwriting.

315 *tending to the great opinion*: Concerning the great respect.

317 *glancèd at*: Alluded to.

318 *seat him sure*: Make his position secure.

319 *worse days endure*: Have to put up with even greater tyranny in the future.

1.3

3 *all the sway of earth*: There is no agreement about the exact meaning of this phrase; the general sense would appear to be 'the whole earthly realm'.

6 *rived*: Split.

8 *exalted with*: Raised up to.

12 *saucy with*: Insolent to.

14 *anything more wonderful*: This may be intended either seriously or sarcastically; that is, 'anything further that inspired awe', or 'anything that was more awe-inspiring than the things you mention'. Considering Cicero's detached attitude, the latter seems the more probable.

15–28 *A common slave . . . shrieking*: This is based on Plutarch's *Caesar*:

For, touching the fires in the element and spirits running up and down in the night, and also the solitary birds to be seen at noondays sitting in the great market-place – are not all these signs perhaps worth the noting, in such a wonderful chance as happened? But Strabo the Philosopher writeth that divers men were seen going up and down in fire; and, furthermore, that there was a slave of the soldiers that did cast a marvellous burning flame out of his hand, insomuch as they that saw it thought he had been burnt, but, when the fire was out, it was found he had no hurt.

Shakespeare's additions are the shrieking women, and the lion, which may have been suggested by Plutarch's account of the escape of the Megarian lions which were a point of difference between Caesar and Cassius (*Brutus*).

18 *Not sensible of fire*: Not feeling the pain of the fire.

20 *Against*: Near to.

21 *glazed*: Neither of the emendations suggested ('glared'

or 'gazed') is necessary; there are many contemporary examples of this word being used to mean 'stared', 'gazed fixedly'.

22 *annoying*: Harming.

22–3 *drawn* | *Upon a heap*: Huddled together.

26 *bird of night*: The screech-owl, which was considered a bird of ill-luck.

29 *conjointly meet*: Happen together.

31 *portentous*: Ominous.

32 *climate*: Area, region.

33 *strange-disposèd*: Abnormally upset.

34 *construe things after their fashion*: Interpret things in their own way; *construe* has the stress on the first syllable.

35 *Clean from the purpose of the things themselves*: Quite differently from their real import.

48 *unbracèd*: This is an anachronism meaning 'with doublet open'.

49 *thunder-stone*: Thunderbolt.

50 *cross*: Forked.

52 *Even in the aim*: At the very spot at which it was aimed.

53 *tempt*: Make trial of (by defiance).

54 *part*: Proper action.

56 *astonish*: Dismay.

57 *dull*: Obtuse. Cassius, in his desire to shake Casca out of his terror, contradicts his own judgement at 1.2.294–9.

58 *want*: Lack.

60 *put on*: Manifest.

in wonder: In a state of astonishment.

64 *Why birds and beasts from quality and kind*: Some editors have suggested that there is an hiatus in the text at this point; but allowing for Cassius' excited state, the meaning is clear enough: 'Why birds and animals seem to act contrary to their very natures.'

65 *Why old men, fools, and children*: This line has been explained in two ways: (1) according to proverb lore these three classes of people have the power of prophecy, (2) that there are so many portents that

fools, dotards and children are able to interpret them. In view of the context, the latter is the more plausible.

fools: 'Naturals' or born idiots.

calculate: Prophesy (originally by astrological or mathematical calculation).

66 *ordinance*: Usual behaviour as ordained by nature.

67 *pre-formèd faculties*: Naturally endowed characteristics.

68 *monstrous*: Unnatural.

71 *state*: State of affairs.

75 *lion in the Capitol*: Perhaps a reference to the lion at 20; but it has been suggested that Shakespeare may have had in mind the lions of the royal menagerie which were kept in the Tower and were one of the sights of Elizabethan London.

77 *prodigious*: Supernatural, threatening.

78 *fearful*: Dreadful, causing terror.

eruptions: Unnatural happenings.

81 *thews*: Sinews.

82 *woe the while*: Alas for these days!

84 *Our yoke and sufferance*: Our submission to tyranny and our patient acceptance of it.

85–8 *Indeed . . . in Italy*: This is an echo of Plutarch's mention of the reason given to Caesar by Decius Brutus why he should go to the Capitol: that the Senate intended 'to proclaim him king of all the provinces of the Empire of Rome out of Italy, and that he should wear his diadem in all other places both by sea and land' (*Caesar*).

89–90 *I know where I will wear . . . Cassius*: This may well be a sincere sentiment based on Plutarch's remark that 'Cassius even from his cradle could not abide any manner of tyrants' (*Brutus*); but see note to I.2.95–6.

91 *Therein*: In the ability to commit suicide.

95 *Can be retentive to the strength of spirit*: Can imprison the resolute spirit.

98 *know all the world besides*: Let everyone else know.

102 *cancel*: This is a legal term meaning 'to annul by legal agreement or bond' and was probably suggested by the legal flavour of *bondman*.

106 *He were*: He would be.

    hinds: Two meanings are implied: (1) 'deer', (2) 'servants', 'lowly born'.

108 *trash*: Twigs, splinters, hedge-cuttings.

109 *rubbish*: Litter (such as results from the decay or repair of buildings).

    offal: Wood chips.

111 *vile*: Valueless.

114 *My answer must be made*: I shall be called to account for my speech.

115 *indifferent*: A matter of indifference.

117 *fleering*: Gibing, sneering.

    my hand: Let us shake hands on it.

118 *Be factious*: Form a party.

    griefs: Grievances.

120 *who*: Whoever.

123 *undergo*: Undertake.

125 *by this*: By this time.

    stay: Wait.

126 *Pompey's Porch*: In Plutarch this porch of the theatre erected by Pompey in 55 BC is the scene of Caesar's assassination (*Brutus*).

128 *complexion of the element*: The visible aspect of the skies. Both of these terms are alchemical in origin.

129 *In favour's like*: In appearance is like. The F reading cannot be defended; for other emendations see An Account of the Text.

131 *Stand close*: Remain concealed.

132 *Cinna*: 'One of the traitors to Caesar was also called Cinna' . . . 'who in an oration he made had spoken very evil of Caesar' (Plutarch's *Caesar*, *Brutus*).

134 *find out*: Look for.

    Metellus Cimber: Shakespeare follows Plutarch's nomenclature in *Caesar*; in *Brutus* Plutarch calls him Tullius Cimber. Historically his name was L. Tillius Cimber and he was a close friend of Caesar's before joining the conspirators.

135–6 *incorporate | To*: In league with.

137 *I am glad on't*: This is a response to Cassius' words
about Casca's joining the conspiracy.

142 *Be you content*: Set your mind at rest.

142–6 *Good Cinna . . . statue*: This is based on Plutarch's *Brutus*:

> . . . his friends . . . by many bills also, did openly call and
> procure him to do that he did. For, under the image of his
> ancestor Junius Brutus, that drave the kings out of Rome,
> they wrote: 'Oh that it pleased the gods thou wert now alive,
> Brutus.' And again: 'That thou wert here among us now.'
> His tribunal, or chair, where he gave audience during the
> time he was Praetor, was full of such bills: 'Brutus, thou art
> asleep, and art not Brutus indeed.'

In his *Caesar* Plutarch notes that these papers were
planted 'in the night'.

143 *praetor's chair*: The chair of the chief Roman magis-
trate; see note to II.4.35.

144 *Where Brutus may but find it*: Where Brutus alone may
find it.

145–6 *set this up with wax | Upon old Brutus' statue*: The prac-
tice of affixing scrolls to statues was an Elizabethan
one. See note to 142–6.

148 *Decius Brutus*: His real name was Decimus. Shakespeare uses North's form of the name.

151 *bestow*: Distribute.

152 *repair*: Return.

156 *yields him ours*: Joins our faction.

159 *His countenance, like richest alchemy*: Casca sees Brutus'
support in terms of alchemical practice, the aim of
which was to turn base metals into gold. Shakespeare
took the idea from Plutarch: 'to have a man of such
estimation as Brutus, to make every man boldly think
that by his only presence the fact were holy and just'
(*Brutus*); however, the image here is more appropriate
in that both Brutus' favour and alchemy were unsuc-
cessful in their operation.

162 *conceited*: The pun is on (1) 'understood', (2) 'expressed
in metaphorical language'.

II.1

    0 *orchard*: Garden.

    2 *the progress of the stars*: The position which the stars have arrived at in their movement across the sky.

    5 *When . . . What*: Both words were often used as exclamations of impatience.

    7 *taper*: Candle.

  11 *no personal cause*: No self-interested reason.
       spurn at: Kick against.

  12 *for the general*: For the common political good.

  13 *the question*: The point at issue; cf. *Hamlet*, III.1.56: 'To be, or not to be – that is the question.'

  14 *It is the bright day that brings forth the adder*: Favourable conditions bring out the latent evil in people.

  15 *craves*: Calls for, requires.

  17 *do danger*: Create harm.

18–19 *Th'abuse of greatness . . . from power*: High authority is misused when its power is exercised without compassion.

20–21 *when his affections . . . his reason*: When he acted under the influence of his emotions rather than his judgement.

  21 *a common proof*: A matter of common knowledge.

  22 *That lowliness is young ambition's ladder*: That an appearance of humility is the way by which the ambitious man climbs to power. Plutarch makes this point about Caesar on several occasions: for example, 'the people loved him marvellously also, because of the courteous manner he had to speak to every man and to use them gently'; and 'But to win himself the love and good will of the people . . . he made common feasts again and general distribution of corn' (*Caesar*).

  24 *upmost round*: Highest rung.

  26 *base degrees*: This refers to both the lower steps of the ladder and, by transference, the means employed in the early stages of his career; the pun is on *base*.

  28 *prevent*: Frustrate by taking anticipatory action.

28–9 *since the quarrel . . . thing he is*: Since the accusation has no validity considering what Caesar is at this moment.

  30 *Fashion it thus*: Let us put the case in this way.

31 *these and these extremities*: Such and such tyrannical extremes.

33 *as his kind*: According to the nature of its species.
    mischievous: Harmful.

35 *closet*: Study.

37 *This paper*: See note to I.3.142–6.

40 *ides*: F reads *first* which is clearly an error, probably due to the compositor reading the abbreviation 'jˢ' (for 'ides') as '1st'. That the error is not Shakespeare's is clear from 59. Some editors have argued that the F reading indicates Brutus' absent-mindedness in practical matters; but this is implausible in view of his reply at 60.

44 *exhalations*: Meteors (which were thought to be caused by the earth's exhaling vapours under the influence of the sun's heat).
    whizzing: Fireworks were sometimes used on the Elizabethan stage for effects, and may have been employed here.

46 *Brutus, thou sleep'st: awake, and see thyself*: See note to I.3.142–6.

52 *under one man's awe*: In awe of a single man.

53 *ancestors*: See note to I.2.158.

56–8 *O Rome . . . Brutus*: This is Brutus' moment of decision that Caesar's death is a political necessity; his debate is forgotten in the face of Cassius' manufactured 'Roman' pleas.

58 *Thy full petition*: Brutus pledges himself to do all that Rome asks of him: speaking, striking and thus redressing.

59 *fifteen days*: Some editors change this to 'fourteen days' on the grounds that this scene takes place on the night of the 14th; but it is obviously near dawn of the 15th; see 101–11.

61–2 *Since Cassius . . . have not slept*: These lines suggest a lapse of time between this scene and I.2 in which Brutus has wrestled with his conscience. The historical time was actually one month; but Shakespeare is telescoping the action for reasons of dramatic pace. The passage is based on Plutarch's description: 'either care did wake

him against his will when he would have slept, or else
oftentimes of himself he fell into such deep thoughts
of this enterprise, casting in his mind all the dangers
that might happen' (*Brutus*).

64 *first motion*: Initial impulse.

65 *phantasma*: Nightmare.

66–7 *The genius . . . in council*: Man's guiding spirit is in
violent debate with his passions. This soul and body
duel was a common Renaissance idea.

67–8 *state of man . . . little kingdom*: The human organism
is viewed as corresponding on the personal level with
the body politic. The F reading *of a man* obscures this
idea.

70 *your brother Cassius*: Plutarch notes that Brutus and
Cassius 'were allied together. For Cassius had married
Junia, Brutus' sister' (*Brutus*).

73 *hats*: Shakespeare was obviously thinking of Elizabethan hats; although the Romans did have various
kinds of headgear.

75 *discover*: Identify.

76 *favour*: Appearance.

79 *are most free*: Most freely wander about.

81–2 *conspiracy . . . smiles and affability*: See note to 225–7.

83 *For if thou path, thy native semblance on*: For, if you
pursue your way, showing yourself in your true colours.
There is no need to emend *path* as many editors have
done, as its meaning 'to go along or tread (a way)' is
well substantiated by contemporary quotations.

84 *Erebus*: The dark region between the earth and Hades
which was crossed by the souls of the dead.

85 *prevention*: See note to 28.

86 *upon your rest*: In disturbing your sleep.

87 *do we trouble you*: This is ironical in view of Brutus'
mental state prior to the conspirators' entrance.

98 *watchful cares*: Worries causing sleeplessness.

101–11 *Here lies . . . directly here*: This is a fine example of
Shakespeare's ability to make a short passage perform
a variety of functions. It is, in stage terms, a device to
cover the whispered discussion between Brutus and

Cassius; it reminds the audience of the gradual drawing
on of the day on which Caesar is to be assassinated;
it is symbolically appropriate that Casca should point
his sword at the Capitol where Caesar is to be stabbed
first by Casca; and it is psychologically true that men
at moments of suspense often talk of trivialities to
keep their minds from the immediate tension.

104 *fret*: Adorn with an interlacing pattern.

107 *growing*: Encroaching.

108 *Weighing*: Considering.

114 *No, not an oath*: This is the first of Brutus' many impo-
sitions of his will on Cassius. Shakespeare deliberately
changes Plutarch's account in making only Brutus
demur: 'having never taken oaths together nor taken
or given any caution or assurance, nor binding themselves one to another by any religious oaths, they all
kept the matter so secret to themselves' (*Brutus*).

the face of men: The F reading may stand although
many editors suggest 'faith' as an emendation, owing
to Plutarch's phrase 'The wonderful faith and secrecy
of the conspirators of Caesar's death', which is printed
in the margin beside the passage dealing with the fact
that the conspirators did not take an oath. The phrase
as it stands comes naturally from Brutus who has been
brooding on the appearance of things and their reality,
the reluctance of the conspiracy to show its face, and
the muffled faces of the plotters. I take it to mean 'the
expression on men's faces' (due to their consciousness
of the time's evils).

115 *sufferance*: Suffering, distress.

time's abuse: Corruption (by Caesar) in these days.

116 *betimes*: At once.

117 *his idle bed*: The bed in which he is idle (or, possibly,
his unused bed).

118 *high-sighted tyranny*: The reference is to falconry, and
Caesar is being viewed as the high-flying bird looking
down on its prey. There may also be the sense of a
tyranny which aims at unlimited power. Flavius sees
Caesar in similar terms at I.1.72–5.

119 *by lottery*: By chance, according to the chance
displeasure of the tyrant.

124 *prick*: Spur, encourage.

125 *Than secret Romans that have spoke the word*: Than the
fact that we are Romans who, once we have given our
word, can be trusted to hold our tongues. See also the
note to 114.

126 *palter*: Deceive, equivocate.

127 *honesty to honesty engaged*: Words of honour ex-
changed.

129 *cautelous*: Crafty, deceitful.

130 *carrions*: This is a term of contempt: 'men who are no
better than dead bodies'.

133 *even*: Uniform, steadfast.

134 *insuppressive*: Indomitable.

138 *guilty of a several bastardy*: Guilty of an act that shows
illegitimate (that is, non-Roman) blood.
several: Individual, separate.

141 *sound him*: Find out his feelings in this affair.

145 *opinion*: Reputation.

148 *no whit*: Not at all.

150 *break with him*: Broach the matter to him.

151–2 *For he will never . . . men begin*: Shakespeare changes
Plutarch's account of this decision to make Brutus the
only dissenter:

For this cause they durst not acquaint Cicero with their
conspiracy, although he was a man whom they loved dearly
and trusted best. For they were afraid that he being a coward
by nature, and age also having increased his fear, he would
quite turn and alter all their purpose, and quench the heat
of their enterprise . . . seeking by persuasion to bring all
things to such safety as there should be no peril. (*Brutus*)

153 *Indeed he is not fit*: Contrast this with 143.

155 *urged*: Suggested, recommended.

156–91 *Mark Antony . . . hereafter*: Plutarch cites this decision
as Brutus' first fault, but gives different reasons for it:

First . . . it was not honest. Secondly, because . . . there was
hope of change in him; for . . . Antonius, being a noble-
minded and courageous man, when he should know that
Caesar was dead, would willingly help his country to recover
her liberty. (*Brutus*)

158 *shrewd contriver*: Malicious intriguer.
    means: Capacity.
159 *improve*: Make good use of.
160 *annoy*: Injure, harm.
    prevent: Forestall.
164 *Like wrath in death, and envy afterwards*: That is, the
    assassination would appear to be the product of
    personal rather than public motives. This motive is
    found in Plutarch's *Antonius*: 'Brutus would in no wise
    consent to it, saying that venturing on such an enter-
    prise as that, for the maintenance of law and justice,
    it ought to be clear from all villainy.'
    envy: Hatred, malice.
165 *limb of Caesar*: A man dependent upon Caesar for any
    importance.
167 *spirit of Caesar*: What Caesar represents, 'Caesarism'.
168 *spirit*: Soul.
169-70 *O, that we then . . . not dismember Caesar*: This is, of
    course, tragic irony in that Brutus does *dismember
    Caesar*, but does not thereby either lay Caesar's *spirit*,
    which appears to him in IV.3, or defeat the Caesarian
    principle, which he recognizes as triumphant just before
    his death at V.3.94–6.
169 *come by*: Get possession of.
171 *gentle*: Noble.
173-4 *Let's carve him . . . fit for hounds*: Shakespeare probably
    derived the hunting imagery associated with Caesar's
    death in the play from Plutarch: 'Caesar . . . was hacked
    and mangled among them, as a wild beast taken of
    hunters' (*Caesar*). Cf. similar references at II.2.78–9;
    III.1.106–11, 204–10.
173 *carve*: Cut up ceremoniously.

176 *servants*: Emotions, feelings.

177–8 *This shall make ... not envious*: This will make it plain
that the murder is one of political necessity and not
the result of personal rancour.

180 *purgers*: Those who heal (originally by bleeding and
purging the patient).

184 *ingrafted*: Deep-rooted.

186 *all*: All the injury.

187 *take thought*: Succumb to melancholy (induced by
sorrow).

188 *were much he should*: Would be far too much to expect
from someone like him.

188–9 *for he is ... much company*: Plutarch has a long account
of Antony's wildness in *Antonius*. See the other allusions at I.2.202–3; II.2.116–17; V.1.62.

190 *no fear in him*: No reason for fear so far as he is concerned.

191 *A clock strikes*: This is anachronistic in that striking
clocks were not invented until the thirteenth century
and were very popular in Shakespeare's day. What is
more important here is that the stage direction reminds
the audience forcibly of the passage of time towards
the moment of the assassination.

194 *Whether*: This is pronounced here 'whe'r'.

195–6 *For he is superstitious ... he held once*: There is no
mention in Plutarch of Caesar's superstition, nor that
he was a follower of Epicurus in ignoring omens and
portents.

196 *Quite from the main opinion*: At odds with the strongly
held belief.

197 *fantasy*: Imaginings.
ceremonies: Portents, omens.

198 *apparent*: Manifest.

200 *augurers*: These were religious officials who predicted
future events and gave advice on public affairs in
accordance with the omens they obtained from sacrifice, bird-flight and so on.

204 *unicorns may be betrayed with trees*: One method of
capturing this legendary beast was for its prey to stand

before a tree to persuade it to charge, and then to dodge behind the tree in which the unicorn's horn would stick.

205 *bears with glasses*: A mirror was supposed to be effective in bewildering wild animals by showing them their own image.

elephants with holes: Like other animals, elephants were trapped by means of specially prepared pits.

206 *toils*: Snares, traps.

men with flatterers: Decius' point is that dangerous men like dangerous animals can be rendered harmless by the use of cunning.

210 *give his humour the true bent*: Influence his nature in the right direction.

212 *all of us*: It is noticeable, however, that according to the stage direction at II.2.107, Cassius is not present.

213 *uttermost*: Latest time.

215–16 *Caius Ligarius . . . speaking well of Pompey*: Cf.:

> Now amongst Pompey's friends there was one called Caius Ligarius, who had been accused unto Caesar for taking part with Pompey, and Caesar discharged him. But Ligarius thanked not Caesar so much for his discharge, as he was offended with him for that he was brought in danger by his tyrannical power. And therefore in his heart he was alway his mortal enemy, and was besides very familiar with Brutus. (Plutarch's *Brutus*)

215 *bear Caesar hard*: Feel enmity towards Caesar.

216 *rated*: Rebuked.

218 *go along by him*: Call at his house.

220 *fashion him*: Talk him into joining our party.

225–7 *Let not . . . constancy*: This is based on Plutarch's remark that Brutus 'did so frame and fashion his countenance and looks that no man could discern he had anything to trouble his mind' (*Brutus*). The reference to actors here retaining their facial composure is anachronistic because Roman actors wore masks.

225 *put on our purposes*: Betray our plans.

226 *bear it*: Carry it off.

227 *formal constancy*: Dignified composure.

231 *figures . . . fantasies*: Imaginings.

233–309 *Brutus, my lord . . . with haste*: In this exchange Shakespeare follows both the ideas and the words of a long passage in Plutarch quite closely (*Brutus*).

237 *ungently*: Disrespectfully.

240 *arms across*: The conventional Elizabethan attitude for someone absorbed in melancholy brooding.

246 *wafture*: Waving gesture.

249 *withal*: Moreover.

250 *an effect of humour*: A symptom of some momentary mood.

251 *his*: Its.

254 *condition*: Frame of mind.

255 *know you Brutus*: Recognize you as Brutus. Some editors emend this to 'know you, Brutus', which weakens its force. The point of Portia's speech is that the description of Brutus is so out of keeping with the Brutus everyone knows and is consequently a measure of his disturbed state of mind.

259 *come by*: Obtain.

261 *physical*: Healthy.

262 *unbracèd*: See note to I.3.48.
    humours: Dampness.

266 *tempt*: Risk.
    rheumy and unpurgèd air: Air which causes rheum and from which the sun has not drawn the moisture. Fear of fog as a cause of diseases was common at the time.

268 *sick offence*: Harmful sickness.

269 *my place*: My being your wife.

271 *charm*: Entreat, conjure.

273 *incorporate*: Make one body. Shakespeare has in mind the Christian rather than the Roman marriage service.

274 *half*: Wife.

275 *heavy*: Doleful.

281–3 *Is it excepted . . . limitation*: These are all legal terms connected with the holding of land, and were probably suggested by the word *bond* at 280.

285 *suburbs*: The London brothels were located in the
suburb of Southwark. The idea is continued in the
phrase *Brutus' harlot* which comes from Plutarch's 'like
a harlot'.

289–90 *the ruddy drops . . . my sad heart*: According to
Elizabethan medical theory, the blood was manufactured by the liver and flowed to the heart where it was
purified and pumped round the body. Sadness was
believed to drain the heart of blood.

295 *Cato's daughter*: Marcus Porcius Cato was Brutus' uncle
as well as his father-in-law. His character and career
were similar in broad outline to his nephew's: he was
an orator and statesman and famous for his rigid moral
code; he fought against Caesar with Pompey, and, after
Pompey's death, continued to fight in Africa. He made
a final resistance at Utica where he committed suicide
rather than be captured.

299 *made strong proof of my constancy*: Put my powers of
resolution to a severe test. This is based on Plutarch:

> . . . loving her husband well, and being of a noble courage,
> as she was also wise – because she would not ask her husband
> what he ailed before she had made some proof by her self
> – she took a little razor such as barbers occupy to pare men's
> nails, and, causing her maids and women to go out of her
> chamber, gave her self a great gash withal in her thigh, that
> she was straight all of a gore-blood; and, incontinently after,
> a vehement fever took her, by reason of the pain of her
> wound. (*Brutus*)

307 *construe*: Elucidate, interpret (accent on first syllable).
308 *charactery*: What is written (in the furrows; accent on
second syllable).
311 *Caius Ligarius*: Both Plutarch and Shakespeare are
historically wrong as the conspirator was actually
Quintus Ligarius. To build up his picture of the well-
beloved Brutus, as well as for obvious practical reasons,
Shakespeare makes the sick Ligarius visit Brutus rather
than vice versa as in Plutarch:

Brutus . . . went to see him being sick in his bed, and said
unto him: 'O Ligarius, in what a time art thou sick!' Ligarius
rising up in his bed and taking him by the right hand, said
unto him: 'Brutus,' said he, 'if thou hast any great enterprise
in hand worthy of thyself, I am whole.' (*Brutus*)

312 *how*: How are you?

313 *Vouchsafe*: Deign to accept.

315 *wear a kerchief*: It was a common practice in
Elizabethan England for the sick to wear a cloth round
the head.

322 *Brave*: Noble.

323 *exorcist*: One who conjures up (and exorcizes) spirits.

324 *mortifièd*: Which was dead.

327 *whole*: Sound, healthy. See Cassius' similar parallel
between political and bodily sickness at I.2.253–4.

328 *make sick*: Kill.

331 *To whom*: To the dwelling of him to whom.
Set on: Advance.

332 *new-fired*: Rekindled (with life and courage).

II.2

0 *night-gown*: Dressing-gown.

2–3 *Thrice hath Calphurnia . . . murder Caesar*: Plutarch is
less specific about Calphurnia's utterance: 'he heard
his wife Calpurnia, being fast asleep, weep and sigh
and put forth many fumbling lamentable speeches. For
she dreamed that Caesar was slain, and that she had
him in her arms' (*Caesar*).

5 *present*: Immediate.

6 *opinions of success*: Judgements on the outcome (whether
good or bad).

9 *You shall not stir out of your house today*: This is based
on Plutarch: 'she prayed him if it were possible not to
go out of the doors that day' (*Caesar*).

10 *Caesar shall forth*: Caesar shall go forth. It is noteworthy
that Caesar uses the third person even in talking to his
wife.

13 *stood on ceremonies*: Attached much importance to

omens. The detail is derived from Plutarch: 'Calpurnia until that time was never given to any fear or super-stition' (*Caesar*).

16–24 *horrid sights . . . streets*: All these portents are Shake-speare's own invention, unlike those recounted at I.3.15–32, most of which he took from Plutarch. It has been suggested that this account may have been based on some popular version of the prodigies which pre-ceded the destruction of Jerusalem. Shakespeare gives a similar account to this later in *Hamlet*, I.I.113–20:

> In the most high and palmy state of Rome,
> A little ere the mightiest Julius fell,
> The graves stood tenantless and the sheeted dead
> Did squeak and gibber in the Roman streets –
> As stars with trains of fire and dews of blood,
> Disasters in the sun; and the moist star
> Upon whose influence Neptune's empire stands
> Was sick almost to Doomsday with eclipse.

16 *watch*: An anachronism since there was no night guard in Rome until the reign of Augustus. Shakespeare obvi-ously has in mind the watches of Elizabethan London of which he gives a comic picture in *Much Ado About Nothing*.

19 *fought*: The F reading *fight* is out of sequence with the other tenses in the passage. However, Shakespeare may have deliberately used the dramatic present mixed with the past tense to suggest Calphurnia's excited state.

20 *right form of war*: In regular battle order.

22 *hurtled*: Clashed.

23 *did neigh*: F has *do neigh*; see note to 19.

25 *beyond all use*: Outside all normal experience.

29 *Are to*: Are as applicable to.

30–31 *When beggars die . . . the death of princes*: This was a common belief in Elizabethan England based ulti-mately on the series of sympathetic correspondences which were perceived between various levels of life and matter in the universe.

31 *blaze forth*: Proclaim.

32–7 *Cowards die . . . will come*: This speech is based on only
a hint from Plutarch: 'And when some of his friends
did counsel him to have a guard for the safety of his
person . . . he would never consent to it, but said, it was
better to die once than always to be afraid of death'
(*Caesar*). Cf. Brutus' acceptance of death at III.1.99.

38–40 *They would . . . the beast*: In Plutarch it is only after
Calphurnia's plea that Caesar 'would search further of
the soothsayers by their sacrifices' that 'the soothsayers,
having sacrificed many beasts one after another, told
him that none did like them' (*Caesar*). Shakespeare
uses Plutarch's earlier description of Caesar's own
sacrifice when he 'found that one of the beasts which
was sacrificed had no heart'.

46 *We are*: The F reading *we heare* would appear to be an
error of palaeographical origin. However, its appearance in the three subsequent Folio editions of the plays
may suggest that Shakespeare was using 'hear' in the
sense of 'to be styled as, to pass for'.

49 *consumed in confidence*: Destroyed by overconfidence.

55 *Mark Antony shall say I am not well*: Plutarch has: 'he
determined to send Antonius to adjourn the session of
the Senate' (*Caesar*).

56 *And for thy humour I will stay at home*: Plutarch also
has Caesar indulging Calphurnia's whim: 'for that he
saw her so troubled in mind with this dream she had'
(*Caesar*).

Enter Decius: Plutarch's 'Decius Brutus, surnamed
Albinus, in whom Caesar put such confidence that in
his last will and testament he had appointed him to be
his next heir, and yet was of the conspiracy' (*Caesar*).

59 *fetch*: Escort, accompany.

60 *happy time*: Opportune moment.

75 *stays*: Keeps.

76–9 *She dreamt . . . in it*: In Plutarch, Calphurnia's dream
is different: 'she dreamed that . . . the Senate having
set upon the top of Caesar's house, for an ornament
. . . a certain pinnacle . . . she saw it broken down'

(*Caesar*). Shakespeare's invention of the statue
spouting blood is the more effective in that it is taken
up verbally by the reference to Pompey's statue at
III.2.189–90, and physically by the action of the
conspirators bathing their hands in Caesar's blood.

76 *tonight*: Last night.
   statue: This is pronounced with three syllables here as
   it is at III.2.189.

78 *lusty*: Vigorous.

80 *And these does she apply for warnings and portents*: As
   it stands this line is Alexandrine; it may, however, have
   occurred owing to the compositor's accidentally repro-
   ducing the *And* from the following line. The accent in
   portents is on the final syllable.
   apply for: Interpret as.

88 *press*: Crowd around.

89 *For tinctures, stains, relics, and cognizance*: Ironically
   Decius sees the Romans treating Caesar as a martyr
   and staining their handkerchiefs in his blood for relics.
   Antony makes the same point to the mob at III.2.134–8.
   tinctures may carry overtones of the alchemical
   meaning: 'a supposed spiritual principle or immaterial
   substance whose character or quality may be infused
   into immaterial things, which are said to be tinctured'.

93–9 *The Senate . . . dreams*: This part of Decius' plea is
   taken straight from Plutarch:

   . . . he . . . reproved Caesar, saying that he gave the Senate
   occasion to mislike with him, and that they might think he
   mocked them, considering that . . . they were ready willingly to grant him all things, and to proclaim him king of
   all the provinces of the Empire of Rome out of Italy . . .
   and furthermore, that if any man should tell them from him
   they should depart for that present time, and return again
   when Calpurnia should have better dreams – what would
   his enemies and ill-willers say . . . ? (*Caesar*)

96–7 *it were . . . rendered*: It would be a sarcastic remark
   likely to be passed.

102–3 *my dear dear love . . . proceeding*: My deep personal
       concern for your career.

104 *And reason to my love is liable*: My affection prompts
     me to utter what my reason tells me is too outspoken.

108 *Enter Brutus . . . and Publius*: See note to II.1.212.
     Publius: Plutarch makes no mention of a conspirator
     of this name, but Shakespeare may have recalled
     Publius Silicius who was sentenced to death by the
     Triumvirate (Octavius Caesar, Mark Antony and
     Lepidus) and was fond of Brutus.

112–13 *Caesar was ne'er . . . made you lean*: See note to
        II.1.215–16.

116 *See! Antony, that revels long a-nights*: See note to
     I.2.202–3.

118 *prepare within*: This is an order directed to servants to
     set out the wine.

124–5 *And so near . . . had been further*: This is inconsistent
        with the events of the assassination, for Trebonius'
        task is to draw Antony out of the Capitol, so he does
        not stab Caesar; see III.1.25–6.

126–7 *Good friends . . . straightway go together*: Shakespeare
        employs the classic symbol of betrayal: the murderers
        taking wine with the victim just before the killing.

128–9 *That every like . . . earns to think upon*: By making
        Brutus comment on the gulf between the appearance
        of their friendship and the reality of their enmity,
        Shakespeare shows his consciousness of his personal
        betrayal.

129 *earns*: Grieves, yearns.

II.3

0 *Artemidorus*: Cf.:

> . . . one Artemidorus also, born in the isle of Gnidos, a doctor
> of rhetoric in the Greek tongue, who by means of his profes-
> sion was very familiar with certain of Brutus' confederates
> and therefore knew the most part of all their practices against
> Caesar, came and brought him a little bill written with his
> own hand, of all that he meant to tell him. (Plutarch's *Caesar*)

1–5 *Caesar, beware . . . Caesar*: Shakespeare may have taken
the idea for the form of this letter from the account
of Caesar given in *A Mirror for Magistrates* (1578 edn):
'Presenting me a scroll of every name; and their whole
device'.

5 *bent*: Directed.

6 *If thou beest not immortal*: This is ironical coming at
this point in the play; but it does also help to build up
a picture of how Caesar was viewed by some Romans.
look about you: Take care.

6–7 *security gives way to conspiracy*: Overconfidence gives
opportunity for treason. This is an admirable comment
on the action of II.2.

8 *lover*: Devoted friend.

11 *as a suitor*: Pretending to be a petitioner.

13 *Out of the teeth of emulation*: Beyond the reach of
envious rivalry.

15 *contrive*: Conspire.

II.4

This scene is based on the following passage in
Plutarch's *Brutus*:

Portia being very careful and pensive for that which was to
come and being too weak to away with so great and inward
grief of mind, she could hardly keep within, but was frighted
with every little noise and cry she heard, . . . asking every
man that came from the market-place what Brutus did, and
still sent messenger after messenger, to know what news. At
length, Caesar's coming being prolonged . . . Portia's weakness was not able to hold out any longer, and thereupon she
suddenly swounded.

6 *constancy*: Fortitude, self-control.

9 *to keep counsel*: So far as the play's action is concerned,
Brutus has told Portia his secret, as he promised at
II.1.304–8. In fact there has been no time for him to
do so.

14 *take good note*: Observe closely.

18 *bustling rumour*: Confused noise.

20 *Sooth*: In truth.

23 *ninth hour*: This is an anachronism; Shakespeare is using modern not Roman measurements of time.

28–30 *That I . . . himself*: These lines have caused some editors to give the Soothsayer's role in this scene to Artemidorus. However, such a change is unwarranted, as the Soothsayer may be merely intending to warn Caesar again. Also *feeble man* at 36 is not applicable to Artemidorus.

35 *praetors*: These were Roman judges of high rank. Brutus, Cassius and Cinna among the conspirators were praetors, Brutus being the chief justice or '*praetor urbanus*'. See I.3.142–3.

37 *more void*: Less crowded.

45 *merry*: In good spirits.

III.1

0 *Popilius*: Although he is not listed in the F stage direction, he speaks at 13.

1–2 *CAESAR . . . The ides of March . . . SOOTHSAYER . . . not gone*: This exchange is perhaps based on two passages. One is in Plutarch's *Caesar*:

Caesar going unto the Senate-house and speaking merrily unto the soothsayer, told him: 'The Ides of March be come.' 'So be they,' softly answered the soothsayer, 'but yet they are not past.'

The other is in *A Mirror for Magistrates*:

(Quod I) the Ides of March be come, yet harm is none.
(Quod he) the Ides of March be come, yet th' are not
    gone.

3 *schedule*: Document, paper.

4–5 *Trebonius doth desire . . . humble suit*: Trebonius has the role later (25–6) of drawing Antony away, and no mention is made of his presenting a suit to Caesar. Decius is merely suspicious of Artemidorus, and manufactures an excuse to distract Caesar's attention.

6–10 *O Caesar . . . mad*: In Plutarch Caesar receives the petition and attempts to read it:

> He [Artemidorus] . . . pressed nearer to him and said. 'Caesar,
> read this memorial to yourself, and that quickly, for they be
> matters of great weight, and touch you nearly.' Caesar took
> it of him, but could never read it, though he many times
> attempted it, for the number of people that did salute him;
> but holding it still in his hand, keeping it to himself, went
> on withal into the Senate-house. (*Caesar*)

Perhaps under the influence of the account of the incident in *A Mirror for Magistrates*, Shakespeare makes
Caesar refuse the paper with a grand gesture which is
consistent with his previous attitudes in the play.

8 *What touches us ourself shall be last served*: Those things
which concern me personally must be last attended to.
Notice the use of the royal plural indicative of Caesar's
arrogance.

10 *give place*: Get out of the way.

12 *Caesar enters the Capitol, the rest following*: Because it
is not known with any certainty how plays were
produced on the Elizabethan stage, it is impossible to
say exactly how the entering of the Capitol was effected
in this scene. However, there is evidence that there
was at the Globe Theatre a large discovery space at
the rear of the stage (intended to serve several staging
purposes) which may here have been utilized for the
Senate House and the attendant senators, with the
front area of the stage being used for the *street* in which
lines 1–11 take place. In Plutarch the murder takes
place in Pompey's theatre: 'the place where the murder
was prepared, and where the Senate were assembled,
and where also there stood up an image of Pompey
dedicated by himself amongst other ornaments which
he gave unto the Theatre' (*Caesar*).

13 *I wish your enterprise today may thrive*: This is taken
from Plutarch's *Brutus*:

Another Senator, called Popilius Laena, after he had saluted
Brutus and Cassius more friendly than he was wont to do,
he rounded softly in their ears and told them: 'I pray the
gods you may go through with that you have taken in hand
. . .' When he had said, he presently departed from them,
and left them both afraid that their conspiracy would out.

17 *I fear our purpose is discoverèd*: This is based on Plutarch's
Brutus:

Popilius Laena . . . went unto Caesar and kept him a long
time with a talk. Caesar gave good ear unto him. Wherefore
the conspirators . . . not hearing what he said to Caesar, but
conjecturing, by that he had told them a little before, that
his talk was none other but the very discovery of their
conspiracy, they were afraid every man of them.

18 *Look how he makes to Caesar: mark him*: In Plutarch's
account Brutus watches Popilius alone and does not
communicate with his companions: 'Brutus marking
the countenance and gesture of Laena, and considering that he did use himself rather like an humble and
earnest suitor than like an accuser, he said nothing to
his companion' (*Brutus*).
  makes to: Goes towards.
19 *sudden*: Prompt, quick.
  prevention: Being forestalled.
20–22 *Brutus, what shall . . . slay myself*: Shakespeare took
the hint for Cassius' panic from Plutarch's *Caesar*: 'But
the instant danger of the present time, taking away his
former reason, did suddenly put him into a furious
passion and made him like a man half besides himself.'
In the account of the assassination in *Brutus* Plutarch
notes that, rather than be apprehended, should Caesar
know of their plan, the conspirators prepare to 'kill
themselves with their own hands'.
21 *turn back*: Return alive.
22–4 *Cassius, be constant . . . doth not change*: In Plutarch

Brutus 'with a pleasant countenance encouraged
Cassius. And immediately after, Laena went from
Caesar and kissed his hand; which showed plainly that
it was for some matter concerning himself that he had
held him so long in talk' (*Brutus*).

22 *constant*: Unshaken, resolute.

24 *Caesar doth not change*: Caesar's expression does not
change.

25–6 *Trebonius knows . . . out of the way*: In Plutarch's *Brutus*
'Trebonius . . . drew Antonius aside as he came into
the house where the Senate sat, and held him with a
long talk without'; in the account of the incident in
his *Caesar* it is Decius who does this.

28 *presently*: Immediately.
   prefer: Present.

29 *addressed*: Ready to do so.

32 *Caesar and his senate*: Caesar's arrogance is reflected
in the word order he chooses.

35 *prevent*: Forestall. Caesar knows what Metellus is to
ask him; see 44.

36 *couchings*: Bowings.
   courtesies: Obeisances.

38–9 *And turn . . . law of children*: And alter by childish
whim what has been decreed by time-honoured and
pre-ordained law.

39 *law*: Although the F reading *lane* has been defended as
meaning 'path, by-way', it is usually taken to be a
compositor's error. Other emendations suggested, 'lines'
(meaning 'goings-on') and 'lune' (meaning 'whim'), are
palaeographically attractive, but they discontinue the
legal metaphor of the previous lines. It has also been
suggested that F's *lane* is a variant pronunciation of
'line', which could mean 'rule, canon, precept'.

39–40 *Be not fond,* | *To think*: Do not be so stupid as to imagine.

40 *rebel blood*: Uncontrollable passions.

41–2 *thawed . . . melteth*: Shakespeare is thinking of blood
as 'mettle' in the alchemist's crucible; Caesar's blood
is thus like gold, in his own eyes, which remains *true*
unlike baser metals. See note to I.2.306–7.

41 *true quality*: The stability proper to it.

43 *spaniel*: Obsequious (hence flattering).

46 *spurn thee like a cur*: This was perhaps suggested by
    Plutarch's account of the incident in *Brutus*: 'Caesar
    at the first simply refused their kindness and entreaties.
    But afterwards, perceiving they still pressed on him,
    he violently thrust them from him.'

47–8 *Know, Caesar . . . be satisfied*: See An Account of the
      Text.

51 *repealing*: Recalling from banishment.

53 *Publius Cimber*: The name is Shakespeare's invention;
    Plutarch gives two accounts of this moment of peti-
    tion in *Caesar* and *Brutus*. Shakespeare seems to follow
    the latter more closely: 'one Tullius Cimber . . . made
    humble suit for the calling home again of his brother
    that was banished. They all made as though they were
    intercessors for him, and took him by the hands and
    kissed his head and breast.'

54 *freedom of repeal*: Permission for his sentence of
    banishment to be rescinded.

58 *be well moved*: Like to be persuaded to change my
    decision.

59 *If I could pray to move*: If I were capable of begging
    other people to change their minds.

60 *constant as the northern star*: As unchanging as the pole
    star.

61 *true-fixed*: Immovable.
    resting: Unchanging.

62 *fellow*: Equal.

63 *painted*: Decorated.

67 *apprehensive*: Capable of reason.

69 *holds on his rank*: Retains his position.

70 *Unshaked of motion*: Movement was the law of every
    star but one.

74 *Wilt thou lift up Olympus*: Will you attempt the impos-
    sible? Caesar's choice of words here, and indeed
    throughout the speech, makes it clear that he is seeing
    himself as something between a god and a natural
    force. The effect of the whole speech is to alienate the

audience's sympathy from him immediately before the
moment he is attacked.

75 *bootless*: Uselessly, unavailingly.

76 *Speak hands for me*: Let the actions of my hands speak
for me!

77 *Et tu, Brute*: This is based ultimately on Suetonius'
account of Caesar, according to which Caesar, at the
moment of death, said to Brutus, 'And thou, my son'
– a reference to Suetonius' belief that Brutus was
Caesar's illegitimate son. The earliest known appearance of the phrase on the English stage is in *The True
Tragedy of Richard Duke of York* (1595), a play believed
to be a version of *Henry VI, Part III*; however, the
phrase appears to have been a stage commonplace at
the time. *Brute* is pronounced with two syllables.
Then fall Caesar: Shakespeare here follows Plutarch's
account in *Caesar*:

Men report also that Caesar did still defend himself against
the rest, running every way with his body. But when he saw
Brutus with his sword drawn in his hand, then he pulled his
gown over his head and made no more resistance.

80 *pulpits*: This is derived from Plutarch's phrase 'the
pulpits for orations' meaning the rostra in the Forum.
Shakespeare may have had in mind London's open-air
pulpits like that at St Paul's.

81 *enfranchisement*: This was probably suggested by
Plutarch's account of the conspirators 'persuading the
Romans . . . to take their liberty again' (*Brutus*).

82–91 *People and senators . . . Publius*: This is Shakespeare's
dramatization of Plutarch's description of the panic in
the Senate:

Brutus, standing in the midst of the house, would have spoken,
and stayed the other Senators that were not of the conspiracy,
to have told them the reason why they had done this fact.
But they, as men both afraid and amazed, fled one upon
another's neck in haste to get out at the door . . . (*Brutus*)

Instead of general reference, however, Shakespeare
effectively focuses the dramatic attention on one aged
senator's reaction to the murder, perhaps suggested by
Plutarch's 'they that were present . . . were so amazed
with the horrible sight they saw, they had no power to
fly . . . not so much as once to make any outcry' (*Caesar*).

83 *ambition's debt*: That which was due to Caesar's ambition.

86 *mutiny*: Tumult.

89 *Talk not of standing*: Talk not of organizing resistance.
This is in answer to Metellus' suggestion that they
defend themselves; and looks ahead to Brutus' miscal-
culation in III.2 where he again assumes that everyone
will understand the assassination when the reasons for
it have been explained.

92–5 *And leave us . . . the doers*: This is based on Plutarch's
general remark that 'Brutus . . . sent back again the
noblemen that came thither with him, thinking it no
reason that they, which were no partakers of the
murder, should be partakers of the danger' (*Brutus*).

93 *your age*: You as an old man.

94 *abide*: Pay the penalty for.

96 *Where is Antony . . . amazed*: Shakespeare changes
Plutarch's information slightly: 'But Antonius and
Lepidus . . . secretly conveying themselves away, fled
into other men's houses, and forsook their own'
(*Caesar*).

97–8 *Men, wives, and children . . . doomsday*: Plutarch
describes the consternation of the citizens at two points:
in *Brutus*: 'when the murder was newly done, there
were sudden outcries of people that ran up and down
the city'; and in *Caesar*: 'the Senate . . . flying filled
all the city with marvellous fear and tumult; insomuch
as some did shut-to their doors, others forsook their
shops and warehouses.'

99–100 *That we shall die . . . men stand upon*: This was a common
Elizabethan proverb. Cf. Caesar's words at II.2.32–7.

100 *drawing days out*: Extending the span of life.
stand upon: Set great store by.

101–2 *Why, he that cuts . . . fearing death*: Some editors give these lines to Cassius on the grounds of greater appropriateness. However, the change is unnecessary; and the sentiment is similar to that expressed by Casca at I.3.101–2.

105–10 *Stoop . . . liberty*: Some editors give these lines to Casca on the grounds that they are inconsistent with Brutus' character. I think they are quite in keeping with his idealistic nature, to which the appeal of such a symbolic action would be irresistible, particularly in view of the way he views the murder at II.1.171–4. The scene also fulfils Calphurnia's prophetic dream in II.2. The whole incident shows Shakespeare taking a vivid detail from Plutarch and giving it a quite different interpretation:

> Then the conspirators thronging one upon another because every man was desirous to have a cut at him, so many swords and daggers lighting upon one body, one of them hurt another; and among them Brutus caught a blow on his hand, because he would make one in murdering of him and all the rest also were every man of them bloodied. (*Brutus*; see also *Caesar*)

108 *market-place*: The Roman Forum.

109–10 *And waving . . . Peace, freedom, and liberty*: This is based on Plutarch's *Brutus*: 'Brutus and his consorts, having their swords bloody in their hands, went straight to the Capitol, persuading the Romans, as they went, to take their liberty again.'

113 *accents*: Languages.

114 *How many times shall Caesar bleed in sport*: How many times (in the future) shall Caesar be killed for entertainment (in plays). This is a common device of Shakespeare's to reinforce the verisimilitude of his historical action by referring to theatrical versions of it; cf. *Antony and Cleopatra*, V.2.216–21:

> The quick comedians
> Extemporally will stage us, and present
> Our Alexandrian revels. Antony
> Shall be brought drunken forth, and I shall see
> Some squeaking Cleopatra boy my greatness
> I'th'posture of a whore.

115 *on Pompey's basis*: The irony of this is brought out
fully in Plutarch's account: '[Caesar] was driven . . .
against the base whereupon Pompey's image stood,
which ran all of a gore-blood till he was slain. Thus
it seemed that the image took just revenge of Pompey's
enemy, being thrown down on the ground at his feet
and yielding up his ghost there' (*Caesar*).
basis: Pedestal.
along: Stretched out.

117 *knot*: Party of men joined in conspiracy.

120–21 *Brutus shall lead . . . best hearts of Rome*: This is based
on Plutarch's *Brutus*: 'Brutus went foremost, very
honourably compassed in round about with the noblest
men of the city.'

120 *grace*: Do honour to.

122 *Soft*: Wait a moment.
A friend of Antony's: In Plutarch it is Antony who
invites the conspirators to come down from the Senate
House to visit him, and 'sent them his son for a pledge'
(*Brutus*).

126 *honest*: Honourable.

127 *royal*: Nobly munificent.

129 *feared*: Antony politicly places this word with *Caesar*
and thus half aligns himself with the conspirators; its
equally skilfully chosen counterpoise is *love Brutus*.

136 *Thorough*: This is a common two-syllable form of
'through'.
this untrod state: This still unknown set of circumstances.

140 *so*: If it should.

142 *presently*: At once.

143 *to*: As a.

144 *a mind*: A presentiment.

145–6 *still . . . purpose*: Always turns out to be uncomfortably close to what actually happens.

146 *Enter Antony*: In Plutarch Antony first meets the conspirators the day following the murder at a meeting of the Senate. By making Antony meet Brutus and the rest immediately after Caesar's death, Shakespeare both speeds up the events and makes Antony the more striking character in his boldness and craftiness.

152 *be let blood*: This was a medical term referring to the removal of superfluous blood for curative reasons. However, it is here used to mean 'be put to death'.
rank: Swollen with disease. Antony continues his medical metaphor.

157 *bear me hard*: See note to II.1.215.

158 *purpled*: Reddened with blood.

159 *Fulfil your pleasure*: This is ironic.
Live: If I should live.

160 *apt*: Prepared, ready.

161 *so*: So well, so much.
mean of death: Manner of dying.

171 *As fire drives out fire*: This was a common Elizabethan proverb.
so pity, pity: So pity for the wrongs of Rome has driven out pity for Caesar.

174 *Our arms in strength of malice*: For the many emendations which have been suggested see the second list of collations in An Account of the Text. However, the F reading preserves and continues the antithesis of the whole speech between the conspirators' bloody appearance and their loving hearts; literally 'our arms which have all the strength which seeming enmity has endowed them with'.

175 *Of brothers' temper*: Full of brotherly love.

177–8 *Your voice . . . new dignities*: Cassius is once again far more politically realistic than Brutus, and offers Antony a share in the power which has come to them by their action in exchange for his support.

177 *voice*: Vote.

178 *dignities*: High offices of state.

181 *deliver*: Report to.

183 *I doubt not of your wisdom*: This is ironic.

188 *my valiant Casca*: This is irony; contrast it with Antony's real opinion at V.1.43–4.

191 *My credit now stands on such slippery ground*: Antony quibbles on (1) his physical position in standing in Caesar's blood, (2) his reputation as Caesar's friend.

192 *conceit*: Judge.

196 *dearer*: More keenly.

199 *Most noble*: This could apply (1) ironically to *foes*, (2) sincerely to Caesar, (3) scornfully to his own action in shaking the hands which had killed his friend.

202 *to close*: To arrive at an agreement.

204 *bayed*: Brought to bay (like a hunted deer).
    hart: For the remainder of this speech, Antony plays on the words *hart* and *heart*. Contrast this speech with Brutus' at II.1.173–4, where Brutus specifically wishes to carve Caesar as a dish fit for the gods and not hack him like the carcass of a hunted beast which Antony here depicts.

206 *Signed*: Marked with, bearing the evidence of.
    spoil: This was a hunting term designating the capture of the hunted animal and its distribution to the hounds; by extension it meant 'slaughter' generally.
    lethe: The pronunciation is with two syllables. This term, originally taken from the name of the river in Hades, the waters of which induced forgetfulness of the past, came to mean loosely 'oblivion'; here its meaning appears to be 'life-blood'.

207–8 *O world . . . heart of thee*: These lines have been questioned as un-Shakespearian; but there are no grounds whatsoever for doubting their genuineness.

213 *modesty*: Moderation.

214 *I blame you not for praising Caesar so*: This is ironical in view of the echo contained in Antony's funeral oration at III.2.75.

215 *compact*: Agreement (accent on second syllable).

216 *pricked*: Marked down by a 'prick' or tick.

224 *good regard*: Sound considerations.

225 *son of Caesar*: See note to 77.

229 *pulpit*: See note to 80.

230 *order of his funeral*: The ceremonies arranged for his funeral.

231 *You shall, Mark Antony*: In Plutarch the discussion concerning Caesar's funeral took place in the Senate two days after the murder:

> When this was done, they came to talk of Caesar's will and testament, and of his funerals and tomb. Then Antonius thinking good his testament should be read openly, and also that his body should be honourably buried and not in hugger-mugger, lest the people might thereby take occasion to be worse offended if they did otherwise . . . (*Brutus*)

> Plutarch also notes that Brutus' decision to allow Antony to speak to the people was his 'second fault . . . when he agreed that Caesar's funerals should be as Antonius would have them; the which indeed marred all' (*Brutus*).

232–5 *You know not . . . utter*: Plutarch notes that 'Cassius stoutly spake against it' (*Brutus*).

236–7 *I will myself . . . our Caesar's death*: Perhaps this is the clearest display in a small compass of Brutus' political weakness, showing (1) his naive conviction that everyone sees situations as he does, (2) his idealistic belief in the obvious rightness of his cause, (3) his conviction that 'sovereign reason' prevails in all men and (4) his blindness concerning the nature of man as a political animal.

238 *protest*: Proclaim.

241 *true*: Fitting, proper.

242 *advantage*: Benefit (by showing our generosity).

243 *fall*: Happen.

257 *tide of times*: Course of history.

260 *dumb mouths*: This is a frequent phrase of Shakespeare's for wounds, particularly those which can 'accuse'; see the passage quoted in the note to III.2.189–90.

262 *A curse shall light upon the limbs of men*: Many

emendations have been suggested for the F reading
limbes, the most favoured being 'lives'. However, there
is no difficulty in accepting the image of the blood and
destruction of civil war afflicting the limbs of men.

264 *cumber*: Burden.

265 *in use*: Common, customary.

268 *quartered*: Hacked to pieces.

269 *with custom of fell deeds*: Because of the commonness
of cruel actions.

270 *ranging*: Roving in search of prey.

271 *Ate*: According to Homer, Ate was the daughter of
Zeus and the personification of moral blindness or
strife. In Shakespeare she is seen as the goddess of
discord and mischief. The word is two-syllabled.

272 *confines*: Regions (accent on second syllable).

273 *Cry havoc*: Antony is here viewing Caesar's spirit as
possessing the kingly privilege of the giving of the
order for general pillage and slaughter. The idea is
taken up from *monarch's voice* at 272.
let slip: Unleash.
the dogs of war: These are listed by the Prologue in
Henry V, 5–8:

> Then should the warlike Harry, like himself,
> Assume the port of Mars, and at his heels,
> Leashed in like hounds, should famine, sword, and fire
> Crouch for employment.

282 *big*: Pregnant with sorrow.

283 *Passion*: Sorrow.

285 *Is thy master coming*: See note to III.2.268.

286 *lies*: Lodges.

287 *chanced*: Happened.

289 *No Rome of safety*: The pun is on *Rome* and 'room',
which were apparently pronounced in a similar way
at the time; cf. I.2.155.

292 *try*: Test.

294 *cruel issue*: Result of cruelty.

295 *the which*: The result of my experiment.

297 *Lend me your hand*: That is, to carry out Caesar's body. According to Plutarch Caesar's body was left in the Senate House when the conspirators went out to address the people.

III.2

0 *Enter Brutus . . . pulpit*: Brutus actually goes into the pulpit at 10.

1 *will be satisfied*: Demand a satisfactory explanation.

2 *audience*: A hearing.

4 *part*: Divide.

7 *public reasons*: This could mean (1) 'reasons concerning the public good' or (2) 'reasons given in public'.

10 *severally*: Separately.

12 *last*: End of my address.

13–34 *Romans, countrymen . . . reply*: Plutarch records that Brutus made a speech immediately following the murder:

When the people saw him in the pulpit, although they were a multitude of rakehells of all sorts and had a good will to make some stir, yet, being ashamed to do it for the reverence they bare unto Brutus, they kept silence, to hear what he would say. When Brutus began to speak, they gave him quiet audience. (*Brutus*)

However, this takes place on the day of the murder two days before Caesar's funeral, and there is no indication in Plutarch of the content of the speech. Shakespeare fashioned its style of oratory from Plutarch's hint that Brutus in some of his Greek letters 'counterfeited that brief compendious manner of speech of the Lacedaemonians. As . . . he wrote unto the Pergamenians in this sort: I understand you have given Dolabella money: if you have done it willingly, you confess you have offended me; if against your wills, show it then by giving me willingly' (*Brutus*).

13 *lovers*: Dear friends.

15 *have respect to mine honour*: Accept me as an honourable man. This is, of course, just the quality Antony stresses for his own purposes in his oration.

16 *Censure*: Judge.

16–17 *your senses*: Your reason.

30 *rude*: Barbarous, ignorant.

37–8 *The question of his death . . . Capitol*: Shakespeare was perhaps recalling Plutarch's account of the meeting of the Senate on the day following the assassination (*Brutus*).

37 *question of*: Considerations which led to.

38 *enrolled*: Recorded in the archives. There has of course been no time for this in the play.

38–9 *his glory . . . offences enforced*: His greatness, which was an honourable attribute, not being devalued, nor his crimes unduly stressed.

43 *place*: Office, position.

45 *lover*: Friend.

50 *ancestors*: See note to I.2.158.

51 *Let him be Caesar*: Shakespeare is perhaps recalling those Romans in Plutarch 'that desired change and wished Brutus only their prince and governor above all other'. The irony of this line stresses the distance between Brutus' high ideals and the mentality of the people for whose good he has slain Caesar.

58 *Do grace to Caesar's corpse, and grace his speech*: Show due respect to Caesar's body, and hear Antony's speech with courtesy.

59 *Tending*: Relating.

64 *public chair*: Plutarch's 'chair or pulpit for orations'.

66 *For Brutus' sake*: In Brutus' name.
    beholding: Indebted.

74–108 *Friends, Romans . . . come back to me*: Plutarch gives two brief accounts of Antony's oration:

Antonius making his funeral oration in praise of the dead, according to the ancient custom of Rome, and perceiving that his words moved the common people to compassion, he framed his eloquence to make their hearts yearn the more. (*Brutus*)

and

. . . he made a funeral oration in commendation of
Caesar . . . When he saw that the people were very glad and
desirous also to hear Caesar spoken of and his praises uttered,
he mingled his oration with lamentable words, and by ampli-
fying of matters did greatly move their hearts and affections
unto pity and compassion. (*Antonius*)

The only hint for the style of Antony's oration provided by Plutarch is that Antony 'used a manner of
phrase in his speech called Asiatic, which . . . was much
like to his manners and life; for it was full of ostenta-
tion, foolish bravery, and vain ambition' (*Antonius*).

112 *I fear there will a worse come in his place*: This was a
common Elizabethan saying.

115 *dear abide it*: Dearly pay the penalty for it.

121 *none so poor to do him reverence*: The lowest member
of society is too high to pay his respects to Caesar.

122–3 *to stir . . . mutiny and rage*: This is based on Plutarch's
remark in *Brutus*: 'the people fell presently into such
a rage and mutiny.'

123 *mutiny*: Disorder, riot.

130 *closet*: Study.
'tis his will: In Plutarch the will of Caesar is first read
in the Senate the day following Caesar's murder: 'they
came to talk of Caesar's will and testament . . . Antonius
thinking good his testament should be read openly'
(*Brutus*). He later notes in connection with Brutus'
mistakes that 'when Caesar's testament was openly read
among them . . . the people then loved him and were
marvellous sorry for him'.

134 *napkins*: Handkerchiefs. The reference is to the practice
of keeping as relics cloths stained in the blood of
martyrs. The idea of hagiolatry may have been
suggested to Shakespeare by Plutarch's remark that
'Caesar's funerals should be honoured as a god' (*Caesar*).

142 *meet*: Fitting, proper.

143 *You are not wood . . . but men*: Contrast these lines with
those of Marullus at I.1.35–6.

150 *stay*: Wait.

151 *o'ershot myself*: Said more than I intended.

168 *far*: Farther.

169 *Bear*: Move.

171–81 *You all . . . or no*: Plutarch gives two accounts of this incident – in *Brutus* and in *Antonius*. Shakespeare's version seems more indebted to the latter: 'To conclude his oration, he unfolded before the whole assembly the bloody garments of the dead, thrust through in many places with their swords, and called the malefactors cruel and cursed murderers'; he combines this with an event related in *Caesar* where the citizens 'saw his body . . . all bemangled with gashes of swords'.

174 *That day he overcame the Nervii*: Antony was not in fact with Caesar at this battle, which was fought at Sambre in the winter of 57 BC. It was one of the most important Roman victories of the Gallic Wars and was likely to be remembered by the Roman people because 'The Senate . . . ordained that they should . . . keep feasts and solemn processions fifteen days together without intermission, having never made the like ordinance at Rome for any victory that ever was obtained' (*Caesar*).

Nervii: In the edition of Plutarch which Shakespeare used there is a marginal note: 'Nervii the stoutest warriors of all Belgae'. The word is three-syllabled.

176 *envious*: Spiteful.

180 *to be resolved*: To learn for certain.

181 *unkindly*: The quibble is on the two meanings (1) 'cruelly', (2) 'not of kind', meaning 'unnaturally'.

182 *angel*: Favourite. The word is Plutarch's.

184 *unkindest*: See note to 181.

189–90 *Even at the base . . . ran blood*: For the passage in Plutarch on which this is based see note to III.1.115. Antony may here be contrasting the hard hearts of the conspirators with the 'sympathy' shown by the statue. The Elizabethan audience, however, may have interpreted the phenomenon in the light of the common belief that a murdered man's wounds bled

afresh in the presence of his murderer; cf. *Richard III*,
I.2.55–9:

> O gentlemen, see, see! Dead Henry's wounds
> Open their congealed mouths and bleed afresh!
> Blush, blush, thou lump of foul deformity;
> For 'tis thy presence that exhales this blood
> From cold and empty veins where no blood dwells.

189 *base*: Pedestal.
  statue: This is pronounced with three syllables here.

193 *flourished*: The quibble is on the two meanings (1) 'triumphed', (2) 'brandished a sword'.

195 *dint*: Stroke, impression.

197 *vesture*: Mantle.

197–8 *Look you here,* | *Here is himself*: See note to 171–81.

198 *marred*: Mangled.
  with: By.

205–6 *Revenge . . . Let not a traitor live*: In Plutarch's *Caesar* when the people 'saw his body . . . all bemangled with gashes of swords, then there was no order to keep the multitude and common people quiet'.

205 *About*: To work!

214 *private griefs*: Personal grievances.

221 *public leave to speak*: Permission to speak publicly.

222–4 *neither wit, nor words . . . To stir men's blood*: Antony lists the qualities of the good orator here: *wit* (intellectual brilliance); *words* (fluency); *worth* (weight of authority); *Action* (gesture and bearing); *utterance* (delivery); effectiveness; results.

222 *wit*: The F reading *writ* has been defended as referring to a prepared oration; but it seems out of keeping with the rest of the passage.

224 *right on*: Just as I think, without art.

226 *poor poor dumb mouths*: See note to 189–90 and to III.1.260.

229 *ruffle up*: Stir up to anger.

243 *To every several man, seventy-five drachmas*: Plutarch refers to Caesar's bequest on three occasions: in *Caesar*,

Antonius and *Brutus*, which last is nearest to Shakespeare's line: 'it appeared that he bequeathed unto every
citizen of Rome seventy-five drachmas a man.'

several: Individual.

drachmas: The drachma was originally a Greek coin.

245 *royal*: Nobly munificent.

249–50 *orchards,* | *On this side Tiber*: For *orchards* see note to
II.1.0. Caesar's gardens actually were situated on the
other side of the river. Shakespeare follows North, who
in his turn was following Amyot's mistranslation of
Plutarch's Greek: 'he left his gardens and arbours unto
the people, which he had on this side of the river of
Tiber (in the place where now the Temple of Fortune
is built)' (*Brutus*).

251 *common pleasures*: Public parks.

255–6 *We'll burn his body . . . traitors' houses*: Plutarch gives
three accounts of this incident: in *Caesar*, *Antonius* and
Brutus, the last of which is the closest to Shakespeare's
words:

> Others plucked up forms, tables, and stalls about the market-
> place . . . and having laid them all on a heap together, they
> set them on fire, and thereupon did put the body of Caesar,
> and burnt it in the middest of the most holy places. And
> furthermore, when the fire was thoroughly kindled, some here,
> some there, took burning fire-brands, and ran with them to
> the murderers' houses that had killed him, to set them a-fire.

255 *holy place*: Where the most sacred temples were situated.

259 *Pluck down*: Tear loose.

260 *windows*: Shutters.

263 *fellow*: This was a term often used either contemptuously or to inferiors.

264 *Octavius is already come to Rome*: Historically it was
six weeks after Caesar's funeral that Octavius returned
to Rome from Apollonia. As elsewhere in the play,
Shakespeare is compressing historical time for greater
dramatic effect.

267 *straight*: At once.

268 *upon a wish*: Exactly as I desired. In Plutarch it is Lepidus
    who enters Rome the night following the assassination.
    Antony at first 'made no reckoning of' Octavius because
    he was young, but later viewed him as a rival. It was
    only in the autumn of the year after the assassination
    that Octavius and Antony settled their differences.
    Shakespeare foreshortens these events for dramatic pur-
    poses, by establishing the Triumvirate immediately after
    Caesar's funeral, and only hints at the antagonism
    between Antony and Octavius in IV.1 and V.1.

270–71 *I heard him say . . . gates of Rome*: Plutarch has in
    Antonius: 'Brutus . . . and his accomplices, for safety
    of their persons, were driven to fly the city.'

272–3 *some notice . . . moved them*: Some information about
    how I had stirred up the people. Plutarch notes that
    'the conspirators, foreseeing the danger before, had
    wisely provided for themselves' (*Brutus*).

III.3

0 *Cinna*: Helvetius Cinna was a poet, and a friend of
    Catullus. The scene is based on the following passage
    in Plutarch's *Caesar*:

There was one of Caesar's friends called Cinna, that had a
marvellous strange and terrible dream the night before. He
dreamed that Caesar bade him to supper, and that he refused,
and would not go; then that Caesar took him by the hand,
and led him against his will. Now Cinna hearing at that time
that they burnt Caesar's body in the market-place, notwithstanding that he feared his dream and had an ague on him
besides, he went into the market-place to honour his funerals.
When he came thither, one of the mean sort asked him what
his name was? He was straight called by his name. The first
man told it to another, and that other unto another, so that
it ran straight through them all that he was one of them that
murdered Caesar. For indeed one of the traitors to Caesar
was also called Cinna as himself. Wherefore . . . they fell
upon him with such fury that they presently dispatched him
in the market-place. (see also *Brutus*)

1 *tonight*: Last night.

2 *unluckily charge my fantasy*: Load my imaginings with ill omen. It was a common Elizabethan idea that a dream of good cheer boded ill luck for the dreamer. Notice Shakespeare's change of Plutarch.

9 *directly*: Straightforwardly.

17–18 *they are fools that marry*: This was an Elizabethan proverb.

18 *You'll bear me a bang for that*: I shall strike you for that (remark).

20 *Directly*: The pun here is on the two meanings (1) 'straightforwardly' and (2) 'in a straight line'.

25 *Briefly*: The pun is on the two meanings (1) 'in brief', (2) 'recently'.

34 *pluck but his name out of his heart*: This is grotesquely related to Brutus' attempt to destroy the implications of Caesar's spirit or name by killing his body. Cf. also Cassius' playing with the names of Brutus and Caesar at I.2.141–6.

turn him going: Send him packing.

36–8 *Come, brands . . . Ligarius*: See note to III.2.255–6.

IV.1

1–6 *These many . . . damn him*: This exchange is based on Plutarch's *Antonius*:

And thereupon all three met together (to wit, Caesar, Antonius, and Lepidus) . . . But yet they could hardly agree whom they would put to death; for every one of them would kill their enemies, and save their kinsmen and friends. Yet at length, giving place to their greedy desire to be revenged of their enemies, they spurned all reverence of blood and holiness of friendship at their feet. (see also *Brutus*)

1 *pricked*: Marked by a 'prick' on the list.

2 *Your brother too must die*: Plutarch notes that 'both of them [Antonius and Octavius] together suffered Lepidus to kill his own brother Paulus. Yet some writers affirm that Caesar and Antonius requested Paulus might be slain, and that Lepidus was contented

with it' (*Antonius*). Lucius Aemilius Paullus had been
consul in 50 BC; and at Caesar's death joined the republican faction and helped declare Lepidus a public enemy
in June 43 BC for having joined Antony. After the
Triumvirate was formed his name was placed first on
the proscriptive list by Lepidus. He escaped to join
Brutus and Cassius, was pardoned after Philippi, but
chose to live and die out of Rome.

4 *Publius*: In Plutarch Antony allows his uncle Lucius
Caesar to be placed on the list; but he has no nephew
Publius. However, immediately prior to the passage
dealing with the Triumvirate's condemnations in
Brutus there is the mention of 'Publius Silicius . . .
who . . . was one of the proscripts or outlaws appointed
to be slain'.

6 *with a spot I damn him*: With a mark I condemn him
to death.

9 *cut off some charge*: Lessen some of the expenditure.
Plutarch says that Calphurnia put Antony in charge
of Caesar's goods, and notes that the Triumvirs 'were
easily agreed and did divide all the Empire of Rome
between them, as if it had been their own inheritance'
(*Antonius*). Shakespeare is contrasting Antony's attitude to Caesar's will here with that in III.2 when it
was a useful political tool.

12 *slight unmeritable*: Insignificant and unworthy of
consideration.

13 *Meet*: Fitting.

14 *three-fold world divided*: This was the Roman world:
Europe, Asia, Africa. Antony was to govern Gaul,
Lepidus Spain, Octavius Africa, Sardinia and Sicily.

16 *voice*: Vote, opinion.

17 *black sentence*: Death sentence.

18 *I have seen more days than you*: I am older (thus more
experienced) than you. In Plutarch 'Antonius at the
first made no reckoning of him, because he was very
young; and said he lacked wit and good friends to advise
him' (*Antonius*).

20 *To ease ourselves of divers slanderous loads*: To divest

ourselves of some of the blame or reproach that may
be laid upon us.

21 *as the ass bears gold*: This was an Elizabethan proverb:
'An ass is but an ass though laden with gold.'

22 *business*: Heavy work.

26 *empty*: Unburdened, idle.

to shake his ears: This was a proverbial expression for
the only occupation for those who have been dismissed.

27 *in commons*: On public pasture lands.

28 *soldier*: The word has three syllables here.

30 *appoint*: Assign.

store: A supply.

32 *To wind*: To turn, to wheel (a term drawn from horsemanship).

33 *His corporal motion governed by my spirit*: His physical
movements controlled by my mind.

34 *in some taste*: In some measure, to some degree.

36 *barren-spirited*: Lacking originality or initiative.

36–9 *one that . . . fashion*: One that takes over outdated
ideas and worn-out fashions of thought, so that all
his ideas are either second-hand or out of date. Cf.
the picture of Lepidus given in *Antony and Cleopatra*,
II.7.

37 *objects*: Wonders, curiosities.

arts: Artificial processes.

imitations: Second-hand ideas.

38 *staled*: Made common or cheap.

39 *Begins his fashion*: Are for him at the height of fashion.

40 *a property*: A mere tool or belonging for cleverer men
to use.

41 *Listen*: Hear.

41–2 *Brutus and Cassius | Are levying powers*: This is based
on Plutarch's *Brutus*, in which Brutus and Cassius meet
at the city of Smyrna and 'were marvellous joyful, and
no less courageous when they saw the great armies
together which they had both levied . . . having ships,
money, and soldiers enow, both footmen and horsemen,
to fight for the Empire of Rome'.

42 *straight make head*: Raise a force immediately.

44 *made*: Made certain.
    stretched: Used to their fullest extent.
45 *presently*: Forthwith.
46–7 *How covert matters . . . surest answerèd*: How hidden
    plans may be found out, and open dangers safely dealt
    with.
48–9 *at the stake . . . many enemies*: Tied to a stake (like a
    bear) and surrounded by many enemies (like barking
    dogs eager to attack us). The metaphor is from bear-
    baiting.
51 *mischiefs*: Schemes to harm us.

IV.2

This scene takes place at Sardis; and is based on
Plutarch's *Brutus*: 'About that time Brutus sent to pray
Cassius to come to the city of Sardis; and so he did.
Brutus, understanding of his coming, went to meet
him with all his friends.'

0 *Enter Brutus, Lucilius . . . them*: It is clear that this scene
    takes place before Brutus' tent into which he retires
    with Cassius at 52, and which may have been the large
    discovery space at the rear of the stage (see note to
    III.1.12). Possibly Brutus enters from the tent attended
    by his servant Lucius, and meets Lucilius at the head
    of his soldiers, bringing in Titinius and Pindarus.
    Titinius: It is odd that Brutus ignores Titinius who is
    Cassius' officer; those editors may be right who suggest
    that he enters with Cassius at 30.
2 *Give the word, ho! and stand*: Lucilius is here passing
    on Brutus' order to his subordinates.
6 *He greets me well*: He sends his greetings with a good
    man.
6–9 *Your master . . . undone*: 'Now as it commonly happeneth
    in great affairs between two persons, both of them
    having many friends and so many captains under them,
    there ran tales and complaints betwixt them' (Plutarch's
    Brutus).
7 *In his own change, or by ill officers*: Whether from his
    changed feelings towards me, or by the misconduct of
    unworthy subordinates.

8 *worthy*: Justifiable, considerable.

8–9 *to wish | Things done undone*: This was a proverbial expression.

10 *be satisfied*: Receive a full explanation.

12 *full of regard and honour*: Meriting all respect and honour.

14 *resolved*: Fully informed.

16 *familiar instances*: Signs of friendship.

17 *conference*: Conversation.

19 *Ever note*: Always observe.

21 *an enforcèd ceremony*: Strained manners.

22 *tricks*: Artifices.

23 *hollow*: Insincere.
   hot at hand: Spirited at the start.

24 *mettle*: Spirit.

26 *fall*: Let fall, lower.
   crests: Ridges of the horse's neck.

27 *Sink in the trial*: Fail when tested.

28 *Sardis*: This was the capital city of the ancient kingdom of Lydia in Asia Minor.

29 *horse in general*: All the mounted soldiers.

31 *gently*: Slowly.

37–41 *Most noble . . . them*: In Plutarch there is no squabble in front of the troops: 'Therefore before they fell in hand with any other matter, they went into a little chamber together, and bade every man avoid, and did shut the doors to them. Then they began to pour out their complaints one to the other' (*Brutus*).

40 *this sober form*: This grave and restrained manner.

41 *be content*: Keep calm. Cf. Cassius' lack of restraint and Brutus' calm at III.1.20–22.

42 *griefs*: Grievances.
   I do know you well: Brutus indicates by this that they are old friends and so need not act like enemies.

45–7 *Bid them move . . . give you audience*: See Plutarch's words in the note to 37–41.

47 *audience*: A hearing.

48 *their charges*: Their troops.

50–52 *Lucius, Lucilius*: F reads *Lucilius* at 50 and *Let Lucius* at 52. The readings are obviously erroneous and need transposing. Lucius, a servant and a boy, and Titinius, Cassius' officer, are ill paired as guards for the Generals' tent. It is far more appropriate that Lucius carry the message for Brutus (as Pindarus, his counterpart, does for Cassius), and that Lucilius make up the guard with Titinius. That this was Shakespeare's intention is demonstrated by the fact that it is Lucilius whom we find on guard at IV.3.126.

IV.3

If the stage arrangement suggested in the note at IV.2.0 is accepted, then at this point Brutus and Cassius would withdraw into the rear area of the stage. Titinius and Lucilius would stand guard at one side of the stage, still in view of the audience. The scuffle between them and the poet (123–7) would take place between the point where they are standing and the stage area representing the interior of the tent.

2 *noted*: Publicly disgraced, slandered. Plutarch's *Brutus* has: 'Brutus, upon complaint of the Sardians, did condemn and noted Lucius Pella for a defamed person, that had been a Praetor of the Romans and whom Brutus had given charge unto; for that he was accused and convicted of robbery and pilfery in his office.'

5 *slighted off*: Slightingly dismissed. A singular verb with a plural subject is frequent in Shakespeare's grammar.

7–8 *In such a time . . . his comment*: Plutarch has: 'This judgement much misliked Cassius . . . And therefore he greatly reproved Brutus for that he would show himself so strait and severe, in such a time as was meeter to bear a little than to take things at the worst' (*Brutus*).

8 *That every nice offence should bear his comment*: That every minor offence should be criticized.
   his: Its.

10 *condemned to have*: Accused of having.
   itching palm: Streak of covetousness in your nature. At one point Plutarch contrasts the extreme covetousness and cruelty of Cassius to the Rhodians with Brutus' clemency towards the Lycians (*Brutus*).

11 *mart*: Deal in or traffic in.

15–16 *The name of Cassius . . . hide his head*: The fact that
the name of Cassius is connected with corrupt deal-
ings endows them with an unwarranted respectability,
so that punishment is impossible (for inferior men as
well as for Cassius). This is based on Plutarch's *Brutus*:
'Cassius . . . himself had secretly, not many days before,
warned two of his friends, attainted and convicted of
the like offences, and openly had cleared them; but yet
he did not therefore leave to employ them in any
manner of service as he did before.'

19 *for justice' sake*: This is the first time justice has been
instanced as one of the motives for the conspiracy.

20–21 *What villain . . . not for justice*: Who of the conspirators was such a villain as to strike Caesar for any other
motive than a desire for justice? This is ironical in that
it is addressed to Cassius, for we know his motive to
have been anything but disinterested.

21 *And not*: Except.

23 *supporting robbers*: There has been no earlier suggestion of this. Its occurrence is due to the fact that
Shakespeare is following his source closely at this point:

Brutus in contrary manner answered that he should
remember the Ides of March, at which time they slew Julius
Caesar; who neither pilled nor polled the country, but only
was a favourer and suborner of all them that did rob and
spoil by his countenance and authority. (*Brutus*)

25 *the mighty space of our large honours*: The high and
honourable offices in our power to confer.

26 *trash*: This was a contemptuous term for money.
graspèd thus: This is presumably an indication to the
actor to make an appropriate gesture.

27 *bay the moon*: Howl against the moon. This was a
proverbial expression indicating a useless activity.

28 *bait*: Worry, harass. Many editors emend this to 'bay';
but there is no need for such a change. The word as
it stands picks up the reference to the dog in the
previous line, as Cassius sees himself as an animal (a

bear or bull) baited by a dog. There may also be a pun
on 'bait'/'bite', for in the sixteenth and seventeenth
centuries words which have *i* + consonant + *e* in
modern English were often pronounced as *a* + consonant + *e*.

30 *hedge me in*: Limit my authority.

31 *Older*: This is derived from Plutarch, who notes 'he
    was the elder man' (*Brutus*).

32 *make conditions*: Manage affairs.

35 *Urge*: Drive, provoke.

36 *health*: Safety, welfare.
    tempt: Try, provoke.

37 *slight*: Of no worth or importance.

39 *way and room*: Free course and scope.
    rash choler: Quick temper.

40 *stares*: Glares.

44 *budge*: Flinch.

45 *observe*: Pay obsequious respect to.
    crouch: Bow.

46 *testy humour*: Irascible temper.

47 *You shall disgest the venom of your spleen*: I will make
    you swallow the poison from your bad temper. The
    spleen was believed to be the seat of the emotions.

49 *mirth, yea, for my laughter*: An object of fun and
    ridicule. Cf. 113, and I.2.72.

52 *vaunting*: Boasting.

54 *to learn of*: To be instructed by.

56 *I said an elder soldier, not a better*: Cassius, in fact, said
    that he was more experienced and a better planner; see
    30–32. Also see the note to V.1.18–20.

58 *moved*: Exasperated, annoyed.

59 *tempted*: See note to 36.

67 *honesty*: Integrity, uprightness.

69 *respect not*: Ignore.

69–70 *I did send . . . denied me*: This is based on Plutarch's
       Brutus:

       Brutus prayed Cassius to let him have some part of his
       money, whereof he had great store . . . Cassius' friends

hindered this request and earnestly dissuaded him from it, persuading him that it was no reason that Brutus should have the money which Cassius hath gotten together by sparing and levied with great evil will of the people their subjects . . . This notwithstanding, Cassius gave him the third part of his total sum.

75 *indirection*: Devious, irregular means.

80 *rascal counters*: Trashy coins.

84 *rived*: Split, cleft, broken.

91 *Olympus*: The legendary home of the Greek gods.

95 *braved*: Defied, opposed, challenged.

96 *Checked*: Rebuked, reproved.

98 *cast into my teeth*: This was a proverbial expression.

101 *Dearer*: More precious.
     Pluto's mine: Pluto, the god of the underworld, and Plutus, the god of riches, were frequently confused in both classical and Elizabethan times.

103 *that denied thee gold*: This seems to contradict 82; but what Cassius is really implying is that although Brutus will have it that he was denied gold, yet Cassius is ready to *give my heart* and so on.

107 *it shall have scope*: Your temper shall have free rein.

108 *dishonour shall be humour*: I shall take your future insults to be merely the products of a whim.

111–12 *Who . . . is cold again*: This was a proverbial expression.

111 *Who*: Which.
     much enforcèd: Struck with force.

112 *straight*: At once.

114 *blood ill-tempered*: Ill-balanced nature.

117 *What's the matter*: This is not intended sarcastically, but shows genuine sympathy for Cassius' distraught state.

119 *rash humour*: Irascible temper. The fact that Cassius inherited his quick temper from his mother is Shakespeare's invention; Plutarch merely notes that he was 'marvellous choleric and cruel' (*Brutus*).
     which my mother gave me: Which I inherited from my mother.

122 *and leave you so*: And let it go at that.

Poet: In Plutarch he is 'one Marcus Faonius, that had been a friend and follower of Cato while he lived, and took upon him to counterfeit a philosopher not with wisdom and discretion but with a certain bedlam and frantic motion, he would needs come into the chamber, though the men offered to keep him out' (*Brutus*). See the headnote to this scene.

126 *stay*: Prevent.

129–30 *Love . . . I'm sure, than ye*: 'This Faonius . . . with a certain scoffing and mocking gesture . . . rehearsed the verses which old Nestor said in Homer:

> My lords, I pray you hearken both to me,
> For I have seen moe years than suchie three.' (*Brutus*)

Shakespeare attributes the couplet to Faonius himself, and, on the strength of this attribution, makes him a poet rather than the pseudo-philosopher of Plutarch.

131 *cynic*: Boorish man.

132 *sirrah*: This was a contemptuous form of address.

Saucy: Insolent.

134 *I'll know his humour, when he knows his time*: I'll put up with his kind of behaviour when he keeps it for a proper time and place.

135 *jigging*: Rhyming, versifying.

136 *Companion*: Here this is used as a term of contempt meaning 'fellow'.

143–4 *Of your philosophy . . . accidental evils*: As a Stoic Brutus ought not to have given way to anger over incidental adversities.

144 *place*: Way.

148 *killing*: Being killed.

149 *touching*: Grievous.

150 *Upon*: As a result of.

150–54 *Impatient of my absence . . . fire*: Some editors have suggested the reading 'Impatience' on grammatical grounds. However, the syntax of the F reading is not uncommon in Shakespeare, and it avoids a clash of sibilants. Plutarch mentions Portia's death, but not in connection with the quarrel:

> And for Portia, Brutus' wife, Nicolaus the philosopher and Valerius Maximus do write that she, determining to kill herself (her parents and friends carefully looking to her to keep her from it), took hot burning coals and cast them into her mouth, and kept her mouth so close that she choked herself. (*Brutus*)

152–3 *for with her death | That tidings came*: The news of Portia's death and that concerning the strength of Antony's and Octavius' forces came together.

162 *taper*: Candle.

163 *call in question*: Deliberate upon.

167–8 *Come down upon us . . . toward Philippi*: These and lines 194–210, 223 suggest that both armies are bearing down on Philippi; but in fact Sardis and Philippi are not close together.

168 *Bending*: Directing.
   Philippi: Accent on second syllable throughout.

169 *tenor*: Purport.

171–6 *That by proscription . . . being one*: This is based on Plutarch's *Brutus*: 'After that, these three, Octavius Caesar, Antonius, and Lepidus . . . did set up bills of proscription and outlawry, condemning two hundred of the noblest men of Rome to suffer death; and among that number Cicero was one.'

171 *proscription*: Condemnation to death.

179–93 *Had you . . . bear it so*: It is generally believed that these lines constitute a first version of the announcement of Portia's death which was imperfectly deleted in the manuscript from which the F text was printed, and that they thus record Shakespeare's first intention of making Brutus display his Stoicism and his ability to subordinate private emotions to public duty. The 'later' version (141–56) shows his gentleness and humanity, accounts in part for his reaction to Cassius, and suggests far more skilfully Brutus dealing with his co-leader while bearing the sorrow of his wife's death. If this theory is correct, then Brutus' *Well, to our work alive* (194) would apply to Cicero's death. Some critics have argued that Shakespeare intended both versions to stand, basing their case on the grounds of their reading of Brutus' character, and of theatrical effectiveness. See An Account of the Text.

189 *once*: Some day.

192 *have as much of this in art*: Have as much of this Stoical fortitude in theory.

193 *nature*: Emotions.

194 *Well, to our work alive*: Let us get on with the work that is our present concern. The choice of the word *alive* has overtones of the importance of matters concerning the living over grief for the dead.

194–223 *What do you think . . . Philippi*: This passage is based on Plutarch's *Brutus*:

> Cassius was of opinion not to try this war at one battle, but rather to delay time and to draw it out in length, considering that they were the stronger in money and the weaker in men and armours. But Brutus in contrary manner did always before, and at that time also, desire nothing more than to put all to the hazard of battle, as soon as might be possible, to the end he might either quickly restore his country to her former liberty, or rid him forthwith of this miserable world, being still troubled in following and maintaining of such great armies together . . . Thereupon it was presently determined they should fight battle the next day.

199 *offence*: Harm.

201 *of force*: Necessarily.

203 *forced affection*: Allegiance out of necessity.

207 *new-added*: Reinforced.

211–23 *Under your pardon . . . at Philippi*: Even as in the matter of Antony's possible assassination, and of his request to speak at Caesar's funeral, Cassius is here overruled against his better judgement. On each of the three occasions Brutus is wrong. Cassius disclaims

responsibility for the present erroneous decision at
V.1.73–5.

218 *Omitted*: Neglected, missed.

219 *bound in*: Confined to.

222 *ventures*: Goods risked in trade.

with your will: As you wish.

226 *niggard*: Supply sparingly, stint.

228 *hence*: Go from here.

229 *Enter Lucius*: In F this stage direction appears before 229,
which is printed there as an unbroken line. It is obvious
that Lucius is summoned, given the order, and exits.

gown: See note to II.2.0.

237 *instrument*: Possibly a lute or a cittern.

239 *Poor knave*: This was a term of endearment, meaning
'poor lad'.

o'erwatched: Tired through staying awake.

245 *raise*: Rouse.

247 *watch your pleasure*: Be awake to anything you wish to
be done.

249 *otherwise bethink me*: Change my mind.

250 *the book*: Plutarch mentions several times Brutus' addiction to reading late into the night; for example, 'if he
had any leisure left him, he would read some book till
the third watch of the night' (*Brutus*).

255 *touch*: Play on.

strain: Tune.

256 *an't*: If it.

260 *young bloods*: Youthful constitutions.

264 *Music, and a song*: Shakespeare frequently uses this
device to provide a peaceful lull before an emotion-
ally highly charged moment; see, for example, the use
of Desdemona's song in *Othello*, IV.3. In the professional theatre the most frequently used song at this
point is 'Orpheus with his lute' from *Henry VIII*, III.1;
another appropriate possibility which has been suggested is 'Come, heavy sleep' from John Dowland's
First Book of Songs (1597).

265 *murderous*: Because it is 'The death of each day's life'
(*Macbeth*, II.2.38).

266 *leaden mace*: The reference is to the mace or staff which was carried by the serjeant or sheriff's officer, and with which he touched the shoulder of the person to be apprehended.

271 *leaf turned down*: This is anachronistic, since Brutus would be reading from a *liber* or *volumen* which was a scroll.

273–5 *How ill . . . apparition*: It was a common Elizabethan superstition that a light turned dim or blue in the presence of a ghost. Shakespeare is here following Plutarch closely: 'looking towards the light of the lamp that waxed very dim, he saw a horrible vision of a man, of a wonderful greatness and dreadful look, which at the first made him marvellously afraid' (*Caesar*).

274–6 *I think . . . any thing*: Shakespeare seems to have in mind here Plutarch's account of Cassius' Epicurean belief:

'In our sect, Brutus, we have an opinion that we do not always feel or see that which we suppose we do both see and feel; but that our senses being credulous, and therefore easily abused, when they are idle and unoccupied in their own objects, are induced to imagine they see and conjecture that which they in truth do not . . .' (*Brutus*)

276–301 *Art thou . . . Nor I, my lord*: Plutarch does not say that the ghost was that of Caesar, but Shakespeare makes it clear that it is both by the stage direction and the lines at V.5.17–19.

So Brutus boldly asked what he was, a god or a man, and what cause brought him thither. The spirit answered him: 'I am thy evil spirit, Brutus; and thou shalt see me by the city of Philippes.' Brutus, being no otherwise afraid, replied again unto it: 'Well, then I shall see thee again.' The spirit presently vanished away; and Brutus called his men unto him, who told him that they heard no noise, nor saw anything at all. (*Brutus*; see also *Caesar*)

276 *upon*: Toward.

278 *stare*: Stand upright.

281 *shalt*: Must.

284 *will*: Am quite ready to.

289 *false*: Out of tune.

302 *commend me*: Deliver my greeting.

303 *set on*: Advance.

    betimes: Early in the morning.

V.I

4 *proves*: Turns out to be.

    battles: Troops in battle order.

5 *warn*: Challenge.

    at Philippi here: The meeting at Sardis actually took place at the beginning of 42 BC, and the battle of Philippi in the following autumn.

6 *Answering before we do demand of them*: Answering a call to battle before we have issued it.

7 *in their bosoms*: In their secret thoughts.

8–9 *could be content . . . places*: Wish they were somewhere else.

10 *With fearful bravery*: With a show of splendour which conceals the fear they are feeling. Shakespeare took this detail from Plutarch: 'In truth, Brutus' army was inferior to Octavius Caesar's in number of men. But, for bravery and rich furniture, Brutus' army far excelled Caesar's. For the most part of their armours were silver and gilt, which Brutus had bountifully given them' (*Brutus*).

    face: Outward appearance.

11 *fasten*: Fix the idea.

13 *gallant*: Splendid. See note to 10.

14 *bloody sign*: Plutarch has: 'The next morning, by break of day, the signal of battle was set out in Brutus' and Cassius' camp, which was an arming scarlet coat' (*Brutus*).

16 *battle*: Army.

    softly: Slowly.

18–20 *Upon the right . . . do so*: In Plutarch this disagreement about the leading of the wings takes place between Brutus and Cassius: 'Brutus prayed Cassius he might

have the leading of the right wing, the which men
thought was far meeter for Cassius, both because he
was the elder man, and also for that he had the better
experience. But yet Cassius gave it him' (*Brutus*).

19 *exigent*: Emergency.

20 *I do not cross you*: I am not opposing you perversely.
    will: Intend to.

24 *answer on their charge*: Meet them when they attack.

25 *Make forth*: Advance.

27–66 *Words before . . . stomachs*: This billingsgate before the
    battle is not in Plutarch, but was a common feature in
    Elizabethan drama.

33 *The posture of your blows*: The nature of the blows you
    can produce; *posture* was a technical term referring to
    the position of a weapon in either arms drill or war.

34 *Hybla*: This is the name of a town and a mountain in
    Sicily which was proverbially famous for the quality
    of its honey. The reference by Cassius is to Antony's
    protestations of friendship after Caesar's death;
    Antony's reply refers only to his eloquence at the
    funeral and its results.

39 *so*: That is, threaten, and so give warning.

41 *showed your teeth*: Smiled insincerely.
    fawned like hounds: See III.1.42–6.

47 *If Cassius might have ruled*: That is, if Cassius had had
    his way about their treatment of Antony after Caesar's
    death; see II.1.155–61.

48 *the cause*: The matter in hand. The term is a legal one
    and this implication is taken up in *proof* and *arguing*.

49 *proof*: Trial or test.

52 *goes up*: Will be sheathed.

53 *three and thirty wounds*: All historical authorities,
    including Plutarch, have 'three and twenty'. The error
    may have been due to a misexpanded numeral in the
    manuscript.

54–5 *or till another Caesar . . . sword of traitors*: Or until
    another Caesar (Octavius) shall have been killed by
    traitors' swords.

61 *peevish*: Silly, childish.

61 *schoolboy*: Octavius was actually twenty-one years old.

62 *a masquer and a reveller*: Plutarch notes in *Antonius* that
    the Roman noblemen disapproved of Antony's

> naughty life; for they did abhor his banquets and drunken
> feasts he made at unseasonable times, and his extreme
> wasteful expenses upon vain light huswives . . . In his house
> they did nothing but feast, dance, and mask. And himself
> passed away the time in hearing of foolish plays, or in
> marrying these players, tumblers, jesters, and such sort of
> people.

66 *stomachs*: Appetites, inclination (for battle).

68 *on the hazard*: At stake. Originally this was a term from
    gambling.

71 *as*: This was a common redundancy in phrases express-
    ing time.

74 *As Pompey was*: At the battle of Pharsalia Pompey was
    forced to fight Caesar against his better judgement.
    Shakespeare is following Plutarch closely in this passage:

> But touching Cassius, Messala reporteth that . . . after supper
> he took him by the hand, and holding him fast, in token of
> kindness as his manner was, told him in Greek: 'Messala, I
> protest unto thee, and make thee my witness, that I am com-
> pelled against my mind and will, as Pompey the Great was,
> to jeopard the liberty of our country to the hazard of a battle.
> And yet we must be lively and of good courage . . .' Cassius
> having spoken these last words unto him, he bade him
> farewell and willed him to come to supper to him the next
> night following, because it was his birthday. (*Brutus*)

set: Stake, gamble.

76 *held Epicurus strong*: Was a convinced follower of the
    philosophy of Epicurus. This postulated that since the
    gods were indifferent to the affairs of human beings,
    then omens and portents could have no significance.
    Plutarch speaks three times of Cassius' Epicureanism,
    and in connection with the omens seen by the repub-

lican armies notes that they 'began somewhat to alter
Cassius' mind from Epicurus' opinions, and had put
the soldiers also in a marvellous fear' (*Brutus*).

79–83 *Coming from . . . gone*: This is based on Plutarch's
Brutus: 'two eagles . . . lighted upon two of the foremost ensigns, and always followed the soldiers, which
gave them meat, and fed them, until they came near
to the city of Philippes; and there, one day only before
the battle, they both flew away.'

79 *former*: Forward, foremost.

84 *ravens, crows, and kites*: These were considered birds
of ill omen since they prognosticate death. This was
probably suggested by Plutarch's 'a marvellous number
of fowls of prey, that feed upon dead carcases' (*Brutus*).

86 *sickly*: Dying.

87 *fatal*: Foreboding death.

89 *but*: Only.

91 *constantly*: Resolutely.

92 *Even so, Lucilius*: Brutus has been talking aside to his
aide while Cassius has been talking with Messala.

92–9 *Now, most noble Brutus . . . to do*: This is a case of
Shakespeare versifying what he found in Plutarch:

Cassius began to speak first, and said: 'The gods grant us,
O Brutus, that this day we may win the field and ever after
to live all the rest of our life quietly one with another. But
sith the gods have so ordained it that the greatest and chiefest
things amongst men are most uncertain, and that, if the
battle fall out otherwise today than we wish or look for, we
shall hardly meet again, what art thou then determined to
do – to fly, or die?' (*Brutus*)

93 *The gods today stand friendly*: May the gods stand
friendly!

94 *Lovers*: Dear friends.

95 *rests still*: Remain ever. The plural subject with the singular verb form is common in Shakespeare's grammar.

96 *Let's reason with the worst that may befall*: Let us consider
what is to be done if the worst happens.

100–107 *Even by . . . below*: Many editors have suggested that these lines are inconsistent with his next speech and with his suicide in V.5. However, Shakespeare is merely showing the philosopher at war with the soldier in Brutus. This is based closely on Plutarch:

> Brutus answered him: '. . . I trust (I know not how) a certain rule of philosophy by the which I did greatly blame and reprove Cato for killing of himself, as being no lawful nor godly act, touching the gods, nor, concerning men, valiant; not to give place and yield to divine providence, and not constantly and patiently to take whatsoever it pleaseth him to send us, but to draw back and fly.' (*Brutus*)

100 *that philosophy*: According to Plutarch, Brutus 'loved Plato's sect best' (*Brutus*).

101 *Cato*: This was Cato the Younger; see note to II.1.295.

104 *fall*: Happen.

104–5 *to prevent | The time of life*: To anticipate the natural limit of life.

106 *stay*: Wait for.

    providence: Fate, destiny.

    some: Whatever. Brutus does not believe in the traditional Roman gods, merely some supernatural power.

108 *led in triumph*: Triumphs were not normally granted to victories in civil wars, the exception being Caesar's victory over Pompey's sons; see note to I.1.32–4.

109 *Thorough*: Archaic form of 'through'.

110–18 *No, Cassius . . . well made*: Shakespeare is here following Plutarch closely:

> 'But being now in the midst of the danger, I am of a contrary mind. For, if it be not the will of God that this battle fall out fortunate for us, I will look no more for hope, neither seek to make any new supply for war again, but will rid me of this miserable world, and content me with my fortune. For I gave up my life for my country in the Ides of March, for the which I shall live in another more glorious world.' (*Brutus*)

119–21 *For ever . . . well made*: This is based on Plutarch:
'Cassius fell a-laughing to hear what he said, and
embracing him: "Come on then," said he, "let us go
and charge our enemies with this mind. For either we
shall conquer, or we shall not need to fear the
conquerors"' (*Brutus*).

122–3 *O, that a man . . . ere it come*: Cf. *Henry IV, Part II*,
III.1.45–6:

> O God, that one might read the book of fate,
> And see the revolution of the times.

V.2

0 *Alarum*: A signal calling to arms.
Enter Brutus and Messala: In F this stage direction
follows immediately after the *Exeunt* at the end of
Brutus' last speech. Thus Brutus and Messala, who
have just left the stage, immediately re-enter *in another
part of the battlefield*.

1 *bills*: Written orders. Plutarch notes that 'Brutus, that
led the right wing, sent little bills to the colonels and
captains of private bands, in the which he wrote the
word of the battle' (*Brutus*).

2 *the other side*: Cassius' wing.

3 *set on*: Attack.

4 *cold demeanour*: Lack of spirit in fighting.

5 *push*: Assault.

6 *them all*: The whole army.

V.3

1–4 *O, look, Titinius . . . from him*: This is based on Plutarch:

> Furthermore, perceiving his footmen to give ground, he did
> what he could to keep them from flying, and took an ensign
> from one of the ensign-bearers that fled, and stuck it fast at
> his feet; although with much ado he could scant keep his own
> guard together. So Cassius himself was at length compelled
> to fly, with a few about him, unto a little hill from whence
> they might easily see what was done in all the plain. (*Brutus*)

 1 *villains*: Cassius' own men.
 2 *mine own*: My own men.
 3 *Ensign*: Standard bearer.
 4 *it*: The standard.
 5–8 *O Cassius . . . enclosed*: This is based on Plutarch:

> Cassius . . . was marvellous angry to see how Brutus' men
> ran to give charge upon their enemies and tarried not for
> the word of the battle nor commandment to give charge;
> and it grieved him beside that, after he had overcome them,
> his men fell straight to spoil and were not careful to compass
> in the rest of the enemies behind. But with tarrying too long
> also, more than through the valiantness or foresight of the
> captains his enemies, Cassius found himself compassed in
> with the right wing of his enemies' army. (*Brutus*)

 6 *on*: Over.
10 *tents*: Encampment.
11 *far*: Farther.
14–32 *Titinius, if thou lov'st me . . . for joy*: This is based on
Plutarch:

> . . . he sent Titinnius, one of them that was with him, to go
> and know what they were. Brutus' horsemen saw him coming
> afar off, whom when they knew that he was one of Cassius'
> chiefest friends, they shouted out for joy; and they that were
> familiarly acquainted with him lighted from their horses, and
> went and embraced him. The rest compassed him in round
> about a-horseback, with songs of victory and great rushing
> of their harness, so that they made all the field ring again
> for joy. (*Brutus*)

19 *even with*: As quick as.
21 *My sight was ever thick*: 'Cassius himself saw nothing,
for his sight was very bad' (*Brutus*).
   thick: Dim.
   Regard: Observe.
22 *not'st*: Observest.
25 *compass*: Full revolution.

29 *make to*: Approach.

on the spur: At a gallop.

31 *light*: Dismount.

32 *ta'en*: Captured.

33–5 *Come down . . . my face*: 'Cassius thinking indeed that Titinnius was taken of the enemies, he then spake these words: "Desiring too much to live, I have lived to see one of my best friends taken, for my sake, before my face"' (*Brutus*).

36–50 *Come hither . . . note of him*: Cf.:

After that, he [Cassius] . . . took Pindarus with him, one of his freed bondmen, whom he reserved ever for such a pinch, since the cursed battle of the Parthians . . . But then casting his cloak over his head and holding out his bare neck unto Pindarus, he gave him his head to be stricken off. So the head was found severed from the body. But after that time Pindarus was never seen more. (*Brutus*)

38 *swore thee*: Made thee swear.

saving of: When I spared.

40 *attempt*: Perform.

42 *search*: Probe, penetrate.

43 *Stand not*: Do not delay.

hilts: This plural form is common in Shakespeare.

46 *sword that killed thee*: Plutarch notes that 'he . . . slew himself with the same sword with the which he strake Caesar' (*Caesar*).

47 *so*: In such circumstances as these.

48 *my will*: What I (rather than Cassius) had wished.

51–3 *It is but change . . . by Antony*: Cf.:

Brutus had conquered all on his side, and Cassius had lost all on the other side. For nothing undid them but that Brutus went not to help Cassius, thinking he had overcome them, as himself had done; and Cassius on the other side tarried not for Brutus, thinking he had been overthrown, as himself was. (*Brutus*)

51 *change*: Exchange of fortune.

60 *O setting sun*: According to line 109 it is three o'clock.

64 *dews*: See note to II.1.266.

65 *Mistrust of my success hath done this deed*: Fear of the outcome of my mission is responsible for this action.

67 *Melancholy's child*: Melancholics (like Cassius) are prone to imagine evils which are non-existent.

68 *apt*: Easily impressed.

71 *the mother*: Melancholy (and, by transference, Cassius, its victim).

78 *Hie*: Hasten.

80–90 *Why didst thou . . . heart*: The details here are taken from Plutarch:

> Titinnius crowned with a garland of triumph . . . came before with great speed unto Cassius. But when he perceived, by the cries and tears of his friends which tormented themselves, the misfortune that had chanced to his captain Cassius by mistaking, he drew out his sword, cursing himself a thousand times that he had tarried so long, and so slew himself presently in the field. (*Brutus*)

80 *brave*: Noble.

84 *misconstrued*: Accent on second syllable.

85 *hold thee*: Wait.

88 *regarded*: Respected, highly esteemed.

89 *By your leave, gods*: He asks permission to end his life before the time allotted to him by the gods.

94–5 *O Julius Caesar . . . walks abroad*: Cf. II.1.167–70; III.1.270–75.

96 *proper*: Own (*own proper* is repetition for emphasis).

97 *where*: Whether.

99–101 *The last of all . . . breed thy fellow*: In Plutarch Brutus 'knew nothing of his death, till he came very near to his camp. So when he was come thither, after he had lamented the death of Cassius, calling him the last of all the Romans, being unpossible that Rome should ever breed again so noble and valiant a man as he . . .' (*Brutus*).

104–6 *and to Thasos . . . it discomfort us*: In Plutarch Brutus
      'caused his body to be buried and sent it to the city of
      Thassos, fearing lest his funerals within the camp
      should cause great disorder'. Thasos was an island
      near Philippi. The F reading *Tharsus* (Tarsus) was the
      name of towns in Cicilia and Bithynia.

105 *funerals*: Usually Shakespeare uses the singular form,
      but he adopts the plural here under the influence of
      Plutarch.

106 *discomfort us*: Dishearten our soldiers.

108 *Labeo and Flavius*: Plutarch identifies these characters
      among the friends of Brutus who were slain in battle
      before his eyes, of whom 'the one was his lieutenant
      and the other captain of the pioneers of his camp'
      (*Brutus*).
      battles: Forces.

110 *second fight*: According to Plutarch the second battle
      occurred twenty days after the first; Shakespeare treats
      the two battles as one.

V.4

0 *Enter Brutus . . . Flavius*: The stage device being used
      here is similar to that at V.2.0.

2–6 *What . . . Cato, ho*: Cf.:

      There was the son of M. Cato slain, valiantly fighting
      amongst the lusty youths. For, notwithstanding that he was
      very weary and overharried, yet would he not therefore fly,
      but manfully fighting and laying about him, telling aloud his
      name and also his father's name, at length he was beaten
      down amongst many other dead bodies of his enemies which
      he had slain round about him. (*Brutus*)

2 *What bastard doth not*: Who is of such base blood who
      does not do so?

4 *I am the son of Marcus Cato, ho*: Therefore he was the
      brother of Brutus' wife; see note to II.1.295.

7–8 *And I am Brutus . . . for Brutus*: There is no speech-
      prefix in F, which has *Luc.* before 9. Plutarch makes it
      clear that it is Lucilius who impersonates Brutus in this

scene (see note to 12–17). If this change in the speech-
prefix is made, and the exit of Brutus indicated at 1,
the action is clear.

12–17 *Yield, or thou diest . . . the General*: Cf.:

Amongst them there was one of Brutus' friends called Lucilius,
who seeing a troop of barbarous men making no reckoning
of all men else they met in their way, but going all together
right against Brutus, he determined to stay them with the
hazard of his life, and, being left behind, told them that he
was Brutus; and, because they should believe him, he prayed
them to bring him to Antonius . . . These barbarous men being
very glad of this good hap, and thinking themselves happy
men, they carried him in the night, and sent some before unto
Antonius to tell him of their coming. He was marvellous glad
of it, and went out to meet them that brought him. (*Brutus*)

12 *Only I yield to die*: I surrender simply in order to die.
13–14 *There is so much . . . his death*: Many editors add a stage
direction after these lines indicating that Lucilius offers
his captors a sum of money to kill him. This is not
necessary as the meaning is: 'There is so much induce-
ment that you will surely kill me at once, and in doing
so win great honour.'
13 *straight*: Immediately.
15 *We must not*: Perhaps because noble prisoners could
be ransomed.
Enter Antony. This is the position of Antony's entry
in F. It is possible that it was placed here in the man
script as an early warning for the prompter; however,
it is more likely to indicate that Antony enters and is
crossing the stage to where Lucilius and the sold-iers
stand, before the first soldier sees him and says line 17.
18–25 *Brutus is ta'en . . . like himself*: Shakespeare is here
following Plutarch very closely:

Lucilius was brought to him, who stoutly with a bold countenance said: 'Antonius, I dare assure thee that no enemy
hath taken nor shall take Marcus Brutus alive. I beseech God

keep him from that fortune. For wheresoever he be found, alive or dead, he will be found like himself. (*Brutus*)

25 *like himself*: True to his own noble nature.

26–9 *This is not . . . enemies*: Shakespeare follows Plutarch closely in these lines:

Antonius . . . looking upon all them that had brought him, said unto them: 'My companions, I think ye are sorry you have failed of your purpose, and that you think this man hath done you great wrong. But, I do assure you, you have taken a better booty than that you followed. For, instead of an enemy, you have brought me a friend . . . For I had rather have such men my friends as this man here, than enemies.' Then he embraced Lucilius and at that time delivered him to one of his friends in custody. (*Brutus*)

30 *where*: Whether.
32 *is chanced*: Has happened.

V.5

1 *poor remains*: Pitiful survivors.
2 *showed the torch-light*: The explanation of this line is found in Plutarch, but not in the play:

Furthermore, Brutus thought that there was no great number of men slain in battle; and, to know the truth of it, there was one called Statilius that promised to go through his enemies, for otherwise it was impossible to go see their camp, and from thence, if all were well, that he would lift up a torch-light in the air, and then return again with speed to him. The torch-light was lift up as he had promised, for Statilius went thither. Now Brutus seeing Statilius tarry long after that, and that he came not again, he said: 'If Statilius be alive, he will come again.' But his evil fortune was such that as he came back he lighted in his enemies' hands and was slain. (*Brutus*)

4–14 *Sit thee down . . . at his eyes*: 'Now, the night being far spent, Brutus as he sat bowed towards Clitus one of his men and told him somewhat in his ear, the other

answered him not, but fell a-weeping. Thereupon he
proved Dardanus, and said somewhat also to him'
(*Brutus*).

5 *a deed in fashion*: The reference is to Cassius' suicide
at V.3.

17 *The ghost of Caesar hath appeared to me*: This is based
on Plutarch's *Caesar*: 'The second battle being at hand,
this spirit appeared again unto him, but spake never a
word. Thereupon Brutus, knowing he should die, did
put himself to all hazard in battle.'

18 *several*: Different.

21–8 *Nay, I am sure . . . run on it*: 'At length he came to
Volumnius himself, and, speaking to him in Greek,
prayed him, for the study's sake which brought them
acquainted together, that he would help him to put his
hand to his sword, to thrust it in him to kill him.
Volumnius denied his request' (*Brutus*).

22 *the world . . . how it goes*: How things are.

23 *the pit*: The hole into which animals are driven (but
also by a quibble 'the grave').

24 *more worthy*: Nobler.

28 *sword-hilts*: See note to V.3.43.

30 *Fly, fly, my lord, there is no tarrying here*: 'And, amongst
the rest, one of them said, there was no tarrying for
them there, but that they must needs fly. Then Brutus
rising up: "We must fly indeed," said he, "but it must
be with our hands not with our feet"' (*Brutus*).

31–9 *Farewell to you . . . at once*: Shakespeare follows Plutarch
closely in these lines:

Then, taking every man by the hand, he said these words
unto them with a cheerful countenance: 'It rejoiceth my
heart that not one of my friends hath failed me at my need,
and I do not complain of my fortune, but only for my
country's sake. For, as for me, I think myself happier than
they that have overcome, considering that I leave a perpetual
fame of our courage and manhood, the which our enemies
the conquerors shall never attain unto by force nor money
. . .' (*Brutus*)

32 *asleep*: Strato does not therefore know what has passed
    between Brutus and Clito, Dardanius and Volumnius.

38 *vile conquest*: Brutus thus dies still believing that
    Caesar's death was necessary; and that the victory by
    Antony and Octavius means the end of Rome's
    freedom, and is therefore *vile*.

39 *at once*: Without further ado.

42 *this hour*: The hour of his death. This is in accord with
    Brutus' Stoic belief that death is not a calamity.

44–51 *I prithee . . . good a will*: Cf.:

> . . . he went a little aside with two or three only, among the
> which Strato was one . . . He came as near to him as he
> could, and, taking his sword by the hilts with both his hands
> and falling down upon the point of it, ran himself through.
> Others say that not he, but Strato, at his request, held the
> sword in his hand, and turned his head aside, and that Brutus
> fell down upon it; and so ran himself through, and died
> presently. (*Brutus*)

45 *of a good respect*: Of good reputation.

46 *smatch*: Taste, tincture.

50 *Caesar, now be still*: In accordance with the revenge
    code, Caesar having now been avenged, his ghost can
    rest peacefully.

51 *Retreat*: This was a military term for a sounding of the
    recall by trumpets of a pursuing force.

52–4 *What man . . . Messala*: 'Messala, that had been Brutus'
    great friend, became afterwards Octavius Caesar's
    friend. So, shortly after, Caesar being at good leisure,
    he brought Strato, Brutus' friend, unto him . . .' (*Brutus*).

53 *My master's man*: In Plutarch Strato was a fellow-
    student of Brutus' when he studied rhetoric.

55 *can but make a fire of him*: Can only put his corpse on
    a funeral pyre.

59 *Lucilius' saying*: See V.4.21–2.

60 *entertain*: Take into service.

62 *prefer*: Recommend.

66 *follow*: Serve.

67 *That did the latest service to my master*: In Plutarch
   Messala introduces Strato to Octavius with '"Caesar,
   behold, here is he that did the last service to my
   Brutus"' (*Brutus*).

68–72 *This was the noblest Roman of them all ... one of them*:
   Cf.:

   Antonius spake it openly divers times that he thought that
   of all them that had slain Caesar there was none but Brutus
   only that was moved to do it as thinking the act commend-
   able of itself; but that all the other conspirators did conspire
   his death for some private malice or envy that they otherwise did bear unto him. (*Brutus*)

71–2 *in a general honest thought ... to all*: Moved by a sincere
   belief that what he was doing was for the public good.
   Cf. II.1.10–12.

73–5 *His life ... man*: This sums up admirably the whole
   impression given of Brutus by Plutarch throughout
   his *Brutus* by such remarks as 'he was a marvellous
   lowly and gentle person ... was well-beloved of the
   people ... was rightly made and framed unto virtue'.

73 *gentle*: Noble and magnanimous.
   elements: The four elements (earth, air, fire, water)
   formed the humours of the body (phlegm, blood,
   melancholy, choler); all had to be in perfect balance
   for physical and spiritual health.

76 *use*: Treat.

77 *respect*: Estimation, regard.
   burial: Shakespeare took this word from Plutarch,
   although he did know the Roman practice of crema-
   tion; see 55 and III.2.255.

79 *ordered honourably*: Treated with all honour. Shakespeare transfers Antony's action in Plutarch to
   Octavius: 'Antonius having found Brutus' body, he
   caused it to be wrapped up in one of the richest coat-
   armours he had' (*Brutus*).

81 *part*: Divide.

Read more in Penguin

PENGUIN SHAKESPEARE